COLLECTION MANAGEMENT IN ACADEMIC LIBRARIES

for our families

Collection Management in Academic Libraries

edited by Clare Jenkins and Mary Morley

Gower

Published by
Gower Publishing Limited
Gower House
Croft Road
Aldershot
Hants GU11 3HR
England

Gower Publishing Company
Old Post Road
Brookfield
Vermont 05036
USA

British Library Cataloguing in Publication Data

Collection management in academic libraries.
   1. Great Britain. Higher education institutions.
   Libraries. management
   I. Jenkins, Clare II. Morley, Mary
   025.19770941

ISBN 0 566 03635 5

Printed in Great Britain by
Billing & Sons Ltd, Worcester

Contents

Illustrations

Tables

Figures

Contributors

Barry Bloomfield has a degree in English from University College, Exeter (1952) and the Postgraduate Diploma in Librarianship from University College, London. He was appointed Librarian at the College of St Mark and St John and then Assistant Librarian in the British Library of Political and Economic Science, London School of Economics, after which he became Deputy Librarian and subsequently Librarian at the School of Oriental and African Studies, University of London (1963-78). Director of the India Office Library and Records, Foreign and Commonwealth Office (1978 to date), he transferred to the British Library in that capacity in 1982, becoming also Director of the Department of Oriental Manuscripts and Printed Books in 1983 and then Director of Collection Management in 1985. He is the author of bibliographies of W H Auden and Philip Larkin and of numerous articles in library and bibliographical journals.

Sharon Bonk is Assistant Director for Collection Development and Research Services at the University at Albany, State University of New York. She has held positions of Assistant Director for Technical Services and Head of Acquisitions at that institution. She has published articles on acquisitions, serials, and resource sharing. She is a member of the Board of Directors of the Association for Library Collections and Technical Services (ALA) and has served on the board of directors and committees of the Resources Section ALCTS. She has enjoyed the privilege of two study leaves in the United Kingdom, based at the College of Librarianship Wales (1981) and at the British Library Document Supply Centre (1989).

Patricia L Bril is currently the Acting Associate University Librarian at California State University, Fullerton, where she was most recently the Collection Development Officer. She has previously held posts responsible for readers' services and bibliographic instruction. She earned a BA in Economics at the University of California, Irvine; an MSLS from the University of Southern California; and an MPA from California State University, Fullerton. She has participated actively in local, national, and international professional associations and has also undertaken several teaching, editorial, and consulting assignments. Her interest in cooperative collection development is a long-standing one which has involved her in Californian cooperative endeavours and which was the subject of her 1989 sabbatical in England.

Ian C Butchart is Chief Librarian at Teesside Polytechnic with managerial responsibilities for the Library Service, Video Production, Graphics Unit and Audiovisual Services. He is a member of the Teesside Polytechnic Steering Group introducing an information skills curriculum as part of the Enterprise for Higher Education Initiative and Vice Chair of the University, College and Research Section of the Library Association. Previous posts include Director of Learning Resources, New College, Durham with responsibility for library, media and computer services and Senior Lecturer at Newcastle Polytechnic, School of Librarianship with particular responsibility for non-book materials in the curriculum. He has written extensively on all aspects of non-book materials in libraries and their educational implications.

Douglas Duchin is currently the Serials/Acquisitions Manager at Baruch College, City University of New York. Previously, he held the position of Vice President, Approval Services, at both Blackwell North America and Yankee Book Peddler. His Master of Library Science degree is from the University of Southern California.

Geoffrey Ford trained as a geologist, but saw the light and became a librarian after graduating. Work as an assistant librarian began to pall, so he switched to research and worked on the PEBUL project, became a systems analyst based in Bristol working on the feasibility study for what became SWALCAP and is now SLS. He moved to Lancaster University Library Research Unit in 1972, and to the Centre for Research on User Studies, where he became Director, in 1976. This butterfly-like progress ceased on his appointment as Sub-Librarian at Southampton University in 1978. After nine years in charge of collection management, and two years as Deputy and head of user services he returned to Bristol as University Librarian in 1990.

Clare Jenkins has been Director of Collection Management at Southampton University Library since 1988. She read French and Spanish at University College, London, where she also obtained her Postgraduate Diploma in Librarianship. Most of her career has been spent in London; she worked in the libraries of University College and Queen Mary College before moving to King's College, where she was Acquisitions Librarian for eight years. Since 1986 she has been a member of the National Acquisitions Group Executive Committee, serving as Education and Training Officer until 1989.

Derek Law is Librarian of King's College London. He spent the first ten years of his career in the Acquisitions and Serials Departments in Glasgow, St Andrews and Edinburgh Universities. In London he has been involved in the merger of the libraries of several institutions and in developing, planning and managing the library of a large multi-faculty college.

Ian Lovecy has been Librarian of the University College of North Wales since 1986, was formerly Deputy Librarian of Reading University and before that UMIST. He is the author of *Automating library procedures: a survivor's handbook*, and has been chairman of the Marc Users' Group and Treasurer of the LA Information Technology Group. Currently he is Chair of the LA Registration Board and a member of the Library and Information Services Council (Wales).

Mary Morley was appointed to the post of Sub-Librarian (Collection Management) at Loughborough University Library in 1989. After reading History at Nottingham University she qualified professionally at the Polytechnic of North London and worked at the National Central Library, Aslib and Nottingham University Library before becoming Acquisitions Librarian at Loughborough in 1975. Previous publishing has been mainly concerned with the development of the National Acquisitions Group with which she has been closely involved since its inception, serving as Secretary from 1986.

J Michael Smethurst has been Director General, British Library, Humanities & Social Sciences since 1986. Prior to his appointment at the British Library, Michael Smethurst was University Librarian of Aberdeen University for 14 years (1972-86); his earlier career included appointments as Deputy Librarian, Glasgow University (1969-72), Librarian of the Institute of Education, University of Newcastle, and Librarian of Bede College, University of Durham. He is a long-serving member of SCONUL Council and was Chairman of SCONUL from 1984 to 1986 and in 1989–90. An ex-President of the Scottish Library Association, he was Chairman of LISC Scotland from its foundation until 1986, and served for many years as a Trustee of the National Library of Scotland. He also served on the various British Library Advisory Committees and the British Library Advisory Council before taking appointment with the British Library. He has written numerous articles in professional journals, and contributions to various books on academic libraries.

Sara Williams is Preservation Librarian at the University at Albany, State University of New York. Prior to this post she held positions in collection management and serials at Kansas State University and at the University of Nebraska, Lincoln. She received her preservation training through a Mellon Foundation internship at the Johns Hopkins University, has published in the areas of serials and preservation and is active in the Preservation of Library Materials Section of the Association for Library Collections and Technical Services (ALA).

Ian Winkworth has been Librarian of Newcastle upon Tyne Polytechnic since 1983. He was previously Deputy Librarian, and before that an Assistant Librarian at Bristol and Leeds University Libraries. He has published and delivered papers on staff management, staff structures, financial management, collection management, library performance evaluation, performance indicators and library cooperation. He is Chairman of the Newcastle Libraries Joint Working Party and was involved between 1987 and 1989 in creating Information North, the innovative library and information development agency. In 1986 he was awarded the Robert Muir Prize by Durham University Business School for his MPhil thesis on the trade unionism of library staff.

Hazel Woodward is Senior Assistant Librarian at the Pilkington Library, Loughborough University. She was Serials Librarian at Loughborough for eight years and is currently in charge of the Information Section, handling literature searching, reference and information enquiries and user education. Hazel has been a member of the UK Serials Group Committee since 1982, serving as Education Officer from 1985-9 and as Chair from 1989. She has contributed many articles and book chapters to the professional literature, and has presented lectures and seminars, both nationally and internationally, on many aspects of serials management.

Helen M Workman has a BSc (Birmingham) and a PhD (Open) in Geography and an MA in Librarianship from the University of Sheffield, 1979. She has held various posts in Sheffield University Library and was appointed Sub-Librarian (Applied Sciences) in 1983. In 1988 she moved to the British Library of Political and Economic Science (the library of the London School of Economics) as Sub-Librarian (Reader Services and Collection Development). She is currently Honorary Secretary of the UK Online Users Group, a special interest group of the Institute of Information Scientists and a member of the SCONUL Advisory Committee on Information Services.

Acknowledgements

We are very grateful to the Librarians of Loughborough and Southampton Universities, Tony Evans and Bernard Naylor, for their support; to colleagues, particularly Jim Burton at Loughborough and Christine Lang at Southampton, for their advice and assistance in producing the manuscript, and Mark Fea for compiling the index; to friends from NAG who helped us to keep things in perspective; and to all our contributors for their professionalism and cooperation which made our editorial tasks relatively painless. Above all we are grateful to our respective families for their patience and forbearance during the time we spent with the book instead of with them.

Introduction

Clare Jenkins and Mary Morley

The fundamental importance to academic libraries of their stock is self-evident; it follows that the effective management of that stock is equally important. It is thus somewhat surprising that there is very little UK professional literature on collection management as a whole, although there is a considerable amount dealing with its constituent activities. The present volume is intended to address this omission by treating the subject from the viewpoint of the academic library manager: the approach is an overview, concentrating on what are seen as current issues and concerns in the area of collection management. While acquisitions, audiovisual, reader services, and serials librarians, among others, should find much applicable to their work, the main audience is assumed to be library managers and library and information science students.

The volume assembles contributions from university and polytechnic librarians, together with perspectives from library supply and the British Library. Several of the contributors are North American, reflecting the editors' perception that US academic libraries have moved further, and more rapidly, along the road towards coordinated collection management than have their British counterparts, and that US experience should be valuable to UK librarians. Equally the experience of UK librarians in meeting challenges posed by economic constraints may benefit colleagues elsewhere.

It is probably fair to say that the term 'collection management' is still establishing itself within the profession. There has been a tendency for practitioners to use 'collection development' and 'collection management' synonymously, although increasingly a distinction is being made between them, and a change of emphasis can be seen in the (mostly American) professional literature away from a former concentration on collection development activities towards collection management. Collection development is perceived as a concept more appropriate to earlier times of expansion in higher education and academic libraries: it implies building and growing, dealing with the selection and acquisition of library materials. Collection management is a more demanding concept, which goes beyond a policy of acquiring materials, to policies on the housing, preservation and storage, weeding and discard of stock. Rather than selection and acquisition, collection management emphasizes the systematic maintenance and management of a library's existing collection: 'the systematic management of the planning, composition, funding, evaluation and use of library collections over extended periods of time, in order to meet specific institutional objectives.'[1] There is, however, at least one example in the recent literature of a different distinction being drawn between the two.[2] The concepts of collection development and collection management, and their history, are further discussed in Chapter 1.

A recent literature search retrieved fewer than fifteen references published since 1980 which contained the term 'collection management' in conjunction with 'academic libraries'. Of these, all but two deal with specific aspects of collection management, and all were published in the US: as already stated, there have been few UK contributions to the professional literature on collection management as a whole. Workman in Chapter 6 reports a similar experience when searching *Library and information science abstracts* (LISA); and Bloomfield observed of collection management at a meeting in 1988: 'that British librarians have an amiable distrust for this type of activity is obvious from an almost complete lack of publication on the subject in the UK.'[3] Yet as early as the 1950s, McClellan[4] was developing systematic bookstock management techniques in the public library context, and collection management, under the guise of stock control, stock management or stock editing, has been a feature of public librarianship in the UK since that time.[5,6]

It is usually held that, to be effective, collection management must be based on an agreed, regularly reviewed collection development policy, formulated after an assessment of user needs and an evaluation of the existing collection. Other aspects seen to contribute to successful collection management are: a senior member of staff having library-wide collection management responsibilities; priority being given to liaison with academic staff and other library users over stock selection and revision; the involvement of professional librarians in these processes; an ongoing programme of collection maintenance – preservation, weeding, relegation and discard – based on agreed written guidelines; library coordination of the materials budget; and planning for cooperation and resource sharing.

In accordance with this view, the premise of this volume is that the management of academic library collections properly consists not of a series of discrete tasks, but of a coordinated programme pervading all areas of the library, which necessarily concerns all academic librarians. The contributions deliberately begin with three chapters on the context of academic library collection management: Law on organization and staffing; Ford on financial management and budgeting; and Winkworth on performance measurement. The themes of these chapters reflect the basic realities and political imperatives under which collection managers currently operate, and receive appropriately thorough treatment. Subsequent chapters discuss specific aspects of collection management, or the implications of managing particular types of material in academic libraries. Serials, for example, although implicitly included by all contributors as part of the totality of the collection to be managed, are also the subject of a separate chapter, by Woodward, to underline the fact that effective collection management involves managing the whole of the library's stock, not just the monographic collections. Similarly, there is a chapter by Butchart dealing with the specific concerns of managing collections of non-book materials.

Current concerns and constraints

Continuing economic constraints, together with such factors as lack of space, curriculum changes, research selectivity, the expansion of higher education, the 'information explosion' and the growth of new information media, lead to higher priority being accorded to planned and coordinated collection management and stock revision than used to be the case. At the same time there has been a move away from an emphasis on building local collections to providing a range of services to users, including access to remote sources of information.

Economic constraints

The economic constraints under which academic libraries have operated for the past decade – and still operate – are too familiar to need much discussion here, and form the background to all the following chapters. Most readers will have experienced the cuts in funding which lead to shrinking bookfunds, fewer staff and insufficient space, together with the difficulties caused by the prices of academic books and serials rising faster than the general inflation rate. In addition, librarians have to face the problems inherent in an ever greater output of publications and the increasing availability of alternative – and usually expensive – electronic information sources. Access to external databases on-line or on CD-ROM is very attractive to library users: the librarian has to decide to what extent such access can be provided – provision which can often be made only from the bookfund.

Accountability and performance measurement

As the purchasing power of academic library budgets decreases, demands for library accountability increase. Academic librarians today are under great pressure to ensure that the financial resources available to them are spent effectively, and to be able to demonstrate effectiveness, efficiency and value for money to their user communities and funding bodies. It is, indeed, 'not an unreasonable requirement that we justify our needs, know what it is we are hoping to accomplish, understand our use patterns, and know what percentage of use we are capable of filling with a given amount of funding'.[7]

Furthermore, government pressure on higher education institutions for greater coordination and rationalization of course provision, leading as it does to mergers of institutions, the closure of departments, the transfer of departments to other institutions and changes to courses offered, has resulted in the introduction of formal monitoring and review procedures. These apply to academic libraries and other central services as well as to academic departments: with the advent of unit costing and bidding for contracts to teach students, the costs of library provision need to be known. In the newly competitive, market-driven environment performance measurement can be vital in ensuring the allocation of adequate resources to the library, an aspect of contemporary library management covered in detail by Winkworth.

New technology

That new technology has had a significant impact on library operations is indisputable, and Lovecy's chapter is by no means the only one in this book to refer to the effect of automation on collection management activities. Automated housekeeping procedures enable librarians to manage daily routines more efficiently, while providing them with detailed and specific management information on library stock and the use made of it, which can be used to assist in the decision-making process and for performance monitoring.

The perceived shift of emphasis in academic libraries from acquisition to access has come about not only in response to economic constraints but, perhaps more significantly, through the availability of an ever increasing number of external databases, including the catalogues of many academic libraries, via JANET and other networks. It seems inevitable that this trend will eventually lead to a broadening of collection management responsibilities to include interlibrary loans, on-line searching and electronic document delivery – areas of the library service which, in the academic sector at least, have tended until now to fall within the remit of those responsible for reader services, an issue addressed by Law in Chapter 1.

In addition to the on-line bibliographic databases, some, such as *BOOKBANK, Books in print*, and *BNB* are now available on CD-ROM. A considerable impetus has been given to collection development activity through the facility to search these tools by subject terms or keywords, and to download the results of such searches into the library's integrated system for other collection management applications. The services marketed by Book Data take this enhanced subject approach a stage further, by offering an abstract of each title included on the database, together with scope notes about potential readership. Detail of the impact that these and similar databases are having on library practice is given by Lovecy in Chapter 4.

New technology has also had an effect on the interaction between the library and the library supplier. As well as enabling libraries to evaluate suppliers' performance more easily, automation, coupled with competition for business, has resulted in an increasing range of services being offered to libraries by suppliers. These services include the supply of information about books, or books on approval, in accordance with subject profiles established for individual libraries; the provision of on-line access to suppliers' potential requirements files, giving details of books yet to be published; and regular data on outstanding orders and on book and journal pricing trends. The contributions from Lovecy and Duchin both cover this aspect of automation.

Library users

There is a recognition in academic libraries, reflected in the chapter by Workman in this volume, of the importance of the library user, and an awareness of the necessity to give attention to the way in which library collections and services are presented and promoted to users and parent institutions. In an environment where institutions expect libraries to be able to justify the level of funding they request, and to be able to demonstrate that their resources are allocated to the best advantage of the institution and its members, it is obvious that the library must attend to the image it projects to its users. Effective presentation and public relations should stimulate use of the collections and encourage feedback from library users, with a view both to improving the collections and gaining support for the library among the academic community. Lovecy's chapter includes further discussion of these points.

An important reason for maintaining close contact with users is the necessity for the library to respond effectively to changing curriculum and research needs. As higher education institutions are increasingly exposed to market forces and competition for students, the changing academic climate means that existing courses are subject to critical review, and new courses are introduced in response to demand. The demographic downturn, too, leads institutions to reinvigorate existing courses and develop new ones, with the intention of increasing the number of those who participate in higher education by attracting students from all sections of the population. Winkworth makes the point that students can now be seen as consumers, rather than 'probationary members of an academic elite, who must gratefully accept what they are given'. The difficulty for most academic libraries is how to accommodate the library stock implications of major course innovations without extra funding: unless reductions can be made in other areas of library spending it may be necessary to choose between providing a range of titles, or multiple copies of fewer textbooks.

In universities, research performance and output have assumed major importance as measures of academic excellence and institutional status. The Universities Funding Council (UFC) policy on research funding and selectivity makes it essential for universities to try to attract research income and improve their output of research publications. Both trends increase pressure on libraries to provide additional serial titles and research monographs. Demand for on-line literature searches also rises as research projects proliferate, as does demand for interlibrary loans. In the longer term, if scholarly publication is to become one of the main measures of performance for academic departments, there will be an even greater increase in published output, which in turn will lead to yet more demands on an ever shrinking bookfund. All these factors have obvious implications for collection managers in their resource allocation decisions.

The current expansion of student numbers in the wake of the lifting of restrictions on the recruitment of additional home students, together with the concern to provide access to higher education for non-traditional students and the modularization of courses, also lead to library collection management problems. The proliferation of course modules and their availability across departmental boundaries results in pressure for increased levels of textbook provision. Furthermore, part-time students, who are a growing percentage of student populations, may need significant numbers of additional copies of texts to be purchased since they often cannot comply with the circulation regulations of short-loan collections. Workman discusses the requirements of part-time students, and the implications for library bookstock, opening hours and lending policies.

If an academic library's collections are to satisfy the teaching and research needs of its users, it is essential that there is close liaison between librarians and academic staff over stock selection and revision. There needs to be effective communication between the library and its users, so that the library has up-to-date knowledge of their subject interests, and is able to make informed materials-selection and service-provision decisions to support the institution's teaching and research. Users can then be confident that their interests drive the library's collection management policies and practice. The library has also to take user needs into account in the exploitation of its stock, maximizing its accessibility by consistent cataloguing and classification practice and the provision of high quality reader services. These areas are covered by Workman, and liaison between library and users receives some attention from Law.

Collection evaluation

It is assumed that effective collection development and collection management policies need to be based on an understanding of the strengths and weaknesses of the current library stock, and an assessment of how well it meets the needs of its present and potential users. Evaluation necessarily involves professional judgement, but subjectivity can be reduced by using a combination of collection- and user-centred measurement techniques and objective data. Collection-centred measures include size, growth, and quality as compared with external standards. User-centred techniques measure the utility of the collection: examples are surveys of user opinion, availability and accessibility measures and circulation statistics. There is an extensive literature on library user and use studies, much of it stressing their difficulty, cost, and labour-intensive nature – with in-library use in particular being notoriously difficult to measure. Nevertheless, such studies can be valuable in enhancing understanding of library collections and how they are used.

Much has also been written recently about the RLG Conspectus, and the adoption and adaptation of its techniques by librarians as a method of codifying descriptions of the strengths of their existing collections and the level of current collecting activity in each subject area. In this volume, Conspectus is discussed in some detail by Bril, Bloomfield and Smethurst, and Lovecy.

Collection development policies

In today's economic climate underfunded academic libraries have to maintain a balance between the provision of learning and research materials; between books and periodicals, print and media; and between current needs and the responsibility – beginning to be questioned by some librarians – to develop collections to meet future requirements. The formulation and production of a collection development policy document is often recommended as a prerequisite for successfully coping with these issues, and is an area to which Law devotes attention in Chapter 1.

Preparation and review of a written policy should also encourage the library and institution to define or refine their goals, and help the library collection to conform to the aims and objectives of the institution and of the library, by translating those aims and objectives into clear and specific guidelines for each stage of materials handling – selection, acquisition, processing, housing, weeding, retention, preservation, relegation and discard. These guidelines should cover all subject fields and all types of library material.

For library staff involved in collection development and stock revision, an agreed policy helps to set quality standards for the inclusion and exclusion of materials and to minimize personal bias while improving consistency in selection and revision practice. It also serves as a good in-service training tool for new staff and helps ensure continuity. Furthermore, written guidelines contribute to operating efficiency in so far as many routine decisions can be made once and for all and need not be considered every time they arise.

A further important benefit is that a policy document can promote improved communication between the library, its users and institutional administrators: librarians gain a better understanding of courses and research, and therefore of the materials they should be acquiring; academic staff are made aware of the library's collecting plans and the constraints under which the library operates. Such a document is also useful as a means of establishing priorities and providing rationale when funding is sought, and in assisting forward planning and budget allocation. Regular review of the document is essential.

Budgeting and fund allocation

The ways in which academic library bookfunds are allocated vary widely. Some are divided into an amount of money for each academic department's library needs, with or without a significant amount being retained by the library; others are divided notionally between subjects, or subject groups, with total control resting with the library. Where funds are allocated to departments, a variety of formulae has been evolved in an attempt to find an equitable method of distributing insufficient funds. The whole area of library budgeting and resource allocation, of fundamental importance to collection management, is comprehensively covered by Ford in Chapter 2.

Technical processes, access and exploitation

An important aspect of collection management practice is ensuring that once materials have been selected, those materials are obtained, processed and made available to the library's users as efficiently and effectively as possible. Thus suppliers should be chosen on the basis of promised performance and services, and their subsequent performance monitored – Duchin considers this in his discussion of acquisition processes, which also deals with the benefits of approval plans as a means of acquiring stock. It cannot be over-emphasized, too, that however carefully and competently materials are selected and acquired the user is not well served if library processes then make it difficult to identify and locate those materials.

In this volume the reader will find little discussion of technical processes, which are well covered elsewhere in the literature. Nevertheless, it should not be assumed that high-quality and consistent cataloguing and classification are seen as less than essential. Good bibliographical control is taken for granted in the succeeding chapters, the editors believing that the automation of traditional library processes, the advent of integrated library systems and bought-in bibliographic records have begun to influence the organization of cataloguing operations in a way that leaves librarians more time to concentrate on other collection management activities. Equally important are the housing, arrangement and exploitation of stock, and lending policies – these matters receive some attention from Workman.

Weeding, preservation, disaster planning

During the years of expansion in higher education in the 1960s and early 1970s there were few pressures on academic libraries to weed or revise stock. In 1976 the Atkinson report proposed the principle of a 'self-renewing library of limited growth',[8] but was much criticized by librarians for advocating a crude measure to deal with a complex problem. Even today, few UK academic libraries appear to practise planned and coordinated weeding of their stock: library procedures tend to be designed to facilitate the acquisition rather than withdrawal of material, which seems most commonly to take place in response to shelf- space crises. There are, of course, other reasons for weeding stock: to remove outdated material, thus enhancing the browsability of the collection and ensuring its continued usefulness, and to take account of changes in, for example, institutional teaching and research interests.   .

As the needs of teaching and research change, and additional library shelf space becomes more difficult to obtain, planned and coordinated stock revision must inevitably receive higher priority than has been the case in UK academic libraries. The experience of academic libraries in America, reported by Bonk and Williams in Chapter 9, is obviously relevant.

Guidelines for weeding collections have to embrace various aspects. For example, what subjects and what sort of material on those subjects should be retained on the shelves, for how long and in how many copies? What should be relegated to remote storage or discarded? To what extent should superseded or revised editions be kept or discarded? Criteria include: publication date, acquisition date, physical condition, circulation history and professional judgement. The application of mechanical criteria becomes much easier for libraries with automated systems, where management information relevant to decisions on stock revision is, in general, readily available; the application of professional judgement tends to be more time-consuming, and, unless exercised with tact, may lead to strained relations between the library and the academic community. There can be considerable advantages in working with academics on stock revision, to which librarians bring knowledge of the collections, and academic staff contribute subject expertise. Also, academic staff involvement in weeding programmes can help overcome the political problems that such programmes sometimes encounter. However, the time and costs involved in such ventures, collaborative or otherwise, should not be underestimated, as Law points out in his comments on the question of stock relegation and disposal in Chapter 1. Bonk and Williams refer to the 'time-consuming nature of collection review', and speculate that this may be a contributory factor to the relative lack of new studies of review methodology appearing in the literature.

The question of preservation also receives some attention from Bonk and Williams in Chapter 9. The development of systematic preservation programmes is, again, one which seems to have progressed more rapidly in the US than in the UK. As with other areas of collection management, there are economic implications which cannot be ignored. For many libraries, such preservation as can be afforded is funded from the general binding fund, with obvious disadvantages; the lion's share of the allocation almost inevitably goes to the binding of current journals, and it is difficult for librarians faced with budgetary cuts to resist the temptation to axe the binding allocation more savagely than other areas of library expenditure. Libraries with written collection development policies may find it easier to achieve some measure of balance in this respect: as mentioned earlier, such policies should provide clear guidelines not only on what material the library should be acquiring, but also on the retention and preservation of that material.

Disaster planning, although not covered in this book, is a related topic. The word 'disaster' in this context is used by archivists and librarians 'to describe an unexpected event with destructive consequences to their holdings', the intention being that the disaster plan should lay down procedures for disaster prevention or reaction. It may be advantageous to develop a disaster plan on a basis of regional cooperation, with the local public library authority, or archive and record offices for example, so that expertise can be shared and a wider pool of people with the necessary skills drawn on, in a situation where speed may be critical if damage to the collections is to be kept to a minimum. For those unfamiliar with the subject, a useful publication by Anderson and McIntyre[1] provides a good starting point for the preparation of a disaster plan for the library.

Cooperation and resource sharing

An inevitable consequence of economic restrictions on the growth of library collections, of shortage of space and the inability of library budgets to keep pace with the publishing output and demands for expensive new information resources, is the exploration of possibilities for cooperation and resource sharing between libraries. There has not been a great deal of progress in this area in the UK, where the unwillingness of academic library users to travel to other libraries or to rely more heavily on interlibrary lending services tends to hamper the development of cooperative ventures. Local availability of material is still much preferred. Bloomfield and Smethurst, Law and Lovecy – library automation being another impetus – all address the issues of cooperation and resource sharing in the present volume. In contrast to UK experience, there have been a number of successful cooperative initiatives in the US, which are described in detail by Bril and will be of considerable interest to many collection managers.

Organization and staffing

The organization of collection management operations in academic libraries – and the extent to which coordinated policies are prepared and implemented – is obviously governed by available staffing and financial resources, but it is also dependent upon the priority accorded to it by the library management. Writers in this area emphasize the importance of central coordination and planning at a senior level in the library, if collection management tasks are not to be neglected as peripheral to the main activities of individual members of staff. There is a continuing debate in the professional literature about the rival merits of technical services-based and public services-based organization. The former model utilizes the skills of acquisitions staff and bibliographers; the second draws on the knowledge reader services librarians acquire of the quality of the collection and the information needs of library users. A related debate centres on the relative advantages of subject specialization and functionally organized academic libraries – the problem of fitting collection management duties in with the primary responsibilities of library staff being particularly acute in functionally organized libraries. Law rehearses the arguments for and against various organizational models in Chapter 1.

Conclusions

The all-embracing nature of collection management makes a degree of overlap between the following chapters inevitable. Many aspects are discussed by several contributors, their different viewpoints offering a valuable range of approaches and interpretations, but all underlining the importance of planned and coordinated collection management in academic libraries today.

A fundamental point not stressed in the book is that a knowledge and understanding of the production and supply of library materials, including an appreciation of the intricacies of publishing and distribution, are essential to effective collection management. Professional education and training in this area, however – at least in the UK – still seem to leave something to be desired, despite the efforts of such groups as the Library Association, the National Acquisitions Group, and the UK Serials Group. Very few library school courses appear to cover collection management or the book trade in detail: it will be interesting to see what influence Line's research, into the need for a common curriculum for people working in the book and information world, has on future development.[10]

As collection managers ourselves, it has been encouraging, while editing this volume, to learn of the various ways in which other library managers are successfully meeting current challenges, and reassuring to be reminded yet again that one's difficulties and problems are not unique. Studying and implementing the lessons derived from experience and research elsewhere may render those of us who are active in collection management in academic libraries better equipped to face present and future challenges in our own institutions.

References

1. Cogswell, J.A. (1987), 'The organization of collection management functions in academic research libraries', *Journal of Academic Librarianship*, **13** (5), p.269.
2. Brindley, L. (1988), Summing up in S. Corrall (ed.), *Collection development: options for effective management*, London: Taylor Graham, p.142.
3. Bloomfield, B.C. (1989), 'How can collection development and management be most effectively organized and staffed?', in *Collections: their development, management, preservation and sharing. Papers from the joint meeting of the Association of Research Librarie and the Standing Conference of National and University Libraries, University of York September 19-22, 1988,* Washington: Association of Research Libraries.
4. McClellan, A.W. (1978), *The logistics of a public library bookstock*, London: Association of Assistant Librarians.
5. Moore, N. (1983), 'Systematic bookstock management in public libraries,' *Journal of Librarianship*, **15**, (4), 262-276.
6. Astin, J. (1982), 'Cheshire: alternative arrangements and beyond' in P. Ainley and B. Totterdell (eds), *Alternative arrangement: new approaches to public library stock*, London: Association of Assistant Librarians.
7. Hitchcock-Mort, K. (1985), 'Collection management in the eighties – where are we now?', *Library acquisitions practice and theory*, **9**, p.8.
8. University Grants Committee (1976), *Capital provision for university libraries: report of a working party* [Chairman: Professor R. Atkinson], London: HMSO.
9. Anderson, H. and J.E. McIntyre (1985), *Planning manual for disaster control in Scottish libraries and record offices*, Edinburgh: National Library of Scotland.
10. Line, M.B. (1990), *Education and training for the book and information world*, London: British Library, (BNBRF report, 45).

1   The organization of collection management in academic libraries

Derek Law

There is no agreed usage for the terms collection development and collection management – in fact the two are used as rather loose synonyms. However, reflection would demonstrate that they do imply different concepts and some distinction is a necessary preamble to any discussion. Collection development relates to the selection and acquisition of material for an expanding collection and decisions on the material to be included in that collection. Collection management may subsume this, but also includes the allocation of the bookfund and the balance between books, journals and conservation; the disposition of stock between open and closed access, between different media and between branches of the library and stores; and, finally, the monitoring and encouragement of collection use. In sum, collection management also includes issues concerned with conservation and disposal, and is aimed more at the presentation of the collection to the user than at the collection itself. It should be clear from this wide definition of collection management that a variety of types of staff will be involved in different ways and at different times. As with all library activities there is no 'right' or 'wrong' way to manage the activity. The library must decide the importance it attaches to the management of its collections and then deploy staff and other resources in the light of local needs and opportunities.

Before considering staffing structures it is necessary to look at the activities undertaken by the library in managing its collections and at the pressures which bear on them. Some of this touches inevitably on the themes developed in other chapters. This chapter will consider the organization and staffing of the various operations within collection management, relationships with academic staff and departments, and where collection management sits as an activity within the organization and in relation to other organizations. Although the divisions are far from watertight, for ease of consideration, the activities will be considered under four heads:

- collection development;
- collection evaluation;
- stock relegation and disposal;
- staff structure.

Collection development

The growth of library collections throughout the expansionist years of the 1960s and early 1970s was spectacular and can largely be attributed to those staff called subject specialists. Libraries appointed staff, in effect as bibliographers, whose role was principally that of guiding the expansion of the collections rather than serving the needs of the majority of readers, although in some libraries there was a real attempt to marry the two activities in one individual member of staff. The end of this era was signalled by the much execrated Atkinson report,[1] but it has taken a further decade of retrenchment and staff losses before the concept of the subject specialist has been brought seriously into question again. Woodhead and Martin[2] conducted a survey which suggested that we may have reached (and now passed) 'the high water mark of subject specialization in British university libraries'. This seems more than likely to be the case. The challenges facing libraries have been changing in the last decade, and it is not obvious that a set of staffing structures devised to cope with the problems and needs of a period of growth in collections and indeed in universities are necessarily the same as those required for a period of contraction, moderated by the growth of technologies which increasingly allow readier access to material and information from outside the collection.

Subject specialists

Subject specialists tend to have highly developed territorial instincts expressed as 'my faculty' or 'my subject' and a much less developed view of the library collections as a whole. Now that possession of information is no longer synonymous with its provision, library managers must increasingly take this into account in developing staffing structures. It will be increasingly important for library staff to possess the technical competencies to access information elsewhere rather than acquire it locally. Advocates of the system of subject specialists also argue that it has been an important element in recruiting high-quality staff, but changes in the ways in which libraries control and manage information may have begun to make functionally organized structures attractive again to good and ambitious staff, who will wish to have information management rather than subject skills. This whole process of the erosion of subject-specialist posts is also perhaps being hastened by the retirement (often regrettably early) of that cohort of staff appointed in the Robbins era of the early 1960s, their posts then being frozen or downgraded.

Even within functional structures it is probably desirable that a sort of hybrid system operates. Matrix management is a fashionable but useful tool which allows staff to perform a variety of tasks without the rigidity and inflexibility of the extreme versions of functional or subject-based organization. It would be a foolish chief librarian who did not take some account of the need for a spread of language and subject skills amongst library staff and, having obtained such subject skills, deploy them to best effect. This can be seen in the area of collection development, where input from library staff who have developed subject knowledge can both originate book recommendations and moderate the aspirations of over-zealous academic staff.

It is also important to consider the role of the acquisitions staff. An acquisitions department with a relatively stable staff possibly has the best overall impression of the way in which collections are developing and the balance obtaining between subject areas. Yet all too often they are employed in a purely technical role as a channel between library and bookseller. To use the acquisitions staff as gatekeepers with an active role in collection development takes full advantage of the expertise they have built up.

Liaison with academic staff

Under most organizational structures there is a member of academic staff within each academic department who is nominated to act as liaison with the library. This practice explains much of the almost whimsical growth of so many library collections. Some of these individuals treat their role very seriously, others see it as an administrative chore; sometimes it is a task for the most junior member of departmental staff and sometimes a senior lecturer. If done well it can play a crucial role in opening a dialogue with the library on how a collection can be expanded. A good relationship with library staff usually ensures that a department will succeed in squeezing out more than its fair share of any spare funds, thus further enhancing both the collections and the relationship. Indeed such departments will often add their own funds to the library grant to expand the collections. Conversely, every institution has its bad departments where no act seems capable of awakening interest in the library. Naturally, such departments tend to be neglected and their collections stultify.

The precise nature of the relationship with academic staff requires careful attention. One of the longest-standing debates in managing collection development is over their involvement. In 1935 Agnes Cuming, then Librarian of the University of Hull, wrote to the Librarian of King's College London that [the teaching staff] 'so often make demands the consequences of which they do not realise and then their last state is worse than their first.'[3] In a paper given at the Newbury Seminar on bibliographic needs, Peasgood produced some firm indicative evidence that academic staff were no better at book selection than library staff.[4] His evidence relates to monographs, but the same view is expressed in relation to journals with less evidence and more cynicism by Broude:

> Though a faculty member may insist that a certain title is crucial to the library, if a librarian can indicate that the journal has no use, is very expensive, is little-related to the curriculum, is unindexed, is available at a nearby library, is never cited by other published articles and is published by an organization with a poor reputation, then at least he has established the basis for a rational discussion about the merits of the journal.[5]

Budgetary allocation

An often unregarded aspect of collection management is budgetary allocation. In most institutions this has broadly reflected the historical strength of different powerbases within the institution, although often masquerading in the gaudy but unconvincing dress of an objective formula. The pursuit of an objective formula for the allocation of bookfunds has been a sort of Holy Grail (more often of library committees than librarians), pursued relentlessly but ultimately fruitlessly. Too many factors conspire to prevent a great truth emerging. Most librarians have compounded this folly by examining cash rather than resources. A budget may be divided more or less equitably, but it can pass more or less unnoticed that a member of staff spends large quantities of time soliciting and then processing gifts in favour of a particular subject. That is not to criticize such initiative, but to note that it is almost universally omitted from any budgetary equation. The whole issue of resource management is considered further in Chapter 2. Another important element in this area is the view which is taken of the library budget. Is it a grant which is allocated to departments to spend, or is it a grant to the library which then seeks advice on how to spend its money wisely? Only if the latter view is adopted can library staff take an active role in collection development.

Collection development policies

The position becomes increasingly complicated with each year that passes and each circular that appears from the Universities Funding Council(UFC). It is now required of libraries by the UFC that they indicate how funds are being applied selectively. This can hardly be done by chance and will require a set of policy decisions. Bloomfield has stressed the importance of collection development policies.[6] Whereas in the past these may have appeared to develop naturally from the work of the subject librarians striving to expand the collections in almost all areas of knowledge, they are now highly charged political issues and inevitably the province of the most senior library management. Issues of resource sharing, which might appear to offer a substitute for a library's own collections, have implications well beyond the narrow boundaries of library efficiency. For a library to declare its intention (as it will increasingly be required to do) to cut back research provision in a subject can, and will, be read as making a statement about academic priorities within the institution. To decide whether the library's mission is synonymous with that of the institution and if not, where and how it should differ, requires a wide perspective which is inevitably found only at the apex of an organization.

Written collection development policies have found much less favour in the UK than in other countries, but the external influences described above may well force a reconsideration of their value. The creation of a written statement of this sort should force the staff involved in its preparation to consider the goals of the organization, both long- and short-term, and the priorities to be attached to different activities. The prevailing view that libraries are, in the main, moving from holdings to access strategies perhaps implies that there will be a need to disseminate information on collecting policies widely. Further, as the generation of staff which has largely built the university collections of today begins to retire, management will perceive the need to record their collecting policies in order to ensure the continuity of collection development independently of the individuals concerned. All higher education institutions are increasingly faced with the discipline of formal planning of all aspects of their activities. It is probably inescapable and perhaps desirable that their libraries will undergo the same process. To state, at least in broad terms, what is to be purchased, what is to be kept and preserved and what disposed of will be a requirement, primarily of the institution and perhaps of the UFC.

Even in the harshest funding climates of recent years there has been in most libraries a vague notion of the equal distribution of resources, however inadequate. This will change, at least at the research level. If funds and collections are to be skewed in their distribution, this will have to be made clear. Gorman[7] sees written policies as contracts between libraries and their users and this useful concept is a way of demonstrating to individuals within an institution precisely what they can expect of the library. Such documents will have little value if seen as once-and-for-all exercises, but if they fall within the planning cycle of the institution, this should ensure that they are regularly and sensibly updated as the needs and priorities of the institution develop. One of the major criticisms of such written collection-policy statements in the past has been their inflexibility. They have been seen as time-consuming and monolithic and libraries are perceived as doing quite well without them.[8] Such static documents certainly exist, but the need for a perhaps less specific rolling planning document may give the desired flexibility which the library – and increasingly the institution – require. It should be stressed that such a policy statement is not a substitute for book selection, whether for acquisition or withdrawal; it is a framework and set of parameters within which staff and readers can work.

The classic view of the development of such policies assumes a committee mainly of library staff, but including academic members of the library committee and perhaps administrators, to ensure a broad consensus and support for the final document. In the harsher world of research ratings and bids for student numbers, it is much more likely that the policy will be a fairly straightforward reflection of the research priorities of the organization as expressed in its institutional plan. Any deviation from that implies a political decision which is unlikely to be taken except at the most senior levels of management. There has been a tendency to recognize this in the appointment of collection-development managers operating at the sub-librarian or deputy-librarian level. Such staff will have a critical role in assembling the evidence to assess the present strengths of the collection and options for sensible collection building. However, even when such a collection policy is seen as a consequence of other documents rather than a free-standing statement in its own right, there is a need to discuss drafts of the document as widely as possible within the institution, especially with groups of users. There may be very little room for manoeuvre in collection policy once it becomes a small building block of an institutional plan, but users still have a right to be heard and considered, and to be kept fully informed of what they may expect from the library in the form of both collections and services.

Equally, if a collection is to be developed beyond the teaching support level within a subject, it would be foolish not to take the advice of academic staff on where emphasis should be placed. It is then the task of the library staff and ultimately the library committee to weld these different special interests into a coherent whole and match grand ambitions with available funds. If such a document is brief and concentrates on the bare bones of subjects, it will allow maximum flexibility within which those responsible for book selection can work and will free the institution from a major review exercise every time a change becomes necessary. Recent developments in practice make it easy to distinguish between such a policy document and the older, fuller type of document which is much closer to a sort of proto-Conspectus exercise.

Resource sharing

The notion of resource sharing cannot really be undertaken until some such framework exists. Administrators will take it almost for granted that library cooperation is entirely logical. Usually this view stems from a belief that such cooperation will result in economy. Long experience in libraries in the UK shows that cooperation is indeed desirable and beneficial, and that there is a string of successes ranging from LASER to SWALCAP, from CURL to SALBIN, but also that identifiable financial savings rarely accrue as a result. Benefits tend ultimately to be for library users rather than libraries. As serial prices continue to spiral and budgets to decline in real terms it seems inevitable that there will be an ever-increasing pressure for interdependence and cooperation. In this respect the reports from LISC[9] which developed the themes of access strategies and local information plans have stimulated an active professional debate.

A recently completed study for the British Library Research and Development Department[10] by Pocklington and Finch showed library collections to be less and less able to meet the needs of academic staff. Collections were seen as becoming narrower, more homogeneous and more limited. Worse, collections were in effect becoming fragmented as staff and departments attempted to compensate for reducing library budgets by purchasing necessary material which was then housed in offices and departments. Libraries compound the problem by organizing cooperative purchase arrangements which expect users to travel to other libraries or rely on photocopies. This was seen as a great disincentive for users and risked making research poorer. As libraries increasingly adopt a utilitarian approach, scarcely aiming to do more than meet the needs of current users, collection building was progressively eroded and gaps created which will damage future research.

Progress in telecommunications, the continuing growth of databases as retroconversion proceeds and the emergence of OSI standards which will link systems and facilitate document delivery open up new possibilities for managing library resources and addressing the gloom of the Pocklington and Finch study. At present interlibrary loans constitute a tiny fraction of any library's total loans, but this will change. It is a paradox that the growth of retroconversion and OPACs makes the library's own catalogue less and less important. From the point of view of the users, a book in a nearby library found on a networked OPAC is more accessible than a copy of the same book in their own library's off-campus store which takes forty-eight hours to retrieve. It is unlikely that libraries can properly forego the collection locally of material required to support teaching programmes, but there is great scope for cooperation in the building of research collections. Stam[11] describes libraries 'linked in a great chain of access', whether they like it or not. The British Library collects only a small percentage of the published output of the world each year and it is quite possible to envisage the sort of planning vision which enlightens RLG's Collection Management and Development Program being applied to the research collections of the UK. It aims 'to expand the universe of materials that can be identified and delivered to scholars in a timely fashion.'[12] A consequence of such a pattern of cooperation is that much of the work of book selection will fall on library staff. It is only within the library that decisions can ultimately be made on whether book recommendations fall in or out of the scope of cooperative agreements.

Collection evaluation

The purpose of collection evaluation and monitoring is the straightforward one of establishing whether a collection is doing its job and whether it is doing so in the most cost-effective way. Although the definition is simple, it makes a number of assumptions which need to be explored about the purpose of collections and how their worth is to be assessed. The simplest aim is, of course, to satisfy the needs of present users. However, any major academic library will also have some regard for building collections for the future, so that there is not a single uniformly sensitive measure and the library will require to take a complex view of what the job of the collection is and how that can best be judged.

Performance measures

A large debate has opened up on performance measures. It can be characterized as having on one side administrators who are interested only in input measures such as pounds spent per student FTE and on the other librarians who are interested only in output measures such as document retrieval rates. Arguably there are two quite different purposes in such measures. Rightly or wrongly, busy administrators want only a very few measures of library performance and usually these are key statistics which can be compared with those of a similar basket of institutions. Here global figures for the whole library are needed and ones which can assess over time whether the library is meeting institutional goals. These will almost inevitably tend to relate to the institution's budgetary spend on the library. Such figures serve an important political purpose within the institution and it is important that the librarian agrees with the administration what the measures are to be and what targets are being set. For example, it may differ between institutions, and over time, as to whether it is desirable to have a rising or falling figure of pounds spent per student FTE. The major characteristic of administrative decision-makers is their wish not to be forced to make decisions. If they can avoid thinking about the library (or the chemistry department or the animal house) and its problems, they would prefer to do so. Good relations with the administration are worth much more than well-argued and large documents, and one or two judiciously chosen macro-statistics which demonstrate that the administration has no need to worry about the library (assuming that to be the case) are what the administration desires.

Within the library a quite different approach is required to measure library performance and then to take action to change or modify outcomes. Not very surprisingly this requires some view of the purpose of the library and its constituent parts, which will vary between institutions. For example, opening hours can be modified to affect collection use. User needs at a campus university may be for long weekend opening hours, whereas in an inner-city area with no resident population, shorter opening hours and a more efficient but expensive recall and reservation system may have a greater effect on the use of collections. Similarly, the balance between closed and open access, and even on-site and off-site storage, can affect the use of collections. In order to assess which variables to alter, the library must have a clear view of its objectives, which may vary over time and in the light of circumstances. It is the role of any professional to determine what clients really need rather than what they think they need and evaluation of the collection in the broadest sense assists in making those decisions. This theme is explored more fully in Chapter 3.

Staffing

One aspect of library management which affects collection use is the availability of staff to assist the user. Two quite distinct schools of thought exist on this – apart from those libraries which offer no real assistance at all. First come those who see the role of the professional librarian as being to act as the first point of contact for users. This model offers immediate access to intermediaries able to interpret and deal with most difficulties, or to channel them to the appropriate quarter if not. The second model offers non-professional staffing of service points, where all enquiries, other than the most basic ones, are channelled up to those particularly qualified to help. Opponents of the first model[13] see the constant interruptions as a distraction from collection development and argue that if a service is too readily available its providers are undervalued, as is the service itself. Opponents of the second model[14] argue that to present enquiries to the inexperienced is a disservice and inconvenience to readers, especially since the inexperienced staff may not really know where to refer questions. This is seen as misrepresenting the potential of the library. As in most debates there is no simple answer. The notion of readers interrupting staff who have more important things to do may seem risible, but in large libraries those charged with collection development may not be the most appropriate staff to help readers. Conversely, non-professional staff with long years of experience may be better equipped to help readers. It is a mistake to consider 'non-professional' and 'inexperienced' as synonyms. Many factors such as the rate of staff turnover and the ability of individuals to deal with the public will in the end determine the best deployment of staff. However, ultimately the decision will depend on whether the librarian and his staff wish to see the library as having a service or a collection-building ethos. The two are not exclusive, but the way in which staff resources are allocated to the two activities will inevitably determine the quality of services to readers.

Stock relegation and disposal

Weeding and stock relegation are too often seen as an unavoidable chore, put off whenever possible and in some sense diminishing the library. However, it is not necessary to go as far as supporting the concept of the self-renewing library to consider weeding as a positive and desirable method of improving service to readers. Thompson[15] comments that 'the unusable library is more familiar to library users than to librarians. For a start most libraries are far too large for ready consultation.' Too many outdated and unused books can hamper access to those which are in demand; they quite literally clog up the shelves. Perhaps part of the problem lies in the emotive term 'weeding' which implies discarding, when that is in fact only one option.

The long-standing concentration in the UK on open-access libraries has obscured the options of balancing collections between open access, closed access and store, as well as simple disposal. The research activity of continental universities is not noticeably hindered by their tradition of closed-access libraries and yet we have tended to take little notice of their experience and achievements. Deciding what to have easily and readily available and what requires more restricted treatment is part of the librarian's professional responsibility. It can be argued, for example, that, as a simple conservation measure, age should be used as a criterion to relegate material to closed access. In some areas of the collection any library may reasonably expect to have an archival function and the attitude to disposal will be quite different from those areas where the library collects to meet use and current institutional need. Here the only question is when, not whether, stock should be weeded. The selection of material for relegation will almost without exception have to be undertaken title by title, as classic studies conducted at Yale University have shown.[16] This makes the task enormously time-consuming and one which probably has to be undertaken with the cooperation of academic staff – although the librarian's knowledge of who uses the collections, and how, is invaluable in determining overlaps of interest. The Yale study showed that the best method was for library staff to select material for withdrawal and then have academic staff validate the selections. Where pressure on space is acute an additional goad can be used, if necessary, through the requirement to clear a fixed number of metres of shelving in order to accommodate new stock.

Criteria

Ford[17] has defined criteria for weeding stock. These are: use; obsolescence; age; death (applies only to series or serials); physical decay; judgement. All but the last two are susceptible to mechanical judgements based on objective statistical or other evidence. Decay is not quite in this category since the library might choose to arrest or reverse the decay and retain the item, while judgement clearly requires other issues to be considered and may even override the objective criteria.

In assessing these criteria for deselection, there can be a problem where it is assumed that the entirety of the collections is to be treated uniformly. It should be clear that different criteria must be used for different parts of the collections. For example, age may be a reason for relegation from an undergraduate collection, but a reason for retention in a history of science collection. At the extremes, the library either relies on the subject expertise of academic and/or library staff or it uses mechanical criteria such as evidence of use from circulation reports. This becomes increasingly possible with the development of management information systems for library computers, as described in Chapter 4. In the former case, the practicality of persuading several academic staff to reach agreement on withdrawing large numbers of books is quite disproportionately time-consuming. An unpublished study of a weeding exercise at King's College London is perhaps illuminating.[18] The pre-clinical collections, which had not been weeded for some time, were examined by two staff from each of the pre-clinical departments. It required twenty hours of academic and library staff time to identify 360 volumes of outdated multiple copy textbooks – some 5.7 per cent of the open access collection – remove them from the shelves, and amend the catalogue entries. Over 40 per cent of the time involved was academic staff time. To repeat this feat across the whole library, for what is perhaps the easiest material to weed, would require the equivalent of one half-time post at senior lecturer level. Since the largest element of the cost lies in the examination of the stock, the cost increases significantly when the percentage of stock weeded falls.

Who selects material for relegation?

The literature is full of careless use of the notion of involving academic staff, as though their judgement were any more general and objective than any other group of individuals. Except in the very rarest of cases, the way in which academic staff specialize reduces rather than enhances their ability to assist in a general weeding exercise. Perhaps the key for the library is that proposed by Routh,[19] to evaluate the advisers rather than the collections. To use library subject specialists assumes a staff structure decreasingly available to libraries. Conversely, to apply criteria, such as current levels of circulation and use, mechanically, negates a fundamental tenet of academic librarianship, that libraries perform the role of Janus, looking to anticipate and guard the needs of the future as well as relying on the evidence of the past. This becomes a little easier once a library has a collection development policy. Few libraries would now aspire to, far less be in, a position to afford universality of collections. At its crudest it is then possible to define major collecting areas where little or nothing but duplicates will be weeded, and teaching collections where use or obsolescence are valid decision-support criteria. There is a large literature on collection weeding methodologies. The techniques which it describes are many and various, but all have to address the issue of whether the weeding is qualitative or quantitative, using objective criteria.[20]

Possibly the largest and most savage stock editing programmes for many years have taken place within the University of London, where the constituent colleges of the University have spent the last five years undergoing a precipitate and radical process of reorganization and merger. Inevitably, similar libraries have been merged and it has proved desirable to rebalance collections through the elimination of duplication and a redefinition of collecting policy. The sheer scale of these exercises has resulted in a very wide range of staff involvement, from relatively junior – but often very experienced – library assistants to library managers more concerned with political issues than stock details. In some cases the process has been simplified by being confined to the disposal of duplicate stock; in others the process of disengaging the stock relating to a transferring department, without damaging the interests of related departments who may be staying in the institution, has proved fraught. Thus in addition to the issue of selecting particular items of stock, the political process has also produced a set of principles for determining the transfer of stock between institutions, to be used when agreement through negotiation has not proved possible. Ironically, the general experience appears to be that the staff of the two libraries between which the transfer is taking place fairly readily reach agreement on what it is practical and sensible to transfer. The involvement of academic staff almost inevitably, and certainly acrimoniously, leads to the sort of difficulties and recriminations which require the imposition of the principles.[21] It is also often the case that, after a due division of stock, the truly contentious areas which remain concern a few hundred pounds worth of books, some of them available in print and some of which the library would probably have rejected if offered as a gift.

Stock disposal is dangerous ground which can arouse fierce passions. The recent experience of the John Rylands Library of the University of Manchester demonstrates the obloquy which can attach to a major stock-disposal programme, no matter how well intentioned. Every library disposes of stock, sometimes unintentionally through theft or accident, sometimes through the transfer or sale of collections to other institutional libraries, sometimes through weeding. Heaney[22] has stressed the importance of preparing a policy on disposal which is approved at the highest level within the institution, preferably before it becomes an issue, and this is undoubtedly sound advice.

Although there has been a great deal of discussion in the literature of why, whether and how to select material for disposal and of who should undertake the activity, the literature is virtually bare of advice on how to dispose of material which no one questions should go. The evidence of this lack of thought is clear in almost all large libraries, where stores steadily silt up with a mixture of unwanted gifts, unprocessed bequests, withdrawn stock, items transferred from branches suffering from space shortages, material awaiting preservation, and perhaps a few bits of special collections. Edinburgh University Library developed and described a policy for controlling disposal over a decade ago,[23] and its main points are worth repeating. Stock disposal should be assigned firmly to one department and be treated as a core activity. Since it is also a revenue generating activity it should be given adequate resources rather than be seen as a chore and in some libraries it may even prove to be self-financing quite quickly. In Edinburgh's case the responsibility for the work lay in the Acquisitions Department, which in effect bore the library's collection-management responsibilities. A critical element is that the management of the stores must be vested in one place. There is a tendency to treat storage areas as common property, which is why they are rarely well managed. If one section has the responsibility for booking material in and out and for assigning space in appropriate areas of store, it is unlikely that over time the library will find that it possesses miscellaneous collections of books of uncertain status and unknown worth. Edinburgh also felt the need to have an agreed set of policies approved by Library Committee in order to protect staff in what is a sensitive area. The need to dispose of some material unobtrusively is also pointed out. One of the laws of librarianship unmentioned by Ranganathan is that, of any pile of books placed in a skip for disposal, one or more will be returned to the library the next day by someone who thinks that he is preventing a tragedy.

Staff structures

Discussions of the staffing and management of resources for acquisitions are rare in the British professional literature, but less so in North

America. Bloomfield[24] ascribes this to an amiable mistrust of modern management theory. There is certainly little outside the North American literature to act as a guide.

Team approach

Bryant[25] has discussed some of the difficulties with the team approach to collection management. There is a major problem in managing personnel who support different subject disciplines, for although the tasks performed are common, assessing productivity is a much more difficult exercise. Yet such issues have to be addressed if there is to be an equitable distribution of the workload. It is also important to determine priorities for the whole collection management team and not leave these to the independent and differing judgements of a series of individuals, leading to fairly anarchic management of the collections. Further, the goals and targets which are set must be attainable or morale can suffer. Woodhead[26] cites the possibly typical subject specialist at the University of Leeds who felt that 'fulfilment of all the duties was an ideal impossible to attain owing to lack of time'. This is a common complaint and Bryant[27] pinpoints the lack of clear evidence on how much time libraries either do or should spend on collection management – this despite the voluminous American literature – and argues that collection development staff must be more assertive in raising the topic through professional organizations and professional literature. She is not in favour of matrix management structures, which are seen as a response to shrinking library staffs rather than a positive attempt to manage the collections more effectively. If the enthusiasm to raise the profile of collection management through the creation of both a theoretical and a practical base for discussion is laudable, the criticism of this style of staff structure seems needlessly prescriptive. No structure can be said to have emerged as normal or even desirable in North America. A survey of seventy members of the Association of Research Libraries[28] describes collection development as an 'organizational step-child' with almost as many structures as libraries surveyed, but with a growing perception of the importance of collection management, usually associated with the allocation of responsibility for collection management at a senior level.

Collection management must not be viewed as a series of narrowly defined and isolated tasks which are the preserve of subject specialists. It has become increasingly pervasive of all library activities and will increasingly demand involvement from all professional staff. Many tasks make up the activity: planning and policy development; collection analysis; materials selection; collection maintenance, including both weeding and preservation activity; budgetary management; liaison with users; resource sharing; appraisal of results.[29] Although many staffing patterns have emerged in North America there are perhaps fewer options for British academic libraries. Smaller libraries, smaller budgets and smaller staffs will almost inevitably prevent a clear division of labour and require staff to be more versatile in their range of duties.

Creth[30] describes a model which avoids the two extremes of subject specialization and a purely functional organization described earlier. She cites Drucker[31] who analyses functional organizations. Their great strength lies in stability, clarity and a high degree of economy. Over time this turns to rigidity, lack of communication between functions and growing inefficiency.

Functional approach

The functional approach involves arranging the work in stages and moving the work to where the staff with the appropriate skills are. This is essentially to treat the work as a sort of assembly line product and in research libraries that is a reasonable model of how many systems operate. Even in reader services where there is not such a visible product as in technical services, departments tend to operate in vertical structures with insufficient communication between groups. Drucker argues that, nevertheless, such a structure can work in small organizations in a stable environment. Creth points out that neither of these conditions obtains at present in higher education and research libraries.

Subject specialization

Subject specialization in its purest form assigns to an individual member of staff, usually with relevant subject knowledge, all the library tasks associated with a particular subject area, but with more routine tasks performed by junior assistants. Book selection, budget control, reader instruction, departmental liaison and teaching, reference work and collection management fall to an individual. This structure is seen as more receptive to the needs of users; problems or issues which straddle traditional departmental boundaries can be treated in a holistic way; it provides a single point where all library problems can be directed; it is a more professionally satisfying job. On the other hand, when universities have perhaps fifty departments and libraries but only a dozen professional subject specialists, the system either has to provide inequitable treatment or assign up to half a dozen subjects to an individual. It is difficult to see how the notion of specialization can be sustained in such circumstances. Equally, paragons are not as common as such a system assumes. Almost inevitably, the specialist will favour one activity over another. Some are accused of avoiding readers and concentrating on book selection; others are accused of spending all their time in departments and not contributing to the library. The structure which results is a necklace, with the librarian in solitary splendour at the centre, rather than the traditional pyramid. This provides the added disadvantage that it is difficult for subject specialists to demonstrate the traditional administrative skills which lead to promotion.[32]

Creth sees collection management as spanning the activities of many of the traditional functional departments and argues that this justifies a team-based approach. Such a management approach is in any case best able to provide the flexibility and innovation required in the dynamic environment which higher education occupies at present. The university itself operates around subject disciplines organized into groups and these can offer the proper model for the library to follow. One senior member of staff should be assigned the role of collection manager with the task of implementing policy, assigning priorities, budget control and staff development and training. Major areas such as humanities or social sciences – broadly the faculties – should have a librarian working to the collection manager, with delegated responsibilities for their own area. Each subject area would then have its own team of librarians drawn from functional departments and having relevant subject or language skills. The subject teams would work together on all aspects of library affairs to do with the subject area. The advantage is that the library focuses all its relevant subject expertise on an area, while library staff benefit from different views and new information. They use the professional skills in which they are strongest, but always within the context of the team. This also improves communication between the functional areas of the library. The doubts over such a structure are: that collection management will have the Cinderella status of a subsidiary duty; that not enough time will be assigned to the task; that staff and their managers will resent giving time away from their main tasks. These arguments essentially relate to the culture of the organization. Improved horizontal communication and the variety provided through working away from the 'home base' can be seen as benefits to staff if treated positively. In larger organizations the structure can be pressed even further so that within the traditional functional departments which remain, staff can be organized in traditional subject groups which mirror the new collection management structure. This provides a much more fluid organizational structure which can be difficult to manage. But such matrix management operates in all sorts of organizations and there is no obvious reason why library managers should be considered any less able than those in industry or commerce to deal with intricate relationships.

Although this model is put forward as a desirable one, each library must make decisions on how to manage collections in the light of the staffing resources which are available. These will differ over time and between libraries, but it is always the acumen, skill and professional judgement of librarians which will build the collections by which libraries will be remembered.

References

1. University Grants Committee (1976), *Capital provision for university libraries: report of a working party* [Chairman: Professor R. Atkinson], London: HMSO.
2. Woodhead, P.A. and J.V. Martin (1982), 'Subject specialisation in British university libraries: a survey', *Journal of Librarianship*, **14**, 93-108.
3. Letter of 11 May 1935. Library Archives, King's College London.
4. Peasgood, A.N. (1988), *Acquisition/selection librarians – academic libraries. Bibliographic records in the book world: needs and capabilities: proceedings of a seminar held on 27-28 November 1987, at Newbury*, London: BNB Research Fund.
5. Broude, J. (1978), 'Journal deselection in an academic environment: a comparison of faculty and librarian choices', *Serials librarian*, **3**, 147-66.
6. Bloomfield, B.C. (1988), 'Collection development: the key issues', in S. Corrall (ed.) *Collection development: options for effective management*, London: Taylor Graham.
7. Gorman, G.E. and B.R. Howes (1989), *Collection development for libraries*, London: Bowker-Saur.
8. Cargill, J. (1984), 'Collection development policies: an alternative viewpoint', *Library acquisitions: practice and theory*, **8**, 47-49.
9. Great Britain, Department of Education and Science, Office of Arts and Libraries (1982), *The future development of libraries and information services. 1. The organisational and policy framework 2. Working together within a national framework* London: HMSO.
   Great Britain, Department of Education and Science, Office of Arts and Libraries (1986), *The future development of libraries and information services: progress through planning and partnership. Report by the Library and Information Services Council* (Library information series no.14), London: HMSO.

10. Pocklington, K. and H. Finch (1987), *Research collections under constraint*. (British Library research paper, 36), London: British Library.
11. Stam, D.H. (1983) 'Think globally, act locally: collection development and resource sharing', *Collection building*, **5**, p.21.
12. Dougherty, R.M. (1988), 'A conceptual framework for organizing resource sharing and shared collection development programmes', *Journal of academic librarianship*, **14**, 287-291.
13. Jestes, E. and W.D. Laird, (1968), 'A time study of general reference work in a university library', *Research in librarianship*, **2**, 9-16.
14. Wheeler, J. and H. Goldhor, (1962), *Practical administration of public libraries*. New York: Harper and Row.
15. Thompson, J. (1982), *The end of libraries*. London: Bingley.
16. Ash, L. (1963), *Yale's selective book retirement program*. Hamden: Linnett Books.
17. Ford, G. (1988), 'A review of relegation practice', in S. Corrall (ed.), ref. 6.
18. Information from an unpublished study conducted by P. Rigby, Deputy Librarian, King's College London Library.
19. Routh, S. (1984), 'Storage and discard' in *Collection management in academic libraries. Papers delivered at a national seminar, Surfers Paradise Queensland 16-17th February 1984.* Library Association of Australia.
20. A good basic guide to the literature is to be found in: A.D. Jarred, (1987), 'The one minute collection manager', *Collection Management*, **9**, 5-12.
21. LRCC Paper (1990), presented to the Advisory Board of Librarians.
22. Heaney, H. (1988), 'The University Research Library', in S. Corrall (ed.), ref. 6.
23. Law, D.G. (1983), 'Managing a stock disposal programme', in J.R. Guild (ed.), *Methods of exchange and disposal of stock*. Edinburgh: Edinburgh University Library.
24. Bloomfield, B.C. (1989), 'How can collection development and management be most effectively organized and staffed?' in *Collections: their development, management, preservation and sharing. Papers from the joint meeting of the Association of Research Libraries and the Standing Conference of National and University Libraries, University of York September 19-22, 1988.* Washington: Association of Research Libraries.
25. Bryant, B. (1986), 'Allocation of human resources for collection development', *Library resources & technical services*, **30**, 149-162.
26. Woodhead, P. (1974), 'Subject specialisation in three British University Libraries: a critical survey', *Libri*, **24**, 30-60.
27. Bryant, B. (1987), 'The organizational structure of collection development', *Library resources & technical services*, **31**, 111-122.
28. Sohn, J. (1987), 'Collection development organizational patterns in ARL Libraries', *Library resources & technical services*, **31**, 123-134.
29. Cogswell, J.A. (1987), 'The organization of collection management functions in academic research libraries', *Journal of academic librarianship*, **13**, 268-276.
30. Creth, S. (1989), 'The organization of collection development: a shift in the organization paradigm', in *Collections*, ref. 24.
31. Drucker, P. (1974), *Management: Tasks, responsibilities, practices*. New York: Harper.
32. Thompson, J. and R. Carr (1987), *An introduction to university library administration*. 4th ed., London: Bingley.

2   Finance and budgeting

Geoffrey Ford

...there is no point at which the marginal value of spending money on the library becomes zero. [1]

Setting the scene

It is easy to be dismissive about money, and it is even easier to adopt this attitude in times of ever increasing budgets. However, in real terms, few publicly funded libraries have seen such affluence since the early 1970s; before entering this period of declining purchasing power, few libraries were funded at a level which, in the opinion of either librarians or users, enabled them to satisfy the legitimate needs of those users. This last may seem a strongly subjective statement, but it can be justified in these terms.

All libraries, in their provision of stock, make some allowance for the anticipated needs of future users: even if the future is defined as next year, it is frequently necessary to acquire documents when they are published to ensure that they are available when needed.

The general trend towards economic instability has led to lower levels of production of individual documents (shorter print runs) and lower levels of stockholding by document distributors (booksellers and publishers are more conscious of storage costs now, and changes in methods of taxation in the USA have had a similar effect). This reinforces the need to acquire documents at the time of publication.

The number of different documents published is increasing: this would not matter if the average price of documents fell in proportion so that the total amount of expenditure necessary to acquire all books published in a given field remained the same; but in practice the average price of books has risen in line with inflation (Table 2.1).

Most university libraries work to long time horizons (which leads to the view expressed in the quotation at the head of the chapter). Prior to 1973, few British university libraries were able to meet the standards of provision considered necessary by librarians (Table 2.2) and there is widespread evidence of under-provision at that time (Table 2.3). Although total expenditure in the 1970s grew with the increase in the student population, this increase failed to keep pace with the inflation in periodical prices and output of books. Since 1979, most universities have suffered an accelerated decline in their book and serial purchasing power.

British polytechnic libraries suffered a decline in book purchasing power of nearly 20 per cent in one year alone (1979/80 to 1980/81), and only two such libraries increased their purchasing power between 1977 and 1981; between 1983 and 1988 the same group suffered a 25 per cent fall in additions to stock.[2]

The same trends seem likely to be applicable elsewhere.[3] Sufficient grounds for suggesting, then, that for a long time libraries really have been short of money for purchasing essential materials.

Table 2.1: Cost of comprehensive collecting: British academic books[4]

	Economics	Music	Engineering	All subjects
1974				
No. published	1 122	116	610	11 832
Average price	£4.83	£3.66	£5.23	£4.58
Cost of 1 copy of each title	£5 419	£425	£3 190	£54 250
1981				
No. published	1 249	171	519	12 284
Average price	£11.35	£9.26	£16.24	£12.16
Cost of 1 copy of each title	£14 176	£1 583	£8 429	£149 373
1988				
No. published	429	136	710	10 413
Average price	£30.75	£20.95	£43.84	£25.44
Cost of 1 copy of each title	£13 192	£2 849	£31 126	£264 907

**Table 2.2: University library acquisition budgets:
recommended and actual, 1964/65**

University	Recommended by SCONUL[5] formula	Actual	Actual as % of recommended
	(£)	(£)	
Bristol	133 810	50 516	38
Durham	67 316	36 438	54
Leicester	58 330	37 110	64
Sheffield	133 140	54 631	41
Southampton	78 250	45 401	58
St Andrews	87 470	59 364	68

Table 2.3: Failure rates in university libraries[6]

University		% Failure rate
Birmingham	1964	12
Lancaster	1968	40
Library A	c.1971	49
Library B	c.1971	39
Library C	c.1971	32

Costs, accounts, budgets and performance

Many libraries and librarians do not recognize the need to think in economic terms. As in all disciplines it takes time for new concepts to permeate the profession; junior professionals have too little influence, senior professionals tend to be conservative. A senior professional who adopts new attitudes will be stigmatized as unstable or (if too eminent to be ignored) tolerated as an *enfant terrible*. As Planck[7] said: 'A new scientific truth does not triumph by convincing its opponents and making them see the light, but rather because its opponents eventually die, and a new generation grows up that is familiar with it.' Unfortunately, economic reality is already here, and since no person or institution can be isolated, libraries have to adapt rather more quickly than Planck's statement suggests.

It is important to recognize the interaction between the *costs* of activities, *accounting practice, budgeting* and *performance*. It is possible to establish the cost of undertaking any library activity: the purchase of a book, the provision of a photocopy, the answering of a user's enquiry. The elements to be included in that cost depend on *accounting practice*, which may vary between institutions or from time to time within institutions. For example, the cost of heating and lighting a building is measurable: should the cost of buying a book include a proportion of the heating, lighting and administrative costs? Table 2.4 shows the effect on costs.

Table 2.4: Acquisition costs per volume acquired

	Acquisition	*Cataloguing*
Price	25.44	–
Labour	2.75	6.50
Computing	0.60	3.40
Administrative overheads	0.18	0.42
Electricity	0.018	0.034
Total	28.988	10.354
Administration as % of total	0.62	4.06
Electricity as % of total	0.06	0.33

The accounting conventions used are dependent on political decisions, and are essentially arbitrary. For example, the library is usually fixed in size, and the cost of heating is only marginally dependent on the opening hours; all academic libraries buy books and the floor area occupied by the acquisitions section is not particularly elastic – the number of transactions handled in a manual system could vary by as much as fifty per cent upwards without increasing the need for space, and in an automated system by even more. Thus, having decided to provide a library and to buy books, there is not much point in calculating the heating and lighting cost of adding a book to stock.

Leaving accounting conventions to one side, the costs of various activities need to be considered when drawing up budgets. To illustrate this point, we must examine briefly the *budgeting* process.

Budgeting and costs

The budgeting process varies considerably between institutions. Most libraries are effectively competing for funds with other services and departments within the same organization; public libraries are competing with fire services, refuse collection services, schools; academic libraries are competing with teaching departments, administrative services, students unions; special libraries are competing with marketing departments, research laboratories, machine tools for new production lines. The library budgeting process typically takes the following form:

1. calculate *this* year's cost of staff, materials, administration;
2. add allowances for inflation in *next* year;
3. add estimates for costs of new activities to be undertaken next year;
4. submit estimated budget to higher authority (Finance Committee, Finance Director);
5. allocation for next year made by higher authority;
6. if allocation is less than estimated budget, revise estimates downwards.

It is rare for actual allocations to exceed estimated budgets at least at the start of the new year. Sometimes in an academic institution supplementary allocations are made later in the year which may make the total allocation exceed the original estimate.

Step 6 above shows the advantage of knowing about the costs of various activities within libraries. It is possible to take a simplistic approach: for example, if the actual allocation is 5 per cent less than the estimated budget, cut 5 per cent from all budgeted expenditure – that is, 5 per cent off staff, 5 per cent off material, 5 per cent off administration. Life is rarely that simple: it may be that the turnover of staff is such that by not replacing those who leave 5 per cent of the total salary bill can be saved. But there may well be factors within the total budget which make this solution difficult. The inflation of serial prices may differ markedly from that of books, so that an 'even-handed' cut will have very different implications for different aspects of the service. Some levels of staff provision are related to user demand which, in the short term at least, is not particularly elastic with regard to the provision for new acquisitions: a cut of 5 per cent in new book acquisition will not lead to the 5 per cent drop in the number of issues which is necessary if one full-time equivalent issue desk assistant in twenty can be disposed of – and how many libraries have twenty full-time equivalent issue desk assistants?

These examples serve to show the complexities of the budgeting process, and of the need for librarians to know the costs of the activities for which they are responsible. The complexities are such that there is considerable scope for modelling the process as an aid to decision-making. One such model was developed at Lancaster University in 1970-71.[8] The model was used to calculate the effects on the allocation of funds, given various overall levels of budget; and to calculate the budget required, given a desirable level of book purchasing some five years ahead. The analysis of the problem showed that, of the many variables in the model, the most sensitive were:

- average book price;
- average serial price;
- number of books purchased;
- number of serials;
- work rate in cataloguing section;
- staff salaries.

While librarians may find little that is surprising in this list, it is the interaction of these variables which is important. The combined effect may be illustrated by Table 2.5.

The increase in total budget of about 25 per cent allows an increase in the materials budget of over 40 per cent while requiring less than 10 per cent increase in the staff budget: a striking illustration of the elasticity of the materials budget. The model works in reverse, of course: a cut in total Budget A of 25 per cent would lead to a cut of nearly 50 per cent in the materials budget, while permitting a reduction of only 3 per cent in the staff budget.

In some libraries the budgeting process is made slightly easier by the fact that there is no annual competition for funds with other activities. Some academic libraries receive a fixed percentage for a useful term of years. A recent example of this is found at Southampton University: in the early 1970s the library's share of the University's income from tuition fees and UGC grant was fixed at 6 per cent; this was altered to 5.5 per cent in 1981 as a result of changes in the basis on which the UGC grant was calculated. A disadvantage of this method of allocation is that no income accrues to the library from research contracts and grants: and a university which attracts an increasing income from these sources places heavier burdens on the library. This was recognized in Southampton, and in 1984 the formula was changed so that a proportion of the University research and contract income was allocated to the library in addition to the 5.5 per cent of the grant and fee income. This method also has its drawbacks, for it makes part of the library service dependent on the most volatile part of the university income; but it makes sense for the library, at least at a time when the traditional sources of university finance (public funds) are being squeezed and the non-UFC income is on a rising trend.

Table 2.5: Alternative library budgets (£000s)

	Staff	Materials	Other	Total
Budget A	125	155.6	15.6	296.2
Budget B	135.8	221.2	15.6	372.6
% increase B over A	8.6	42.2	0	25.8

This overall formula approach was widely canvassed by British university librarians in the late 1960s, and the basis for the calculation was published in the Parry report.[9] The share of university budget which was thought necessary to support an adequate library service in a 'medium sized' university was 6 per cent. This figure has since often been quoted out of context as a desirable minimum for all university libraries, although this was never intended. Some libraries did achieve a fixed allocation – Southampton, already mentioned, 6 per cent of a proportion of the total grant and fee income; Newcastle, 4.5 per cent of the university income. However, this fixed percentage approach has its dangers: it ignores the absolute size of the budget. It is important to remember how the figure was originally arrived at: a group of experienced librarians drew up a model budget for a library, with no branches, and with no special collections, intended to serve a medium-sized university, to show how it compared with the average amount actually spent on university libraries. The model budget was 6 per cent, the actual average only 3.8 per cent. In a later part of the report, the same group of librarians indicated another way of calculating a model budget which, although they did not make the calculation, implied that for the same medium-sized university, the proportion spent on the library should be closer to 10 per cent. The perpetuation of the 6 per cent myth (which surfaced again in 1984) [10] is an interesting example of the misinterpretation of figures.

Budgeting and performance

If the global formula approach is unsuited or unavailable to the library in question, what are the alternatives? How can the librarian justify his existence? There is no single answer, and any solution depends to a certain extent on politics – institutional and national. Librarians may be able to influence their own institution, but these factors are essentially outside their control. Library performance *is* under the librarian's control to a certain extent, and that performance must be monitored, measured and finally presented in such a way as to keep the funds rolling in. Something will be said in Chapter 3 of the necessity to relate performance measures to objectives: but it is obvious that when objectives have been set in terms both of priorities and targets, and when costs and performance have been measured, the formulation of budgets necessary to meet agreed objectives in service provision becomes increasingly easier, and the resulting figures become easier to defend. When objectives are ill-defined, costs unknown and performance inadequately measured, then the budgeting process is like playing darts in the dark: the target is obscured, the degree of accuracy is unpredictable, and there may well be unpleasant surprises for some of the participants. Joking aside, there is one important measure of performance: the degree to which a library meets its financial targets. In those libraries where unspent balances are carried forward, it is wise to avoid major deviations from the estimated budget.

Allocation of materials budgets

Our prime concern in this book is with library stock: and in this section I consider how materials budgets may be sub-divided, given that the total materials budget has been arrived at by some undefined means. Later, I will consider the ways in which materials budgets may be built up from first principles.

Most libraries sub-divide their budget in some way: a public library may have sub-divisions called Central Reference, Central Lending, Children's Books, Branches; and an academic library may have sub-divisions called Books, Periodicals, Audio-visual. The major sub-divisions may be further divided – perhaps even to the level of an individual book selector. Some sub-divisions are more formal than others: for example, a university library may formally allocate a certain amount of money to each teaching department, and informally set a target amount of money to be spent each month in order to keep an even (or predictable) flow of materials through the system. Opinions are divided as to the value of formulae in budgeting for library materials. In academic institutions, where academic staff undertake much of the book selection, there is great pressure to have formulae to ensure fair shares for all. But sub-division of a budget can be inefficient: there is a tendency for most controllers of funds to keep a little in reserve for a rainy day, and to underspend over the whole year. When the total budget is divided into fifty or more bookfunds, each of which underspends, the overall out-turn looks poor. However, there are often strong political pressures to maintain these separate funds; and the pressure is (naturally) strongest where funds are shortest. The key is to have central funds, under the control of the Chief Librarian, which are large enough to outweigh the inefficiencies inherent in the minute sub-divisions of the rest of the materials budget. The late Joe Lightbown, sometime Deputy Librarian at Bristol University and a master of collection development, had a rule of thumb which, on translation from his native Lancastrian went: 'if the amount available for purchase of books is £x, then at least £0.5x should be centrally controlled.' Lightbown's Rule may be considered as the first step in applying a formula, the subsequent sub-division of the non-centrally controlled funds being left to any political process considered suitable. Before examining some examples of allocation formulae in action, I must briefly explore factors affecting the process of allocation.

Factors in the allocation process

Since most libraries operate with a mixture of overlapping and interlocking systems, it is important to recognize the influence of these systems on the allocation process. Some of these factors are quantifiable, some are uncontrollable – but they exist. The least controllable are external factors – economic, political, social – which may have very specific effects. Economic factors, principally inflation and exchange rates, are explored in more depth in a subsequent section (see section on financial trends). Political initiatives have implications for libraries: legislation on equal opportunities, against racial discrimination, on the handicapped, for example, has led to the allocation of library funds to build up stocks to support services to minority groups not specifically catered for previously. A more tangible factor is that of professional orientation. Librarians' attitudes arise from a complex mixture of opinions, prejudices, education and philosophy; traditionally, librarians were biased towards building up balanced stocks and retaining them for posterity. Now there is much more of a trend towards the user-oriented service and providing access to information, rather than buying it. This shift in professional thinking gives rise to debates about what should be included in a materials budget. The cost of interlibrary lending? The cost of on-line searching of computerized databases?

Closer to home are the factors deriving from a library's place in its own institution: the influence of institutional objectives is important, but the way in which these affect the budget may differ. The organization of an academic institution is an important determinant of library allocations; this may be a considerable handicap at the operational level when academic departments want 'their' books to be shelved together, regardless of the classification scheme adopted by the library. Handel quotes some examples from the field of operational research at Lancaster: of 250 books of interest to the Operational Research Department, only 58 were classified as operational research; 17 different departments had ordered the books in this sample, and only one-third (8 out of 24) of the books ordered by the Operational Research Department had been classified as operational research.[11] The financial regime of an institution may also be of importance in allocating budgets: the regime may affect the ways in which certain items in the budget are grouped. Finally, although most library funds come from one major source, there may be grants and endowments for specific purposes. Within the library itself, the organization of the library – the number of branches or subject divisions, the level of responsibility for book selection – is a determinant, as is the history of the library – particularly as reflected in the beliefs and traditions of the library staff. It is no good suddenly asking library staff to select books in anticipation of use when for many years they have been accustomed to reacting only to established user demands.

The combined effect of these factors may be an historical-cum-political approach to the materials budget: everyone gets what they had last year, plus a bit extra (or minus a bit). A better approach is to plan forward in some way: budgeting related to the library objectives, user needs, institutional developments. These may be encapsulated in a formula (see examples in later sections), but formulae can be stifling. The ideal, perhaps, is a flexible approach based on institutional priorities, responding each year to new developments and observed use – though this is more demanding, open to criticism of bias, and perhaps politically unacceptable.

Political pressures in institutions often lead to the adoption of allocation formulae: sometimes these formulae are introduced at the initiative of librarians as a defence mechanism. From time to time, surveys of libraries are undertaken to identify whether they use such formulae, and the results can usually be summarized as:

- some do;
- some are looking for or are about to adopt one;
- some have just given one up.

In numerical terms, in the United Kingdom:

- 7 university libraries out of 37 used formulae in 1978;[12]
- 21 polytechnic libraries out of 24 used them in 1985;[13]
- 7 university libraries out of 28 used them in 1988.[14]

An optimist (or pessimist) could detect from these figures a slight trend in favour of formulae in university libraries, but the evidence is weak.

The search for a perfect system of resource allocation, whether initiated by a librarian or by another, is likely to have three stages:[15]

- the search for a formula;
- the failure to agree;
- the averaging of the results.

The search is complicated by the existence of the large number of variables which may be considered relevant to the process of resource allocation:

- actual users;
- potential users;
- levels of use;
- interlibrary loan activity;
- level of research activity;
- size of existing stock;
- previous levels of expenditure;
- price;
- publishing output;
- rate of obsolescence;
- relative importance of books and serials;
- need to cover split sites;
- type of subject eg 'hard' versus 'soft' disciplines;
- importance of library resources for the study of the subject;
- importance of the subject.

It is quite easy to identify a list of criteria relevant to resource allocation; it is extremely difficult to transform this list into a formula. The first set of problems arises in finding numeric indicators for these criteria. The questions that arise include the following.

Actual users Divide by category? Undergraduates, postgraduates on taught courses, postgraduate research students, academic teaching staff, research workers, external users? Full time equivalents or actual numbers?

Potential users As above, but how is the potential defined? Current enrolment at, or employment by, the institution? Current planning numbers up to five years ahead? Ten years ahead?

Levels of use Records of loans and 'in-house' use? How should the latter be measured? Should a 'short' loan count as much as a 'long' loan? Do limits on the number of items which may be borrowed affect demand and hence use? Are citations evidence of use?

Interlibrary loan activity Does a photocopy supplied for retention by the user count the same as an original which has to be returned? Does a rationing system affect demand?

Level of research activity   How is this to be measured? By number of staff and students engaged? By the number of publications produced?

Size of existing stock   How is this to be measured? Metres or numbers of physical units? And how is it to be categorized? By mapping the library classification onto the institution's academic departmental structure? What about interdisciplinary studies, and such basic subjects as mathematics?

Previous levels of expenditure   Should past decisions be included in an analysis of current and future requirements?

Price   Average price of books published or books bought? If the former, which index, and what about foreign language materials? If the latter, would this not be constrained by the money available? Over what period should prices be averaged?

Publishing output   Where are the data?

Rate of obsolescence   Where are the data?

Relative importance of books and serials   Who will decide?

Need to cover split sites   How is this to be quantified?

Type of subject e.g. 'hard' or 'soft' disciplines: How is this to be quantified?

Importance of library resources for the study of the subject   How is this to be quantified?

Importance of the subject   To whom – the nation or the institution? Who is to decide, and how is this to be quantified?

The absence of answers to some of these questions may have the effect of reducing the number of variables quite substantially. The absence of data is a poor reason for excluding a variable from a formula, but such exclusions illustrate well the point that resource allocation is a political process. There remains the question of how to combine the remaining variables in a satisfactory manner to produce a workable formula. There is no escape from a further subjective process, and this process is most likely to lead to the 'failure to agree' mentioned above. In practice, the results derived from the operation of a formula may be less sensitive than might be supposed to variation in the weightings applied to the variables.

Constructing materials budgets from first principles

Most formulae have as their basis some attempt at the enumeration of basic principles. For example, in the simplest terms, a librarian decides, using some rational criteria, that £200 000 must be spent on periodicals and £300 000 on books to provide the desired level of service: a total of £500 000. The library is actually allocated by a higher authority £450 000; and the librarian then allocates £180 000 to serials and £270 000 to books – that is, the actual allocation is made in the same proportions as the 'ideal' budget. A budget constructed from first principles has been used to derive a formula which is then applied to an actual allocation. A budget constructed from first principles should, however, be organized so that if the total allocation is less than that required, the reductions made in each component of the budget are in accordance with a system of previously determined priorities and constraints, and not simply *pro rata*. The basic principle which must be stated is that libraries need to acquire stock in order to maintain their relevance to users. This involves an element of prediction, but basically it boils down to the question 'how many books should be acquired?'

There has been a considerable amount of work on stock management in public libraries which has had implications for budgeting for materials purchase. This approach to stock management is not directly applicable to academic libraries, but the analysis may offer some insights on the problem of supply of books for students on taught courses. McClellan[16] offers some guidance on the basic problem. In a public lending library he identified three factors which affect the decision on the appropriate size of the budget. These are: physical deterioration, obsolescence, and 'reader exhaustion', the last of these referring to the fact that after a certain time users will have read all the items in stock which interest them.

All three variables are equally relevant in an academic library. The first two factors can be quantified: it might be established that a book will last (say) eight years on average before becoming physically unacceptable to readers; and in non-fiction, some guidance is possible (for example, a superseded edition of a new text is by definition obsolete; books on

World War Two based on research done since the secrets of 'Ultra' were revealed have made many earlier works obsolescent). 'Reader exhaustion' is more intractable. In a given category, it might be thought that the ratio

$$\frac{\text{Average number of books borrowed per year}}{\text{Total number of books}}$$

would give the proportion of the total number which needs to be purchased each year in order to keep the stock fresh. However, this ratio ignores the different rates of reading between readers. McClellan preferred the formula, again for a given category,

$$\frac{100 \times \text{number of issues per year}}{\text{Total number of books} \times \text{total number of books on loan}}$$

to indicate the percentage of books needing to be replaced annually. As Betts and Hargrave[17] point out, this formula cannot be tested directly. They prefer a measure related more directly to usage. They suggest that so long as a book continues to achieve a given level of usage, it should be considered to be still of current interest. Research will be needed to establish the average shelf life of a book, and it will be necessary in this research to distinguish between the effects of McClellan's three factors; but assuming this can be done, then the annual replacement rate of stock becomes

$$\frac{\text{Number of issues per year in category}}{\text{Average shelf life (measured in issues) of each book.}}$$

In the academic library context, Buckland and others examined the effects of demand, loan periods and levels of duplication on availability (defined as the proportion of users who obtain the books they want).[18] The number of issues per year was used to determine the loan period necessary to achieve a given level of availability, with duplication becoming necessary at higher levels of demand. Unfortunately, the measure of performance – availability – proved to be homeostatic, or nearly so: that is, as supply improved, demand grew so that availability remained approximately constant. Although there is some evidence that improving the supply does increase the availability,[19] the measure is rather too crude to be used as a factor in a formula demanding precision of allocation.

The concept of availability is taken further in some work done in Cheshire County Library. There the 'threshold of choice' has been used to indicate the shelf stocks needed to maintain a given level of lending activity. The threshold established is 'one in twenty': that is, the reader should have a stated probability of finding one book in twenty acceptable. This threshold of choice is achieved, with a 95 per cent probability, if the shelf stock is sixty volumes – say, two standard shelves. In passing, it is worth noting that 'two shelves full' is about the maximum number of books with the same class number which an average user can be expected to peruse if the books are not sub-arranged by author. Having set a performance level – to maintain the present level of issues – and a control variable – the threshold of choice – the librarian is in a position to establish a minimum budget for annual additions to stock. The success of this approach is illustrated by the fact that when Cheshire had to reduce its overall budget in 1981/82, the book fund was not cut at all – the 'minimum book fund to maintain existing lending activity had been identified'.[20] This approach is of course, only possible where a high degree of substitutability between books is possible; the formula has been developed to take into account differences in demand and usage patterns. There is scope for examining the 'threshold of choice' in the academic library context and its potential as a guide to decisions on purchase and on relegation.

A more fundamental approach to budgeting involves concepts from the field of economics. Gold proposes a model in which the budget is allocated so that marginal benefits equal marginal costs for each competing budget head, and considers the case for an academic library.[21] He argues that an explicit value judgement must be made about the contribution of each budgeting unit to the overall institutional objectives, and that the prospective usage of material should be included in the formula. The marginal costs can only be measured if a satisfactory definition of 'library resource units' is used: Gold argues that the United States Office of Education's definition of a volume is inadequate for this purpose since it ignores differences between subjects. At present, in the absence of any such adequate definition, Gold's model cannot be made operational. This seems to be the fate of many economic models, but its true value is in the debate it opens up as to the objectives of budgeting: Gold is for efficiency, whereas Kohut and Walker, in a reply to Gold argue for equity.[22] They argue that library resource allocation is a problem of welfare economics – a point made earlier by Morley.[23] They also point out some conceptual deficiencies in Gold's model. Whatever the views of economists, there is no doubt that librarians tend to prefer equity and to apply rules of thumb when deciding what factors to include in a formula, and when deciding how to weight those factors.

The relationship between institutional objectives and budget allocation was taken up in the research project reported by Handel.[24] He recommended the division of the university library budget between teaching and research, without indicating the relative proportions; some indications of these can be gleaned from data from Sussex University Library,[25] where expenditure on course-related materials varied between 15 and 20 per cent of the total, with wide fluctuations for individual subjects. Thus, in biology, course-related materials accounted for up to 50 per cent of the books purchased; in history the proportion was as low as 8 per cent. In principle the division of a budget according to function is a good one.

An earlier quantification of the needs of a library to support its institutional activities is found in the Parry report.[26] A sub-committee of SCONUL drew up a model budget for an established university library. They began their assessment by sampling the literature in various subjects, and consulted a number of experienced university librarians. This stage led to the proposal of 'basic minimum standard annual allocations' for a number of subjects. These allocations were intended to cover current publications, both books and serials. An addition was made for the provision of duplicate copies of text books: this figure was set at £3 per student (the then current standard at Cambridge University Library), and it was stated that, generally, 'multiple copies should be provided on the basis of one for ten students'. Binding costs were then added: at that time most libraries spent between 10 and 12 per cent of the total bookfund on binding, and this was 'generally regarded as inadequate'. So the sub-committee decided that 25 per cent was essential for binding, while a further 10 per cent for sundries was thought 'reasonable'. The final sum looked like this for a university with 4 000 students:

	£
Books – 16 000 vols @ £2.10	40 000
Serials – 3000 @ £7	21 000
Multiple copies @ £3 per student	12 000
Binding	15 250
Sundries	9 805
	98 055

Although this exercise started with basic principles, it will be seen that a certain degree of arbitrariness (or rules of thumb) crept in. This was the sum of money which represented 6 per cent of the average university budget and has been so widely quoted since.

The same SCONUL sub-committee later produced, with some degree of reluctance, a formula based on the principle that potential user numbers should be the basis for allocation: 10 units for each undergraduate and 75 units for each postgraduate or member of academic staff. Each unit at that time was supposed to be £1. This formula (reluctantly, presumably!) would yield a book grant of £142 500 for the same notional university library.

More recently, Emsley and Jenkins proposed a very simple formula, also based on potential user numbers in conjunction with the principle that the use of the library varies between subjects.[27] To these basic principles were added some rules of thumb. The annual book fund allocation was calculated as:

$x =$ Subscription cost of abstracts and indexes + (for each science subject) average cost of 1 book per undergraduate + (for each non-science subject) average cost of 3 books per undergraduate + (for all subjects) average cost of 1 serial subscription per postgraduate and member of academic staff.

$0.2x =$ Cost of general reference works, special purchases, binding, interlibrary loan, cataloguing, on-line equipment.

$0.05x =$ Contingency fund

Total = $1.25x$

The weighting of 3:1 for non-science:science in the books part of the formula reflects circulation statistics for undergraduates in the library of King's College London. There is an implicit assumption that postgraduate and staff use reflects the same pattern. Similarly, the use of postgraduate and staff numbers for the serials part of the formula assumes that undergraduate use of serials is either insignificant or reflects the same pattern as the chosen groups. There is an assumption also that circulation use is an adequate indicator of need. The choice of weights in the books part has a basis in use, but the choice of units – one book per science student, one periodical per member of academic staff, and so on – is completely arbitrary.

A more thorough investigation of basic principles of allocation was undertaken at Newcastle Polytechnic Library.[28] This investigation identified 13 fundamental criteria. For books, five criteria were chosen as relevant, and for periodicals three. Table 2.6 lists the criteria and the reasons for adopting or rejecting them.

These criteria were then examined in detail. For books, the criterion of obsolescence was abandoned (no suitable data), as was the criterion of publishing output (inadequate data, and no clear link between output and purchasing). Prices, student numbers and six measures of use were combined to give overall indexes. For serials, the existing stock and the publishing output were compared, and a balance was struck, yielding theoretical numbers of titles to be bought for each subject area. Combined with the average price this gives a theoretical allocation. The relevant point here is that an examination which could have led to a basic minimum standard budget in fact led to a pragmatic formula – a transition made necessary because of the inadequacy of data and the difficulties of measurement. An example of the formula in action is given in the next section.

A rather similar exercise at Southampton University Library gave rise to the SOULBAG (Southampton University Library Budget Allocation Game). A working party of academic and library staff identified six factors as the most relevant to the allocation process:

- size of community served;
- importance of library to subject;
- publishing output;
- price;
- breadth of subject;
- importance of subject to University.

Allocations were made at the Faculty level: each Faculty representative on the Library Committee distributed 4 800 points across a 48-cell matrix (six factors, eight Faculties; each point was in effect worth about £135). That is, each representative had complete freedom to weight the factors and the Faculties at will. This approach gave freedom of choice when it came to quantifying some of the factors, for which no measure met with universal approval. While the individual weights selected in this way

Table 2.6: Criteria for determining book fund allocations

Criterion	Measure	Books		Serials	
		Relevant	*Reason*	*Relevant*	*Reason*
Actual users	Student Numbers	Y	Good indicator of demand level	N	Not available for loan
Potential use	As above	Y	Similar to above	N	Not available for loan
Level of use	Various	Y	Unequal demand made by users	N	Difficult to measure
ILL activity		N	No reason given	N	No reason given
Research activity		N	Not relevant in polytechnic	N	Not relevant in polytechnic
Existing stock		N	Does not reflect demand	Y	
Previous expenditure	Money	N	Arbitrary	N	Arbitrary
Price	Money	Y	Wide variations between subjects	Y	Wide variations between subjects
Publishing Output		Y	Wide variations between subjects	Y	Wide variations between subjects
Obsolescence		Y	Wide variations between subjects	N	
Book/serial split		Y		Y	
Split sites		N	Against library policy	N	Against library policy
Type of subject		N	No reason given	N	No reason given

varied considerably, the allocations when summed for each Faculty showed a remarkable degree of agreement, so that it was reasonable to strike an average. The result was to suggest that five Faculties should have their allocations increased and three reduced. Subjectively, the resulting allocations favoured Education rather more than was justified (see Lovecy's comments on the Bangor formula, below), but this was not sufficient to explain why the method – developed with the aid of the decision-makers in the allocation process, and representing their view of the fundamental criteria – was found politically unacceptable. Perhaps the use of 'Game' (although strictly accurate) in the name of the method was the stumbling block.

Arising from this abortive effort was a more systematic and objective analysis of the allocation process. An operational research study helped to make explicit the political choices involved.[29] The method has the following stages:

1. identify variables in allocation process (23 in this case);
2. identify suitable measures for each variable and collect or collate data;
3. perform multiple linear regression on variables (to identify which pairs of variables are closely correlated and can thus be used as substitutes for one another);
4. use principal components analysis to identify which (small number of) variables can safely be used to represent the whole (the three identified were total number of students, size of collections, research citations);
5. select weights for the three variables to be used in the next stage;
6. for each allocation unit (= Faculty in this case), multiply the weight by the appropriate variable etc;
7. use the results of this calculation in a linear programme to calculate the allocations in order to maximize the benefit.

Although the method displays a level of rigour often absent from the discussions on allocation formulae, its application proved no easier than its SOULBAG predecessor: the Library Committee was unable to agree on a political process for weighting the variables (stage 5), preferring to receive instead the considered judgements of the Librarian and a few other 'wise persons', who are of course able to use any method they choose.[30]

The political imperative of the introduction of cost centres may lead to demands for rather more explicit allocation methods than the judgements of individuals or small groups, however wise. Revill[31] has developed a response to this new situation which includes the fundamental principle of establishing the needs for each cost centre using basic data such as student numbers, usage, price, present size of collections and research needs (using interlibrary loan transactions as a measure). However, resources are then allocated 'taking into account all known, identifiable, objective and subjective factors.'[32]

To summarize, academic libraries have not yet adopted systems which relate budgets directly to defined performance levels, which in turn relate to stated objectives. With the possible exception of the original SCONUL 'basic minimum standard', there are no published statements which make this connection: such formulae as exist, even when derived from first principles, have usually applied to slicing a given cake, rather than determining the appropriate size of cake. Emsley and Jenkins proposed a formula for determining the cake size without indicating how they arrived at the arbitrary weights in their formula; and Gold's model of economic efficiency, even if it is appropriate, cannot be made operational. There are then still conceptual gaps between objectives, performance and needs, which academic libraries must bridge if they are to achieve materials budgets based on needs, rather than allocation formulae based on pragmatism.

Some examples of allocation formulae are examined in the next section.

Examples of allocation formulae

It should be clear that there are no universally acceptable allocation formulae; but it should also be clear that there are some variables which are commonly accepted as being relevant to the allocation process. These include student numbers, average prices of books and periodicals, levels of publishing output, use of existing stock, and some indicator of research needs. In general formulae, there is no need for further sophistication: academic staff numbers are highly correlated with student numbers, use is often highly correlated with existing stock levels, and so on. Where an allocation process is based on a definition of (say) research and teaching needs, different variables may be appropriate for each portion of the budget. The following examples show how these variables have been used in some institutions. Further examples can be found in the COPOL compendium.[33]

At least one university[34] adopted an allocation formula based on the SCONUL work reported in the Parry report. The formula was then used to allocate whatever sum was available. The formula was:

> 20% to General fund
> 40% split between Boards of Studies (Faculties) by subject formula
> 15% split between Boards of Studies by staff/student numbers
> 25% split between Boards of Studies equally.

The subject formula was derived from the basic minimum standards of the SCONUL sub-committee, with adjustments from time to time to allow for changes in the pattern of publishing. The staff/student numbers element was calculated each year using a points system:

> 1 for every 10 undergraduates
> 1 for every 5 postgraduate advanced course students
> 1 for every postgraduate research student, or member of academic staff.

The formula was not used for allocating money for serials. However, in 1982, it was decided to bring serials into the arrangement. The new formula was:

10% to General fund			
90% divided between Boards of Studies using 100 points			
Book element:	by subject formula	25	
	by staff/student numbers	5	
	equally divided	<u>15</u>	45
Serials element:	by subject formula	40	
	equally divided	<u>15</u>	55

The 55:45 split between serials and books reflected the then current position; and the weighting of the components in the various elements was similarly chosen to achieve, using this new formula, the same allocations as had been made using the old formula. In the future, the

balance between books and serials could be varied between different Boards of Studies. All in all, an interesting example of the evolution of a formula, working originally from first principles.

The second example of an allocation formula comes from Newcastle Polytechnic Library.[35] This formula was developed from first principles and was first used in 1983/84 to allocate a sum fixed by higher authority. The steps in the process were as follows:

- set aside Development and Contingencies Fund, subscriptions to HMSO publications, abstracts and indexes, and other general money;
- set aside Binding Fund (same percentage of total as last year);
- calculate theoretical number of serial titles relevant to each Faculty, and multiply by average price of serials in that subject area; add up total to give total serials budget;
- remaining sum available divided up among Faculties using a weighted index based on student numbers, price and use.

This formula was based on an analysis of fundamental criteria, from which a comparatively small number was chosen. This analysis was fairly objective, up to a point – the point at which pragmatism determined which criteria could be used in practice (as opposed to theory); and a little later, more subjectivity entered the exercise when various measures were combined to produce a single index number. For example, at Newcastle when making the book allocation, the Student Number Index, the Price Index and the Use Index were combined using weights of 2, 1 and 1 respectively; and the Use Index was made up of six separate indexes, weighted 2, 2, 2, 2, 1 and 1. Table 2.7 shows the effect on the allocation of altering all the weights to 1 in the Use Index and the overall index. It is perhaps worth questioning in this case whether the differences in allocation which result from using the more sophisticated system of weights are worth the trouble.

Most book allocation formulae have been derived for use in academic libraries. McGrath proposes a general formula for use in academic and public libraries.[36] This is based on two simple parameters: the amount of use of the existing stock and the average cost. The procedure has seven steps:

- describe the scope of each book fund – for example, by subject, form of material, location or whatever;

- tabulate annual circulation figures using the same categories as used for the book fund;
- calculate the average cost of books within each category, using the library's own cost data;
- multiply the average cost by the circulation to obtain cost-use for each category;
- add up the cost-uses to give total cost-use;
- divide each category's cost-use by the total, to give percentage cost-uses;
- multiply percentage cost-use by total book fund to get allocations for each category.

This formula clearly has general application where books are able to circulate: it could perhaps also be used for reference libraries if a reliable method of assessing use was found. McGrath suggests a test of the effectiveness of the allocation formula which compares the rank order of size of the book collections in each category with the amount of circulation and number of books acquired. This test depends on the assumption that the buying programme should be solely related to circulation: if this assumption matches the library objectives, then the test may be appropriate.

Table 2.7: Bookfund allocation using differently weighted indexes: Newcastle Polytechnic Library 1983/84

Faculty	1.Using actual index	2.Using alternative index with equal weights	Percentage difference (2-1)
Art & Design	16 284	17 112	+ 5.1
Business & Management	22 080	20 976	− 5.0
Community & Social Studies	18 630	19 734	+ 5.9
Construction & Applied Science	21 114	20 838	− 1.3
Engineering, etc.	18 354	19 734	+ 7.5
Humanities	19 872	18 492	− 6.9
Professional Studies	21 666	21 252	− 1.9

McGrath's formula is appropriate only for one part of a library's stock – the monographs. Kohut suggests a formula which allows for serials as well.[37] The basic model assumes that each fund is allocated a proportion of 'library resource units' – or volumes, if you like. This presumes that the value of a given collection is directly related to its size – questionable to say the least. This allocation has to be made in accordance with library objectives: it might be based on the number of users, or size of existing collections, or might allow for some priority to be given to areas of new development. Within each fund, a decision is made on the proportion to be spent on serials. Each year, adjustments are made for inflation: since this varies from subject to subject and between monographs and serials, the calculations are made separately for each fund and type of material. These calculations affect the percentage of the total money allocated to each book fund, but preserve the balance of resource units established in the first year of operation.

In recent years a number of academic libraries have adopted formulae which recognize the differing needs of teaching and research. Characteristically, these formulae include a proportion (around 20 per cent) of the total for use as a central fund. The remainder of the money is then allocated using a variety of simple formulae.

At the University College of North Wales, Bangor, the primary division between Arts and Science is proportional to the actual numbers of staff and students in each group. In the Arts Faculty 80 (and in the Science Faculty 70) per cent of the available money is then allocated to cost centres (= subject groups) using the 'teaching' formula. The remaining sum is divided by the 'research' formula. The 'teaching' formula is as follows:

let sum available to each faculty be T

for each cost centre calculate average book price $= p(i)$

for each faculty calculate average book price $= P$

for each cost centre express average book price
as proportion of faculty price $= \dfrac{p(i)}{P}$

for each cost centre add numbers of staff and
students $= n(i)$

for each cost centre calculate $\dfrac{n(i) \times p(i)}{P}$ $= C(i)$

for each faculty add these products $= F$

divide allocation T by F to get unit allocation $= t$

for each cost centre calculate $C(i) \times t$

This figure will be the cost centre allocation for teaching/book-based elements. The 'research' formula is much simpler:

assume total allocation available to each Faculty is R.
Staff and student numbers are weighted as follows:
    Undergraduates   = 0.25
    Postgraduates   = 1.5
    Research staff   = 1.5
    Academic staff   = 3
for each cost centre calculate weighted numbers   = w(i)
for each faculty add these numbers   = W
divide allocation R by W to get unit allocation   = r
for each cost centre calculate w(i) x r

This figure will be the cost centre allocation for research requirements and activity.

The particular formulation was chosen because Lovecy, the Librarian at Bangor, 'thought it accorded with subjective assessments'.[38] In the Librarian's opinion, one department (Education) is consistently overfunded, and one is too small to receive adequate funds. These phenomena are common. In British universities, departments of education have no undergraduates, and thus are relatively overweighted in the research formula; and their undergraduates spend one term on teaching practice and make fewer demands on the library's collections than more conventional students, so that the teaching formula is also over-generous. Also, small departments are liable to fall short in any formula based on averages and may thus need protection. On the other hand, large departments do not seem to be underfunded in these formulae: this may be due to the fact that they are usually science-based, and there is a large amount of material common to these subjects; or to the lesser dependence on books on the science side; or to the existence of economies of scale.

The problem of small departments has been catered for in at least one formula. At Lancaster University, Mackenzie introduced the following procedure. The primary division was between central funds and departmental funds. The amount allocated to central funds was decided on historical principles: at some time in the past a sum was allocated to cover the cost of certain serials and continuing bibliographic works, and the cost of these was a first charge on the budget. In addition a fairly large contingency fund was agreed, to provide for the purchase of desirable items not bought by departments, duplicate copies of textbooks in heavy demand, and gap-filling: this contingency fund was increased each year by the percentage by which the total materials budget was increased. The balance remaining after covering these central funds was available for distribution to departmental book allocations. The allocation to each bookfund was determined by formula. Each department received an equal basic allocation, except in language departments which received twice the normal sum to allow for the need to purchase items in two languages. The remaining sum was distributed according to weighted numbers of staff and students:

each full-time equivalent undergraduate counts 1
each full-time equivalent taught course postgraduate counts 1
each postgraduate research student counts 3
each member of academic staff counts 6

Table 2.8 is a worked example showing the resulting allocations in a given year. In the table, the column headed Total Allocation (1) is calculated using the weights described above; Total Allocation (2) is calculated using a revised weight of 3 for each undergraduate and taught course postgraduate in arts departments in recognition of their greater reliance on library materials. The results show that in that case, considerable difference to the final allocation can be made by this kind of adjustment. Note that no mention is made in the formula at this stage of a split between books and serials. In fact, in this library, a department could spend up to 10 per cent of its allocation on periodicals. The overall proportion of the budget (including central funds) spent on serials is a matter of considerable interest and will be discussed later. The idea of having a uniform basic allocation for each department, combined with a variable element to give the total allocation resurfaced at St Andrews University, to which Mackenzie moved from Lancaster. Each department receives a 'floor' allocation, and variable elements for teaching and research are added.[39]

Another formula based on the teaching/research split is in use at Sheffield University.[40] Here the teaching and research allocations are calculated for each subject and the totals are expressed as percentages of the total sum needed. These percentages are then applied to the sum actually available for subject funds.

Table 2.8: Example of formula allocation in a university materials budget

Subject	Undergrads +PG course	Research students	Staff	Basic alloc	Weighted numbers	Total alloc (1)	Total alloc (2)
French	117	2	11	1 600	189	4 244	5 950
German	57	1	6	1 600	96	3 943	3 760
History	152	5	17	800	296	4 563	6 700
Physics	138	8	24	800	306	5 030	3 950
Education	50	0	7	800	92	2 087	1 750

The sum needed for support of teaching is calculated as follows:

for each department calculate weighted teaching load
undergraduate load + 1.5 x postgraduate course load $= w(i)$
for arts and law faculties teaching need (1989) $t(i)$ $= 75w(i)$
for other faculties teaching need (1989) $t(i)$ $= 50w(i)$
the total teaching need is then T.

The sum needed for support of research is based on the concept of 'library units'. These are defined as:

arts based   1 unit = 125 books and 30 periodicals
science based   1 unit = 40 books and 30 periodicals

For each department calculate entitlement to library units using weighted numbers:

0.02 x postgraduate research students
+ 0.05 x academic and research staff $= u(i)$

Having converted $u(i)$ to numbers of books and periodicals, use average book and serial prices to calculate the research need, or $r(i)$. The total research need is then R. If the total sum available for distribution is B, then each department is allocated

$$\frac{t(i) + r(i) \times B}{T + R}$$

Table 2.9 illustrates the allocations which would be made to typical departments by some of the formulae described above.

Table 2.9: Formula allocation in three libraries

The results of applying three different formulae
to the same department in one university:

Formula	Variables	Allocation
Bangor	book price, staff and student numbers	17 304
Bradford	staff and student numbers, publishing pattern	23 147
Sheffield	book and serial prices, staff and student numbers	16 235

The books/periodicals split and other allocation problems

There are no adequate theoretical bases for dealing with the problems described in this section. The problems just exist. For academic libraries, the proportion of the total budget spent on serials is a significant measure: and there is no 'right' figure which can be set. Table 2.10 illustrates the range of values which this measure has taken in some university libraries in recent years. Note the trend, in general, for the percentage to increase; and also that the differences between universities of similar type – technological, large civic, small civic and new – can be quite marked.

Table 2.10: Proportion of total materials budget spent on serials

University	1968/69	1971/72	Year 1976/77	1981/82	1987/88
Brunel	34	45	44	70	66
Loughborough	50	44	40	41	54
Birmingham	47	53	51	62	na
Leeds	23	34	37	51	49
Leicester	31	36	40	48	63
Nottingham	48	33	58	69	60
East Anglia	1	27	47	44	52
York	40	44	46	65	56

For some years past, the rise in prices of serials has exceeded the general rate of inflation of retail prices. Since there is a tendency for publicly funded libraries to have their budgets linked to the general rate of inflation, maintaining the same number of serials subscriptions requires an increasing proportion of the materials budget (see Table 2.10), with a corresponding decline in the amount available for book purchase. Since most libraries are expected to buy at least some books, some limit must be placed on the total devoted to serials. Some librarians think that 60 per cent is the maximum that should be spent on serials: but the actual value in any institution must depend on the range of subjects covered. Most academic libraries have, since 1972, had one or more rounds of serial subscription cancellations, with varying degrees of trauma: to give one example only, in 1983 University College Cardiff cancelled 30 per cent of its serial subscriptions.

The balance between subjects is an arbitrary one. In an academic library, the number of books purchased in the social sciences is likely to be large compared with the number purchased in science. The publishing and usage patterns are important influences on these variations between subjects. Few libraries manage to acquire all they want at the time of publication; this may be due to lack of funds, or to the fact that new developments create the need for retrospective purchasing – back-runs of serials, classic monographs, old government publications. It is important to relate these retrospective purchases to institutional objectives, the availability of interlibrary loans and conservation policies; there is a tendency for librarians to fill in gaps in serial runs to make holdings look tidy, when a little more thought would lead to the discarding of an unused, broken set. Many libraries have special collections which need looking after. These may be related to special responsibilities undertaken by libraries as part of cooperative acquisition schemes; collections of local history materials or subject-related collections, perhaps based on past gifts of material. Libraries have an obligation to maintain the value of such collections – but there are no rules to govern allocation of funds to such activities.

Book and serial prices and other financial trends

Librarians need up-to-date information on prices. It is a key factor in planning – and all budgets must be planned. The librarian is both aided and hindered by the existence of a variety of published price indexes for books and periodicals. The most directly useful are the periodicals price indexes published annually by Blackwell's in the *Library Association record* and by Faxon in the *Serials librarian*. These two international subscription agents, handling subscriptions to thousands of serials, are well placed to calculate average prices and to predict trends. For most libraries in the UK the Blackwells index is a good indicator. Table 2.11 shows how the index has moved since 1974.

Table 2.11: Index of serial prices 1974/89

Year	Index
1974	100
1977	194
1980	237
1983	368
1986	557
1989	693

Books present more of a problem. There is no international index available. For British books, there have been four published at different times. *Average prices of British academic books*[11] was originally derived from the prices of those British books acquired by Cambridge University Library under the terms of the Copyright Act, and considered to be of academic worth. From 1985 the source of data has been Blackwells. This index is now published by the Library and Information Statistics Unit (LISU). The index is analysed by subject and is a good indicator of trends. The second price index covers all British books recorded in Whitaker's database, and is published in *The Bookseller*. Like the LISU index it relates to new editions and new titles. A third index, published in *Financial statistics*, shows a higher rate of increase than either of the other two. It is apparently based on the prices of books available for sale, but the actual details of the sample on which it is based are not clear. A fourth index, representing the average prices of books recorded in the *British national bibliography*, was published regularly in the *Library Association record* until 1981, with an update in 1984.

A price index which relates only to British books is not particularly useful in libraries buying significant amounts of foreign material. Here it is necessary to refer to currency exchange rates. Economists distinguish between real exchange rates, which make allowance for different rates of inflation in the two countries whose currencies are being exchanged, and market exchange rates, which are the rates experienced from day to day. Librarians are mainly concerned with market rates, and since 1973 the British pound has declined in value relative to most currencies. Table 2.12 illustrates these trends. There is little comfort to be gained from these figures for British librarians purchasing material from overseas – except for those interested in the Romance languages.

Table 2.12: Exchange rates 1973/89: value of £ sterling against major currencies

Currency	Index 1989 (1973=100)
French franc	104
(West) German mark	54
Italian lira	155
Netherlands guilder	54
Spanish peseta	138
Swiss franc	38
US dollar	67

US book prices are published in *Publishers weekly,* and exhibit similar trends to those already described. From 1984, *Average prices of USA academic books,*[42] based on data supplied by Blackwells has provided data parallel to that for British books. A related set of indexes is the CVCP *Indexes of University costs.* These relate to actual expenditure – they are indexes of what universities can afford to buy. Data on trends can also be extracted from the statistics compiled by SCONUL[43] and COPOL.[44]

Future trends in budgeting

The interactions between the factors described briefly in this section have been treated in various ways by different institutions: the balances struck are largely the result of political decisions. Since the number of combinations of factors is so large, computer modelling of budgeting is a powerful aid; using a suitable model, the effects of varying different rates, or of introducing new factors, can be shown without the tedium of numerous manual calculations. Leicester Polytechnic Library has a model which accepts as input student numbers and average prices of books and serials and permits variations of weighting according to student use and research demands on library resources. This is only one illustration of the use of microcomputers in situations where the calculations are, while simple individually, tedious to undertake; the widespread availability of spreadsheet packages has made it easy for librarians to experiment with formulae, and to compile their own price indexes to reflect the balance of acquisitions in their own library. It can be expected that such applications will spread. We can also expect that more libraries will be pushed towards explicit formula allocation as more people recognize the limitations of historical budgeting, particularly in times of economic recession when the real purchasing power of libraries declines; and that the whole basis of library budgets in publicly funded libraries will change as the impact of electronic publishing becomes felt, and as the technologies of libraries, computers, communications and teaching media converge. Finally, we can also expect that librarians and others will become more interested in the effects of their budgeting and allocation policies: what happens to the books that are acquired with the funds allocated? At least one university library has published details of the changes in budget allocation made as a result of studying use patterns.[45]

References

1. Simpson, M. et al. (1972), *Planning university development*, Paris: OECD, p.64.
2. Council of Polytechnic Librarians, *Statistics of polytechnic libraries*. Oxford: COPOL.(Published annually.)
3. Bryan, H. (1976), 'The perpetuation of inadequacy', *Australian academic and research libraries*, **7** (4), 213-221.
4. *Average prices of British academic books, 1974* Loughborough: Library and Information Statistics Unit. Published successively by LMRU, CLAIM and LISU.
5. University Grants Committee (1967), *Report of the Committee on Libraries*. [Chairman: T. Parry], London: HMSO.
6. Urquhart, J. and J. Schofield (1972), 'Measuring readers' failure at the shelf in three university libraries'. *Journal of documentation*, **28** (3), 233-246.
7. Planck, M. (1937), *Scientific autobiography*, London: Williams & Norgate pp.33-34.
8. Simpson, M. et al. ref. 1.
9. University Grants Committee, ref. 5.
10. Law, D. (1984), 'No simple formula for library funding', *Times higher education supplement*, 9 March.
11. Handel, A. (1977), *Developing an acquisitions system for a university library*. London: British Library. (BLR&DD Report, 5351.)
12. Larkin, P.A. (1978), *The use of formulas in allocating the library grant*, [London]: SCONUL.
13. Payne, P. (1985), 'Polytechnic library financing', in: Council of Polytechnic Librarians, *Working papers on bookfund allocation*, 10.

14. Goffin, K.R. (1989), *Summary of responses to the survey of the use of formulas used for allocating book funds in UK universities.* [Canterbury]: University of Kent at Canterbury Executive Sub-committee of the Library Committee.

15. Ford, G. (1985), 'Review of: Council of Polytechnic Librarians, *Working papers*' in: *Library & Information Research News,* **31/32,** 38-39.

16. McClellan, A.W. (1973), *The reader, the library and the book: selected papers 1949-1970.* London: Bingley.

17. Betts, D. and R. Hargrave (1982), 'How many books?', *Library management,* **3** (4).

18. Buckland, M. et al. (1970), *Systems analysis of a university library,* Lancaster: University of Lancaster Library Research Unit.

19. Handel, A.(1977), 'A theoretical note concerning the adaptivity of demand for library documents', *Journal of documentation,* **33** (4), 305-307.

20. Astin, J. (1982), 'Cheshire: alternative arrangement and beyond' in: P. Ainley and B. Totterdell. *Alternative arrangement: new approaches to public library stock.* London: Association of Assistant Librarians, pp.13-33.

21. Gold, S.D. (1975), 'Allocating the book budget: an economic model', *Library resources & technical services,* **36** (5), 397-402.

22. Kohut, J. and J. Walker (1975), 'Allocating the book budget: equity and economic efficiency', *College & research libraries,* **36** (5), 403-410.

23. Morley, R. (1969), 'Some welfare economics' in: *Project for Evaluating the Benefits from University Libraries,* Appendix 4, Durham: Durham University Computer Unit.

24. Handel, A. ref. 11.

25. Lewis, P. Private communication.

26. University Grants Committee, ref. 5.

27. Emsley, J. and C. Jenkins (1984), 'A question of bookkeeping', *Times higher education supplement,* 17 February, 16.

28. McDowell, E. et al. 'Bookfund allocation working party: final report', in: Council of Polytechnic Librarians, *Working papers on bookfund allocation,* 95-107.

29. Abdinnour, S.F. (1987) '*Allocation of library funds to the different faculties at Southampton University.*' M.Sc. dissertation, Southampton University.

30. Abdinnour, S.F. and G. Ford, 'Resource allocation for library materials purchase', (in preparation) .

31. Revill, D.H. (1989), 'Cost centres and academic libraries', *British journal of academic librarianship,* **4** (1), 27-48.

32. Revill, D. ref. 31.

33. Council of Polytechnic Librarians (1985), *Working papers on bookfund allocation.* [Oxford]: COPOL.

34. Ayres, F.L. Private communication.

35. McDowell, E. et al. ref. 28.

36. McGrath, W. (1975), 'A pragmatic book allocation formula for academic and public libraries with a test for its effectiveness', *Library resources & technical services,* **19** (4), 357-367.

37. Kohut, J. (1974), 'Allocating the book budget: a model', *College & research libraries,* May, **35,** 192-199.

38. Lovecy, I. Private communication.

39. University of St. Andrews Library (1986), *Annual report for 1985/86,* St Andrews: University of St Andrews Library.

40. Paterson, A. Private communication.

41. *Average prices of British academic books,* ref. 4.

42. *Average prices of USA academic books, 1984-,* Loughborough: Library and Information Statistics Unit. (Published successively by CLAIM and LISU.)

43. SCONUL. *University Library Expenditure Statistics, 1980/81– and Statistical database part II: library operations 1984/5-*, London: SCONUL.
44. Council of Polytechnic Librarians, ref. 2.
45. Peasgood, A.N. (1986), 'Towards demand-led book acquisitions?: experiences in the University of Sussex Library', *Journal of Librarianship*, **18** (4), 242-256.

3 Performance measurement and performance indicators

Ian Winkworth

The possibility of producing performance statistics of impressive arithmetical precision should not delude anyone into thinking that performance measurement is an exact science. It is not. Performance measurement is about logic and judgement. Thinking through the logic of using particular performance indicators is far more important than precise calculation or acres of computer-produced data. There is a plentiful technical literature on performance measurement for libraries. What is lacking is a convincing rationale to persuade libraries to use the measures and indicators proposed. The intention here is therefore to outline possibilities, to provide a framework for selecting suitable performance indicators for collection management, and to provide initial guidance to the literature.

Traditionally the size and variety of its collections were the main measures of the excellence of an academic library. Because scarcity was the problem – it was a question of acquiring one of the few copies known to exist of any title – the notion of too many books was inconceivable. That belief still has deep roots in academic communities. It seems common sense that a library with one million titles is better than one with 500 000. What further performance measures are needed? Yet when there are several hundred thousand books published in the world each year and an institution could spend half its budget on its library, how big is big enough? And is adding more books the best solution? Lancaster[1] and others demonstrate that a probability of 90 per cent that the library owns a book routinely translates into a 45 per cent probability that the user will actually retrieve the volume from the shelf.

In 1975 it was estimated that the world output of book titles to date was 35 million to 40 million.[2] By 1990 that figure has probably passed 50 million. How far can the holdings of one library, be they 10 000, 100 000, 1 million or more, go towards representing this world of knowledge? And how are you sure that you really have the right selection? If libraries have chosen the right books, why is it that stock overlap surveys (for example as reported by Ford[3]) repeatedly show such low overlaps of stock between academic library collections?

Collection management is about balancing additions and withdrawals, and about the storage, display and accessibility of collections, what Buckland describes as 'managing the physical availability of books'.[4] The term 'books' is intended to include periodicals, audio-visual items, electronic and other media. In the last two decades it has become clear that there are severe operational penalties for size, penalties deriving from the administrative structure needed to operate a large library and the higher proportion of unused stock. These offset the economies of scale. Users of large libraries have to come to terms with the sophisticated systems needed to organize a large library. And the easy manipulation of records in automated catalogue systems means that arguments from administrative convenience for retaining every book once it is acquired no longer suffice.[5] What is a 'good' performance for a library collection? To what extent is the optimum performance of an academic library related to the size of its stock? What performance measures should determine the resources put into collection-building? In an age of accountability these are questions which have to be confronted by collection management librarians.

Accountability

There is growing demand from government, within academic institutions and within academic libraries, for evaluation or 'performance measurement'. In the UK this includes the Jarratt enquiry into university efficiency[6] and the 1990 exercise by Her Majesty's Inspectors for higher education which involved special two-day visits to 45 polytechnics and colleges solely to discuss the performance indicators the institutions are using. It is probably fair to assign the main impetus for this to the wish of funders to be assured that they are receiving the best possible value for money, that funds are being spent on the purposes for which they were intended, and that managements are actively managing. However, another source of impetus may come from the steadily growing power of the consumer movement. From this point of view, students (and those who pay their fees) become consumers of services provided by the academic institutions. As such, the students have a right to expect certain standards of quality and facilities in the education they receive. They are no longer probationary members of an academic elite, who must gratefully accept what they are given. This description overstates the contrast, but there is nonetheless a strong trend towards greater accountability of institutions, both to governments and to their students. It is therefore no surprise that academic libraries should find themselves subject to the same pressures for accountability, and if libraries are to be accountable then so must their collection management be.

Studies, most famously at the University of Pittsburgh,[7] have repeatedly shown the traditional belief of academic librarians – that there will eventually appear a reader for any book stored in any location – to be substantially untrue. Meanwhile, accessibility, display, and costing of the benefits achieved have been generally neglected. Academic libraries need a better collection management framework, one which links what is done more closely with the current, specific purposes of the institutions served, produces real outputs, balances the conflicting demands on the library from researchers and students, and does not result in apparently limitless claims for money and accommodation. Performance measurement is the key to achieving such a framework.

Library objectives

Accountability requires an agreed basis of assessment related to objectives and activities. Only the very largest and most famous research libraries – the Bodleian Library, the British Library Reference Collections, for example – may be able to justify their existence independently. But even libraries such as these, enjoying the benefit of legal deposit, are facing difficulties in persuading their funders to provide adequate resources. For most academic libraries there is a quite proper need to demonstrate responsiveness to particular institutional needs and objectives as a condition of funding.

For the academic institution the library provides one of many inputs to the education of students and the advancement of knowledge. The objectives of the library have on one side to be linked to the objectives of the institution and on the other to be made concrete as some part of the outputs of the institution. The activities of the library form the link between the objectives and the outputs. Table 3.1[8] illustrates the relationships. This overall framework is the context within which the place and role of collection management within the overall library operation has to be clearly located.

Table 3.1: Aims, activities and outcomes

Polytechnic Objectives
↓
Library Objectives
↓
Library Activities
↓
Library Outputs
↓
Polytechnic Outputs

Objectives of collection management

Another paper,[9] based on an analysis by Buckland and Hindle,[10] summarizes the tangled trains of thought about the objectives of library collection management. Six major variations are identified. These are shown in Table 3.2. The character of the different objectives can be crudely outlined as follows.

Table 3.2: Objectives of collection management

Completeness
Document availability
Browsability
Circulation and reference use
Reading
Awareness

Completeness

Completeness is not necessarily the uncritical pursuit of quantity of stock; it may alternatively refer to completeness in the sense of representing quality literature. However, the main emphasis in such views inevitably tends to be on increasing the number of titles in a collection. Certainly withdrawal of titles, once added, is wholly alien. The library stock is seen as an independent work of art in itself. A rather lower priority is accorded to the expressed needs of actual current users.

Document availability

The concept of document availability was invented to deal with the difference between theory and practice in the comprehensive collection, where all the required titles are in theory available but, if lending is allowed, a very large part of the potential demand is never met because of the uneven distribution of demand and no duplication of high-use titles. Document availability as an objective results in more emphasis on duplication of titles in order to bring the stock holdings more in line with the actual (short-term) pattern of demand. Performance of the collection against this criterion is also affected by the loan regulations.

Browsability

In browsability the representative nature of the complete collection and the hard-headedness of document availability are combined. A 'good' collection would always have a reasonable selection of the most popular titles to offer and a lower proportion of little-used or unused titles. Browsability is perhaps the objective which most nearly fits the goals of the classic open-access, subject-classified, academic library. It is arguably the case that a reference collection would better achieve the browsability objective than a lending collection.

Circulation and reference use

Circulation is probably the objective for which performance is most easily measured and understood. Data are cheap to collect and the concept is straightforward. One disadvantage is that additional, and much less easy, analysis of reference use is required for a full picture. Secondly, maximum measured performance could be achieved by increasing purchases of cheap, high-use books (conceivably of little or no relevance to the academic objectives) and by shortening loan periods.

Reading

Reading tends to be defined for this purpose as 'document exposure': the hours of use of a book by the reader. This is nearer to an assessment of the value to the reader of the book, but is difficult and labour-intensive to measure, requiring detailed information about the behaviour of readers over long periods. The 'value' is still only represented by a surrogate quantitative measure – hours of reading – which clearly may not represent in any real sense the value to the reader: one key idea or fact can be worth more than 300 pages of text or many hours of reading.

Awareness and document supply

Lastly, there are the notions of 'awareness' and 'document supply', which are perhaps the traditional objectives of many industrial libraries. The aim here is to achieve the maximum knowledge of relevant litera-ture by readers, whether or not the library owns the stock in question, and then to provide access to any items requested, by loan from stock, by purchase or by interlibrary loan. This objective represents the ultimate 'access' approach and the complete antithesis of the 'completeness' objective. There is deliberately limited effort put into building up stock in advance of need, and reliance on a network of information provision agencies is essential. Against this objective the in-house collection may no longer be the main vehicle for satisfying readers' needs, and collec-tion management may seek mainly to minimize the resources invested in collection building.

Formulating practical collection management objectives

To be useful, objectives need to be phrased as targets against which performance can be measured. A statement such as 'supporting the teaching and research of the University' is an inadequate formulation as a collection management objective. How is success defined? Is it simply lack of complaints? But in that case is it known what standards the readers are using to judge the adequacy of the stock? And do they not adjust their demands to the supply? Certainly this is what research, for example at Lancaster University[11] and at Newcastle Polytechnic,[12] suggests. To be practical, objectives must be conceived in terms which allow performance measurement. The appropriate measures of performance depend on the objective or balance of objectives selected. A library whose objective is primarily document availability might decide:

> To make available to readers the literature or information they require:
> > 60% immediately
> > 90% within one week
> > 99% within one month
> all at least cost.

If completeness were the goal, then the objective might be something like the following:

> To attain as representative as possible a collection of the literature of lasting importance, within the constraints of the resources available and the priorities established in the collection policy statement.

The critical features of the objective are, however, the same: clarity, relevance, and measurability. It should also be noted that most of these types of collection management objectives involve other library activities also, for reasons which are explored further below. Only completeness arguably can be measured without including in the assessment an evaluation of other aspects of library services.

The performance context of collection management

Most academic libraries undertake at least twenty different services and activities, including many which depend on the quality of collection management. In these circumstances, together with the many aspects of performance (see below), it seems unwise to seek, as some writers have done,[13] a single performance indicator. There is a tendency for the quality of a collection to be measured primarily in relation to availability and borrowing of particular titles. Yet borrowing is a minority part of the total use of an academic library. Annual surveys carried out in a number of libraries for the Council of Polytechnic Librarians (COPOL)[14] suggest that reference use may account for three or more times as much consultation as borrowing, even from collections which might be thought to be aimed primarily at lending (though it should be noted that other studies have produced widely varying results[15]). The role of the collections in supporting enquiry work and other services is also significant. Table 3.3 demonstrates the range of activities and attempts to group the varied activities into a manageable number of categories for performance review purposes. Collection management is one activity within those relating to provision of stock.

Table 3.3: Library activities

1   Provision of stock (3 activities)

     collection management; acquisition; cataloguing and indexing; covering books, periodicals, AV and computerized sources

2   Document access (6 activities)

     borrowing; reference access; reshelving and collection tidying; photocopying service; interlibrary loans; and reservations

3   Information services (4 activities)

     enquiries; current awareness; information provision; teaching information handling skills

4   Providing study facilities (3 activities)

     study places; equipment for using non-print sources; other facilities

5   Income-earning library services to clients outside the institution (3 or more activities)

     examples: subscription members; consultancy projects; publications

6   Contributing to general institutional management

     through input to institutional policy-making and shared tasks (such as organizational structure, budgetary systems, staff appraisal policy)

7   Management and evaluation

     examples: liaison with customers, library policy-making, target-setting, management, staff training, administration, and monitoring and review of activities

The library collections support a number of direct services to users. Table 3.4 shows the relationships of the activities and the proportion of budget each consumed in one UK polytechnic library in 1988/9. The overheads include all general liaison with clients, staff training and communication, evaluation, and so on. Buildings costs are excluded, since they are frequently contained in a central institutional budget and separate library buildings costs are unobtainable. An estimate of annualized building costs in the polytechnic library added some 25 per cent to total costs, of which half might be attributed to study facilities and half to stock provision. An analysis of spending at Stirling University Library in the 1970s by Peacock[16] confirms the broad picture, except for a higher proportion of expenditure on bookstock provision and less on direct services. This is likely to be typical of many university libraries.

Table 3.4: Library activities: relationships and inputs

Financial category	Activity grouping	Percentage of budget
Direct services	Document access	17%
	Information services	14%
	Study facilities	1%
	Income generating	5%
Capital investment	Bookstock provision	4%
Overheads	Management and evaluation	17%
	Contribution to institutional management	3%

Collection management, and its associated stock provision activities, consume a high proportion of the budget, but have no direct outputs. Table 3.5 shows the main outputs of the library from the four 'direct service' areas of activity. The benefits of the collections are always mediated via the direct services. It is therefore important to stress the interrelationship between collection management and other library activities.

Table 3.5: Specimen library outputs

Document access	issues; reference consultations; photocopies; interlibrary loans; reservations
Information services	enquiries; readers instructed; literature searches; current awareness services
Study facilities	reader visits; reader hours
Income generating services	external use; sales income

Maintaining the collections may reasonably be regarded, like buildings and equipment, as part of the essential capital investment base of the library service. Regarding the library bookstock as a capital item provides a suitable framework both for costing library collection-building decisions and for performance measurement. Like other capital investment, bookstock provision yields its returns over a long (but finite) period and incurs substantial maintenance costs. Spending on the collections is, however, easier to apportion year-to-year, since the investment is naturally spread over a large number of years and is automatically self-renewing. There is therefore no need to resort to accounting devices such as depreciation. The exact timing of bookstock expenditure in one year or another is only occasionally critical (to support specific new initiatives, for example) but consistent neglect is likely in due course to affect the effectiveness of the operation. (This is, by the way, a good description of what happened in UK academic libraries in the 1980s.)

Libraries and performance measurement

At first sight libraries are better prepared than many other departments in the institutions for the new emphasis on performance measurement. Libraries have collected statistics of collection size, annual additions, issues, funding and so on for many years. There are also established methodologies and a large literature devoted to more sophisticated measurement of various aspects of library use. Lancaster's two books on performance measurement,[17,18] Goodall's survey of recent literature,[19] and Revill's article in the *Encyclopedia of library and information science*[20] provide an excellent general introduction.

An examination of the real world, for example through library annual reports, reveals a less encouraging picture. Little effort is made to relate the statistics to the objectives and outputs of the institutions. Most of the statistics routinely collected – except the ubiquitous issue statistics – relate to inputs of resources rather than delivery of services. There is almost no measurement of quality of service. The sophisticated use measures are rarely applied beyond the institutions and research projects where they were developed.

Efforts to gain acceptability for standardized performance measures make only slow progress, as individual librarians seek to frame measures in ways which they feel will show their own operations in the best light and frequently fail to take advantage of research and development already carried out. Thus in the UK the interlibrary comparison exercises for academic libraries conducted by the Centre for Inter-Firm Comparison[21] have begun to impact on collective thinking only in the late 1980s.

Performance measurement

There are also some objective difficulties in performance measurement of any activity. The first of these is that there are many aspects of performance. Cheapness, effectiveness and quality are all part of good performance, but they cannot all be measured in the same way. A typical representation of aspects of performance and their relationship to activities is shown in Table 3.6. A problem with this model is that it rather implies that everything can be reduced to a neat set of simple statistics, fitting the cynical view of one academic manager, who described performance measures as 'devices which permit the ignorant to pretend to make judgements'. In practice, the desired outcomes may be difficult to measure, may not be readily quantified at all, or may be very indirect. How is the quality of activity to be assessed? There may come to be an undue emphasis on economy and efficiency simply because they are more readily quantified. If staff genuinely pursue the measures as stated, will the outcomes be those desired?

Table 3.6: Typical performance measurement schema

Inputs   >>>   Throughputs   >>>   Outputs   >>>   Outcomes
       ↓   ↓   ↓
    Economy   Efficiency   Effectiveness

A standard set of performance measures cannot replace judgement based on local aims and objectives. Evaluation should be ongoing; should incorporate input from clients, peers, funders and the operators of the service reviewed; and should compare achievements with the objectives of the library and of its parent institution. Hence the adoption of the term 'performance indicators', which implies a less deterministic relationship between the measure used and the resulting judgement, in preference to 'performance measures'. Performance indicators are a necessary part of the process of evaluation, but no more. The role of performance indicators is to provide some systematic evidence, which can hopefully be compared with evidence from other institutions or on a year to year basis. Indicators do not supplant judgement. Whether any differences or trends observed are 'good' or 'bad' remains a matter of judgement and interpretation.

Performance indicators for libraries

Performance indicators may be used in one or more of three linked stages of review:

Monitoring: What are the objectives? What is produced? What is its value? What is the cost? Which leads on to –

Comparison: Overcoming or taking account of local circumstances in an apparently objective and fair way. Which leads on to –

Judgement: Of one operation against another; of one time period against the next; about relevance; about quality; about appropriate size of resources.

In the academic library context, the government funders, the managers of the institution, the users of the library, the library managers, library section heads, other library staff – all these are likely to have different requirements. Different types of indicators, and different levels of detail especially, may be appropriate to different purposes and of interest to different people, even when the same operation is being considered.

Those setting performance indicators usually seek indicators which are simple and economical to collect. They need also to ensure that the indicators used are relevant, reliable and consistent year by year. Putting caveats on the reliability or relevance of figures published is rarely effective. The pressures for simplicity are likely to lead to the caveats being overlooked at the comparative and judgemental stages. Thus both partial and over-complicated indicators are to be avoided and care must be taken not to rely over much on single indicators.

A problem at the comparative and judgemental levels is that different institutions may legitimately have set different objectives and policies or may have given their libraries wider or narrower responsibilities. The performance indicators must therefore also be capable of dealing with the varying balances of emphasis in the objectives and activities of different libraries.

Significant comparative data about academic libraries have generally only been available about inputs (money, number of books, staff, balance of spending between stock and other headings) and straightforward outputs (issues, interlibrary loans). Typical are the series of statistics collected and published for UK academic libraries by COPOL,[22] and the statistical database created by the Standing Conference of National and University Libraries (SCONUL).[23] These series of statistics were originally conceived primarily as a measure of resource input and allocation, and as a tool to assist individual libraries in persuading their institutions to provide more funding. Shifting the emphasis first towards measurement of outputs and then towards measures of performance has therefore been a slow process.

There are a number of aspects of performance, and a useful distinction can be made between base data, on which generally applicable performance indicators can be built, and the actual indicators, which allow meaningful comparison over time and between institutions. The indicators are generally best expressed as a ratio of some kind, to control for variations in the nature of the environment, but not all the indicators are quantitative. The suggested main base data elements are given in Table 3.7, below. The actual performance indicators are created by relating various elements of the base data together. The current state of knowledge suggests five, or perhaps six, useful indicators for various purposes. Table 3.8 lists these and relates the definitions to the base data in Table 3.7. These concepts can be applied to most library activities, including collection management. Whatever the shortcomings of this particular framework, which is still being developed, the consistent use of such a schema helps to ensure that the multi-faceted nature of performance is kept in mind, that the interrelationship between different library activities is considered, and that some degree of balance is maintained between different aspects of performance.

Table 3.7: Base data

Data element	Explanation
D1. Clientele	Number of students and staff
D2. Institutional objectives	As stated in mission statements, plans, and so on
D3. Library objectives	General aims and specific targets as stated in library plans
D4. Inputs	Cost of library services/volume of input
D5. Outputs	Issues, reference consultations, enquiries and so on (see below)
D6. Staff hours	Hours per week or year

Table 3.8: Aspects of performance.

Indicator	Definition
P1. Relevance	Library objectives (D3) related to polytechnic objectives (D2) and including assessment of client satisfaction
P2. Delivery	Outputs (D5) related to library objectives (D3)
P3. Effectiveness	Outputs (D5) related to clientele (D1) and including assessment of client satisfaction
P4. Cheapness	Inputs (expressed as costs) (D4) related to clientele (D1)
P5. Cost efficiency	Outputs (D5) related to inputs (D4)
P6. Staff efficiency	Outputs (D5) related to staff hours (or throughput) (D6)

Automated library systems offer some potential for provision of relevant data. Rates of borrowing for different stock areas, borrowing patterns of students on particular courses, and lists of used and unused titles can all be produced from current library computer systems. The systems are less help in calculating the actual performance indicators – no doubt because it is only recently that suitable computing power has been available at reasonable cost and comprehensiveness, and it is only recently that librarians have begun to press for more sophisticated management information.

Statistical packages such as SPSSX and Minitab are generally available on mainframe computers in academic institutions for both number crunching and the application of tests of statistical reliability. Some data can be adequately dealt with on microcomputer spreadsheets and database software, and microcomputer versions of the statistical packages are also now available.

However, those without access to suitable computer facilities or lacking the skills to use them (the learning curve for which should not be underestimated) are not wholly disadvantaged. Sample surveys based on manual consultation of date labels or of books returned are an adequate source of borrowing data for policy-making, and worthwhile analysis of user interviews and questionnaire data can be carried out manually, though this is easier and a larger range of usable information can be extracted if a statistical package is applied.

Performance indicators for collection management

Tables 3.9 and 3.10 below provide a suggested outline framework of performance indicators for collection management based on the structure outlined in Tables 3.7 and 3.8. There is a deliberate emphasis in the suggested indicators on the outputs of the library (D5), relating output to clientele (D1), institutional objectives (D2), library objectives (D3), inputs (D4) and staff hours (D6). A definite shift is advocated away from the traditional emphasis in collection statistics on inputs and on proportions of budget spent on staff and materials. There is no such thing as a 'correct' size of library budget or 'correct' balance of spending. Such comparisons may illuminate differences in output or efficiency, but the key feature is meeting the objectives of the parent institution at least possible cost, not achieving some idealized model of library operation.

Table 3.9: Base data relating to collection management

D1. Clientele	At an overall level student and staff numbers; numbers studying/using particular subject areas are applicable to detailed analysis
D2. Institutional and library objectives	What sort of institution the university or college is seeking to be is clearly vital in determining appropriate collection management objectives; at an individual subject level the corporate plan and departmental plan (if they exist) should provide guidance about depth of collection
D3. Collection objectives	Book availability targets; collection bias targets; collection objectives
D4. Inputs	Materials expenditure, binding costs, staff costs, shelving costs (and, if available, building construction and maintenance costs)
D5. Outputs	None directly; issues, reference consultations and other outputs can be used provided the possible influence of storage, circulation and other policies is allowed for
D6. Staff hours	Staff hours spent on collection management

Table 3.10: Collection management performance indicators

P1. Relevance (D3 : D2)	Comparison of collection management objectives with library and institutional objectives; user judgements
P2. Delivery (D5 : D3)	Meeting book availability or other targets; issues and so on per book and similar measures
P3. Effectiveness (D5 : D1)	User satisfaction with collections; plus issues and so on per FTE student
P4. Cheapness (D4 : D1)	Collection management costs related to student numbers
P5. Cost efficiency (D5 : D4)	Library outputs related to inputs (costs) of collection management
P6. Staff efficiency (D5 : D6)	Task units completed per staff hour

The remainder of this chapter discusses how the performance indicators suggested can be applied to the six different types of collection objectives outlined earlier, and provides examples of and references to the methods of evaluation which have been developed.

Assessing relevance

Relevance (P1 in Table 3.10) is an example of a performance indicator which is predominantly not quantitative. It is possible to invent scaling systems but these will be difficult to apply outside one institution, given the great variation in the way in which institutional and library objectives are formulated. The basic approach is to set the collection management objectives (D3 in Table 3.9) alongside the broader objectives and targets of the library and of the institution (D2 in Table 3.9) to see the extent to which an overall relationship is apparent and the same priorities are in use. This apparently simple exercise can be surprisingly informative, and the very fact of undertaking it can illuminate the causes of long-standing conflicts within the library.

At a more detailed level collection development policies can be useful in likewise clarifying balance of effort and resource between subject areas. In recent years, especially in North America, there has been growing interest in collection development policies, which lay out clearly the type and depth of collection which the library seeks to provide in particular subject areas. The aim of policies such as those advocated by the American Library Association[24] or the Research Libraries Group[25] is to make collection building more consistent and systematic by allocating each subject area a collecting level (such as: comprehensive, research, study, basic, minimal). The Association of College and Research Libraries has also published a step-by-step guide to evaluation of performance which begins with setting out the objectives.[26]

Increasingly, UK academic institutions have followed in the wake of their North American relatives and developed explicit mission statements and corporate plans, with which the priorities outlined in library collection policy statements can be compared. In the past it was sometimes difficult to obtain the detailed planning data from the institution. Within the UK all publicly funded higher education institutions are now required by their funding bodies to have more explicit academic development plans. It is useful also to seek direct input from library users (and non-users), through surveys, small group discussions and formal meetings, about how they view institutional priorities and goals. If there is no written mission statement then the library can use these methods to help it create a statement of what it understands the institutional mission to be.

One problem with mission statements is their tendency to be 'all things to all persons' and therefore to allow variation in emphasis to suit the interests of the interpreter. The direct input from staff and students provides a useful check on the degree of acceptance which the official mission statement enjoys. Thus a mission statement may talk of research 'in support of teaching', but the teaching staff may seek to interpret that phrase very widely because in practice research for its own sake influences career prospects. The otherwise illogical insistence of teaching staff on protecting research journal subscriptions (if necessary at the expense of multiple copies of texts and journals of teaching and learning) is explained and the true nature of the dispute as an institutional one, which the library cannot hope to resolve, is exposed for the institutional leaders to handle.

Lancaster[27] summarizes attempts to use a different test of relevance: matching the subject profile of the library collection with the subject profile of the institution, as indicated by courses and enrolments. But this may prove both more laborious and less successful at capturing the specific goals of the individual institution than the techniques outlined above.

A consideration of Relevance (P1) indicates which (and what balance) of the six different types of collection objective outlined above are appropriate. Most academic libraries in practice operate on a mix of objectives – to be comprehensive or representative in fewer or more areas, to achieve reasonable levels of availability and browsability, to attain high levels of circulation and reference use (to prove that resources are being well spent), and at least to make passively available means of awareness of what exists outside the library. This mix of objectives is also reflected by the users. The same user – approaching at different times as an individual, the member of a class or study group, teacher, researcher, resource allocator, and performance commentator – will at different times subscribe to each of these as the major objective of the library!

However, these objectives cannot all be fully delivered, without enormous resources far beyond those available to most libraries. This can result in disappointment and disillusion for the client community and odium for the library. Indeed, it is arguable that most academic libraries in part survive on the fact that potential users adjust their expectations in the light of disillusioned experience, thus automatically limiting expressed demand to a level not far above what can be delivered. This has the unfortunate consequence of tending to make whatever balance of service the library provides apparently acceptable, when it may be that significant shifts in service orientation would represent better value and a higher level of service. The real priorities will not necessarily emerge from study of use of present services.

A clearer statement of which objectives have priority, justified by reference to the goals of the institution, can offer great liberation and improved use of resources. It may, of course, also challenge some treasured but erroneous beliefs and perspectives. If the library development plan is non-existent or shows little sign of relationship with institutional plans then it is quite likely that the library is failing to offer the positive support it should. Table 3.11 offers a specimen analysis of Relevance. It is strongly recommended that Relevance (P1) is the very first performance indicator investigated, since this checks on the overall direction of the library and provides a much-needed perspective. Without getting this right, quite sophisticated performance measurement exercises can rapidly vanish down blind alleys of little value to practical collection management.

Table 3.11: Assessing relevance (extracts)

A. Policy level

Institutional mission statement

. . . outstanding quality of its teaching and supporting research . . . concern for extension of access . . . continuing education . . . development of the full potential of students . . . harmonious and satisfactory learning and working environment . . . cost-effective operation

Library aims

. . . to disseminate information and ideas in order to meet the literature and information needs of students and staff . . . in ways such that maximum educational benefit is obtained . . . to be responsive to the corporate plan

Collection development policy

. . . to maintain the quality, relevance and up-to-dateness of stock as specified subject by subject in the collection-development policy statement . . . financial resources to be spent to achieve optimum benefit . . . formula for allocating funding . . . initial investment to support new developments . . . purchases related to the teaching and research programmes . . . changes in teaching methods . . . avoid private collections for particular research workers . . . assess expected use before purchase and retention decisions . . . no censorship . . . average availability of 75%

B. Strategic planning

Corporate plan 1990/91

. . . to expand student numbers by 15% over the next four years including new course developments as listed in the attached appendix . . . to improve access to polytechnic courses via various open learning methods . . . to increase consultancy income by 50% . . .

Library targets 1990/91

. . . to review the nature of library services to be offered given higher student numbers and less funding per student . . . to review loan regulations . . . to improve effectiveness of library teaching . . . to develop more varied study facilities . . . to review and develop special support services for open-learning students . . . to complete conversion of all catalogue entries to computerized form . . .

Collection development targets 1990/91

. . . to support agreed new course and consultancy developments as listed . . . to purchase duplicate stock and reallocate stock to match planned relocations of subjects between sites . . . to overhaul general reference collection . . . to improve average immediate availability of lending stock to 65%

Assessing Delivery

Second priority is given to Delivery (P2 in Table 3.10): to checking whether the collections are actually delivering what the objectives assert and what the library staff imagine. Delivery is technically defined as Outputs (D5 in Table 3.9) compared with Collection Objectives (D3 in Table 3.9). At any one time most of the 10 per cent most popular books will not be on the shelves. Special collection provision for students, such as undergraduate collections, short loan collections or reference collections, may compensate in part. But there is always an element of 'collection bias' – defined non-technically as the extent to which the books most in demand are/are not available on the shelves. Buckland[28] provides an explanation of the term and a methodology for applying it. Collection bias afflicts all library collections, always making the collection look less attractive to users than the library staff envisages. However hard they try, it is difficult for library staff to adjust fully to this perspective and to take fully into account the time pressures which characterize much library use, especially by students. Assessing delivery is also an essential corrective to the library tendency to recognize problems and take some action without properly assessing how far the action is successful. The tendency is exacerbated by the likelihood that most users, failing to find what they want, simply accept a less adequate substitute, try another source of supply outside the library or seek to do without.

For the comprehensive library, delivery is achieved as long as the item sought is in stock. The delivery test is a comparison of holdings against lists of desirable titles which are based on academic judgement at a particular time. Standards for library collections based on a list of desirable titles[29,30] or criteria of size[31,32,33] may be helpful. Another approach is to check the stock against bibliographies of published works, or the subject catalogue of a library acknowledged to be excellent in relevant areas.

A traditionally common delivery test of a sort has been the annual stock-check to make sure the books in the catalogue really are on the shelves or on loan and that the catalogue is correct. It is interesting that many comprehensive-minded university libraries who would feel they could not afford the effort to do a user survey annually, found time for an annual stock-taking. The main benefit of library stock-taking is often no more than tidying up of obscurities in the record keeping (or each year rediscovery by a new member of staff of the same obscurities), since it is readily apparent without a stock-check (from reservations and user enquiries) which sought items have been lost. Such an approach is, however, logical enough if the main objective is comprehensiveness as defined above.

If an availability objective has been adopted, then there is need to employ one of the established techniques for testing availability – based on satisfaction interviews with users; based on factual user-experience interviews; or based on testing the actual availability of a suitable sample of titles drawn from reading lists or other lists of sought titles. Lancaster[34] provides methodological details. The use of actual user-experience data is generally recommended, since those data are closest to the actual behaviour of library users. Reading-list-based collection provision can be as ineffective in achieving high availability of the items actually sought as comprehensive provision. Analysis of use of reading-list titles shows that some reading lists appear to be almost totally ignored by students, even though other lists prove a good guide.[35] This point illustrates the way that library policies must be tied properly to the teaching strategies adopted by teaching staff and the learning strategies adopted by students.

Browsability might require a mixture of both comprehensiveness and availability indicators. Alternatively one could also use up-to-dateness, defined as proportions of stock of varying ages. Surveys have shown that newer books are, in general, more heavily used.[36] By way of example, data from Newcastle Polytechnic show that books five years old are used twice as much as books ten years old and three times as much as books which are 15 years old.[37] If the proportion of newer books falls because ageing stock is not replaced and supplemented, then the browsability of the collection is bound to suffer. The best measure of browsability is, however, collection bias, because it most closely reflects actual user experience.

Specific levels of circulation and reference use are unlikely objectives. Comparative data year-to-year are frequently available to show trends, but levels of use are more a test of Effectiveness (P3 in Table 3.10) than of Delivery.

Reading or document exposure is rarely an explicit academic library objective, although the techniques of measurement have been available for nearly twenty years.[38] There is the conceptual difficulty that the availability or not of a book in a library, while a basic essential, may have relatively little influence on the number of hours reading or document exposure by the reader. And researching the document exposure involves going deep into readers' lives, with consequent difficulties in data collection and interpretation. Such surveys are likely to be practical only to an indicative extent, giving very broad guidance. They may be useful indicators of overall library performance, but they are not of great help in assessing collection management performance *per se.*

Awareness as an objective will impose particular and conflicting priorities on collection management. The collection management goal under 'awareness' as a library goal is really the lowest level of stock compatible with user satisfaction. Collection management is only incidental to the main objective. It is immaterial whether more or less of the demand is met from the in-house collections, unless cost of supply from in-house collections is markedly different from the cost from external sources. Measuring success can be either via user satisfaction or via measuring the proportion of users' information input which is gleaned from the library. But in either case the library's own collections may sometimes have only a small influence on delivery performance.

The main performance indicator adopted for assessing Delivery will vary greatly depending on the objectives of the library in question. Whatever the objective it is appropriate to include some test of user satisfaction also. This involves some type of sample survey. A number of methodologies exist, using questionnaires, interviews and small-group sessions. To obtain a full picture, the sampling frame should include all the potential clients, not just those who currently use the library. For a general purpose academic library, the best indicator of overall collection performance with regard to Delivery (P2) is one assessing the availability of the items actually sought by users. Thus one might set objectives and report results as in Table 3.12. On the basis of these results this (hypothetical) library is performing satisfactorily on secondary availability, but needs to take action either to moderate the instant availability targets it advertizes or to improve stock provision or loan regulations to achieve its instant availability target. However, availability is not solely determined by collection quality, but depends also on loan regulations, catalogue effectiveness, display of stock, and so on, so care is needed in drawing conclusions. The use of the quantified target nonetheless draws attention to failings in library service which would otherwise simply be ignored.

Table 3.12: Assessing delivery

Objective	Performance indicator and result
65% instant availability	user interview survey revealing 85% availability for periodicals and other reference items, 48% availability of books for lending
75% availability within two weeks of item being requested (for items not instantly available)	output results showing that 70% of reservations and 85% of interlibrary loan requests are supplied and collected within two weeks
90% of users rate the collections as satisfactory or better	user satisfaction survey reporting 40% of users rate collections as very good and 80% as satisfactory

Assessing effectiveness

The Effectiveness of the collections (P3 in Table 3.10) was defined as levels of Output (D5 in Table 3.9) achieved per potential client (D1). This is judged in two ways – use per student and user satisfaction. Both aspects are important because of the tendency discussed above for user expectations to be influenced by what is provided, including users' previous experience of other libraries. The underlying purpose of this type of performance indicator is to try to evaluate what contribution is made by the collections to the work of the institution.

Levels of use per client are derived by dividing the number of issues, reference consultations, and so on, per year by the client base. Within the thirty UK polytechnic libraries, which serve predominantly teaching institutions with a large proportion of part-time students, government standard definitions for converting into full-time equivalent (FTE) student numbers the actual numbers of students on courses of various types (full-time, sandwich courses involving lengthy work placements, part-time day, evening only, and so on) have been found to be a satisfactory way of defining the client base for performance measurement purposes, with teaching staff numbers used only in a subsidiary way. More heavily research-oriented institutions, particularly where there are few part-time students, may prefer simply to aggregate student, staff and other user numbers, with or without some weighting for different client categories such as is used in the FTE conversion above.

The outputs most closely related to the collections are borrowing, reference consultations and enquiries. Overall visits to the library might also be considered. Borrowing statistics are regularly compiled in most libraries. Reference consultations are not, but can be estimated on the basis of user survey data from sample days, which are then scaled up to provide approximate annual figures. Other techniques for measuring reference use include placing slips in volumes and checking for disturbance, and self-completion slips attached to the books for users to tick or sign. Once again, Lancaster[39] provides a helpful outline of methods.

The successful answering of enquiries depends a great deal on the staff concerned, but many enquiries require reference to the stock, and enquiries are therefore one of the collection-dependent outputs of the library service. The number of visits – for any purpose – to the library is the most generalized measure of library output and hence not discriminating with regard to the library activities responsible. But the quality of the collections is certainly one of the key attractions for many users. The proportion of user visits attracted by the collections, as against study or other facilities, can be assessed by user-activity surveys.[40]

The objective of most collections is to support a variety of direct services, as outlined in Table 3.4. The collection is part of the capital investment of the library. The effectiveness of the collection has to be judged via the outputs of the direct services (unless the collection is seen as a goal in its own right, independent of use). Therefore care has to be taken when using outputs to assess the performance of the collection in order to control for any ways in which the direct services are operated. Changes in the client population, loan regulations, study facilities or the staffing of enquiry points can all affect the outputs independent of any change in the collections themselves. Likewise, differences between libraries may obscure comparisons of collection performance. But at an indicative (rather than explanatory) level, it is reasonable to use the outputs of the library as indicators of the performance of the collections.

It is useful to complement this with a survey of users which asks them specifically to describe what they were seeking and whether they were successful. Such surveys can show up, for example, that books may be available on the shelves but users are not finding them. Table 3.13 illustrates how some performance indicators for Effectiveness might be calculated. In the case of this hypothetical library, the outputs seem to be high. It would be interesting to put these ratings alongside the inputs, as in the cost-efficiency indicator (P5).

Table 3.13: Assessing effectiveness

Client base calculation:

4 600	full-time students x 1	=	4 600
1 350	sandwich course students x 0.9	=	1 215
3 800	part-time students x 0.5	=	1 900
2 600	part-time students x 0.2	=	520
	Total client base (full-time equivalent students)	=	8 235

Output	Total p.a.	per FTE student	average
Borrowings	476 000	58	52
Reference consultations	1 999 000	243	240
Enquiries	237 000	29	32
User satisfaction (as Table 3.12)			

The comprehensive or representative collection will be less worried by low scores on effectiveness than collections with other objectives, since the main objective of the comprehensive collection is long term rather than relating to current clients. For any other collection objective, low scores on amount of use or user satisfaction should be a major cause for concern. Reference to other performance indicators will show whether the problem is lack of recent investment, wrongly directed investment, poor cataloguing or display, sub-optimal loan regulations, or whatever.

Assessing Cheapness

Performance indicators for Cheapness (P4), Cost efficiency (P5) and Staff efficiency (P6) are generally thought to be easier to understand and implement than the indicators for qualitative aspects of performance (Relevance (P1), Delivery (P2) and Effectiveness (P3)). Cheapness is usually defined as Inputs (costs) (D4 in Table 3.9) divided by Client numbers (D1). At an overall, library-wide level, most libraries already have available broadly comparable figures for the financial inputs they receive. Comparative data on clients are also readily available, provided the client base is described in the same way. Such measures are well established in, for example, the COPOL and SCONUL statistical series. Thus COPOL figures[41] show an average cost of £142 per FTE student in 1987/88 and SCONUL figures £244 per student.[42] Comparison against inflation rates for previous years shows that the libraries have been becoming steadily cheaper in real terms. (Other indicators will show whether the level and quality of services have been maintained.)

Assessment of the cheapness of the collection management function is no more difficult. In relation to expenditure on books, periodicals and other materials, few libraries would have any difficulty in calculating the sum spent on materials per client per year. However, there may be an absence of data when it comes to determining the staff costs of collection management. There is often a reluctance to tackle the allocation of staff costs, fuelled by the reports in the literature of mammoth diary-recording exercises used to allocate staff time. This is one of the points where the sense of proportion encouraged by having a schema to cover all aspects of performance is useful. Given the imprecision of much of the data available for performance indicators, there is no great value in seeking to allocate staff time with an accuracy of +/- 15 minutes for each activity of each member of staff. In practice, relatively crude, judgement-based methods for allocating staff time are adequate for the purpose intended.

One approach devised at Newcastle Polytechnic Library and now being tested in several polytechnic libraries estimates the allocation of staff time between activities for a typical current week, by agreement between the staff and their section heads, to the activity headings used in Table 3.3 above. The discipline that all the time has to be allocated somewhere ensures accuracy down to the nearest half-day, which is accurate enough. Approximate costs can be derived by using average salaries for each grade and verifying the totals against actual salary expenditure. It is then possible to indicate proportions of time and staff cost (not at all the same thing) spent on each activity.[43] The calculation can be done within ten person-days of staff effort.

Adding together the materials and staff costs covers 90 per cent of the costs usually included in the library budget. The remainder can be apportioned but it is important to be clear which overhead elements are included. It may be helpful to try to clarify a few key concepts about costs. At least four different variants of cost may be relevant, as shown in Table 3.14.

Table 3.14: Costing terms

total costs	the full costs including capital investment, overheads, maintenance, buildings, and direct costs
direct costs	the costs which can be directly linked to the activity – excluding all general overheads but including a suitable share of any clearly attributable costs
marginal costs	the additional costs over and above what might be incurred for existing activity
chargeable costs	costs actually charged against a budget

Rational collection management has been hindered by the absence of proper consideration of the cheapness of alternative policies. Firstly, it is rare for any library budget to show the total cost of any activity. Building costs and institutional overheads are usually unrecognized in library budgeting. Marginal costs of some courses of action may be assessed, as may the chargeable costs, but these can sometimes provide a dangerously incomplete picture. Thus additional collection enhancement projects in a library, even if they bring marginal funding, will tend, for example, to occupy space and management time that would otherwise have been devoted to different activities. A concentration on chargeable costs can distort decision-making: librarians would perhaps be more cautious in their demands for ever more space in which to store unused books, if the cost of building the space were to be directly deducted from an annual total grant for library provision.

It is important to keep clear the basis on which cheapness is being assessed. Total costs are preferable, but the reality for the present is that most library budgets as identified by institutions include only the direct library costs.

Having determined the total costs of the activity, these can be related to client numbers to provide a comparative indicator of cheapness (fictional data in Table 3.15), which can then be the basis of comparison over time or between institutions. Cheapness may readily be compared on a year-to-year basis for an individual library. It is, however, important when comparisons are made between libraries that common definitions are used. A frequent problem in comparison is that, for example, what comprises 'collection management' or 'stock editing' or 'selection' as defined in different surveys varies greatly. Achieving some sort of agreed standard at this level is much more important than a high level of accuracy in the actual cost estimates.

Table 3.15: Assessing cheapness

Conventional library budget heads	Cost p.a. (£)	Cost per client (£)
Materials	1 300 000	156
Staff	125 000	15
Other (computing, etc.)	38 000	5
Conventional total	1 463 000	176
Other overheads		
Library management etc.	15 000	2
Buildings (costed over 20 years)	130 000	16
Building maintenance	150 000	18
Full costs	1 758 000	212

Cheapness and the measurement of the inputs on which cheapness is based can also be expressed in non-financial terms – as number of books per client, library staff to client ratio, and so on. Library standards have often been expressed as minimum resources required per potential client.[44,45] The UK Atkinson report specified metres of books per student.[46] Thus, assuming an average width for a book of 30 millimetres, each linear metre of books would contain an average of 33 items. On this basis the stock of UK university libraries in 1976 varied between 30 and 195 books per student, with an average of 114. Were some libraries six times better or worse than others? Were some over-provided or some totally inadequate? Perhaps this is because 'How big?' is an inappropriate question. To define the optimum library in terms of size or books per student is to measure only inputs, and that very crudely. Such a measure may be a helpful guide in setting up a library, but it says nothing about local objectives, collection organization, performance or quality, and provides no guarantee whatever of a good library service. The use of financial measures of input – cheapness – is much more amenable to meaningful comparison related to library objectives and allows adding up the total resource costs of a particular activity. It becomes possible to say 'we achieved these objectives at a cost of £x per student', for example, and then to offer a number of possible changes – either seeking to achieve higher objectives with the same resources, or maintaining standards on lower resources, or adjusting both objectives and resources in the same direction up or down.

The methodology used for assessing Cheapness (P4) varies little depending on what the collection management objective is. What may vary depending on the prevailing culture is whether a high score or a low score is seen as 'good'.

Cheapness of alternative collection management strategies

For many years, academic librarians automatically assumed that a high level of resourcing (that is, an expensive collection) was automatically a good thing, and statistics about levels of resourcing (income under various heads, number of books, space occupied by the library, number and grades of staff) attracted far more interest than any others. One of the benefits of the recent greater emphasis on accountability and other aspects of performance has been more scepticism about the assumed automatic link between more resources and a better collection. It is time that collection management librarians recognized the need to take a more balanced view and to consider whether alternative strategies might deliver either the same services more cheaply or better services for the same investment.

Before looking at the costs of alternative policies such as high-density storage, cooperative storage, weeding, relegation or disposal, it is important as a baseline to try to establish the costs of holding stock. These costs will vary between libraries, between locations, between countries, between times. A useful model for determining the cost of holding stock or alternative policies was put forward in 1980 by the UK economist, Professor A.J. Brown.[47] This is based on the concept of a 'cost per book per year', derived from adding together the annual cost of:

- initial cost of the building which houses the stock – infrequent capital cost to be spread over many years;
- cost of heating, lighting, maintenance – revenue cost;
- cost of buying and cataloguing the book – normally funded as a revenue cost but arguably a book is a capital asset like a building, whose cost should likewise be spread over its useful life.

This approach has been further developed as 'life cycle costing' by the British Library,[48] as the costs of even 'free' material obtained through legal deposit are appreciated.[49] Attention should also be paid to the opportunity costs of various courses of action – what other use might be made of the same resources – and there is need to be aware of the influence of external costs on calculations of cheapness. By external costs are meant those costs which are part of the operation but which are borne outside the accounting unit. Thus library costing usually takes no account of the costs to the library user, usually in time, of one policy or another. The 'lazy' reader who fills in a reservation request rather than look on the shelves personally is simply reversing the process of externalizing costs. These are all important concepts for proper judgement of collection management policies.

Assessing Cost-Efficiency

Cost-efficiency (P5 in Table 3.10) relates the Outputs produced (D5 in Table 3.9) to the Inputs (costs) incurred (D4 in Table 3.9). Applying cost efficiency as defined to collection management is uncommon, because of the indirect, mediated relationship between building the collection and users receiving benefits.

If stock provision, including collection management, is recognized as an overhead on the whole library operation, a part of the capital investment, then the cost-efficiency of collection management can only be expressed in relation to generalized overall output measures. But how do you add book issues, enquiry answers and current awareness products together? Library outputs, which generally have no direct price attached, are unlike library inputs and cannot be converted to financial terms and summed together as money.

One possibility is to use visits to the library as the output measure. Analysing collection performance in this way throws into sharp relief the other-worldliness of the traditional comprehensive collection. Thus, interesting comparisons on the basis of cost per library visit can be made between the British Library Reference Division and a polytechnic library, as seen in Table 3.16. Clearly the functions of the two types of libraries are quite different and may justify a considerable discrepancy. Every nation needs at least one library of last resort, but the hundred-fold difference indicates the real cost of a comprehensive collection as compared with an availability-based one.

Table 3.16: Cost per visit, 1987/88[50]

Library	Operating costs	Visits p.a.	Cost per visit(£)
British Library	68 200 000	343 866	198.00
Teesside Polytechnic Library	770 000	341 610	2.25
Newcastle Polytechnic Library	1 480 000	960 000	1.54

An alternative approach, instead of adding the outputs together, is to try to allocate a relevant part of the total collection management costs to each of a group of outputs – document accesses, information units supplied and study hours supported. Once again the discipline of having to allocate all the costs somewhere means that the overall cost efficiency of the resources spent on collection management is reflected, but there is need for further work to try to define principles for allocating collection management costs if sensible comparison between libraries is to be possible.

Given the difficulty of attributing monetary value to the outputs, a further alternative is to assess inputs in a non-monetary way and relate, for example, the frequency distribution of use to the number of books added or in stock. A number of studies, for example by Kent and others,[51] Trueswell[52] and Hardesty,[53] have confirmed the '80 to 20' rule – that a minority, approximately 20 per cent, of any collection generates the majority of use, approximately 80 per cent. And Kent's study showed that 40 per cent of the books added were not borrowed at all in seven years. A variant of these studies compares use rates for different subject areas. This technique has been employed, including at Newcastle Polytechnic,[54] to help allocate collection development funds.

At this point in time there is insufficient experience to determine unequivocally which indicator is the best, but some general conclusions about application can be drawn. The comprehensive collection might almost be defined as seeking the highest possible level of capital investment and a correspondingly low level of cost-efficiency. For collections with availability and other types of objective, a higher level of cost-efficiency, represented by low cost or low volume of input per unit of output, is clearly desirable, since either implies high outputs in proportion to the inputs.

Assessing Staff Efficiency

Staff efficiency or throughput (P6 in Table 3.10) is a familiar concept in evaluating those aspects of stock provision where the output of the section is easily counted in standard units and can be matched against the staff time input – acquisitions and cataloguing, for example. The general definition is Outputs (D5 in Table 3.9) divided by Staff hours (D6).

This was an area where the Centre for Interfirm Comparison exercise made some headway in obtaining comparative data.[55] There is more practical difficulty in assessing the time spent on collection management – selection, stock editing, and so on – because these tasks may be carried out in between enquiry or other work or to a greater or lesser extent by teaching staff, whose time does not count against the library budget (it is an external cost). One might also query what is the output of a stock editing exercise: is it the number of books reviewed, the number withdrawn or transferred to storage, or the average use level of the books remaining?

However, measuring staff efficiency is probably the least critical aspect of performance measurement. This is not because staff efficiency is not to be sought, but because marked inefficiency is likely to emerge anyway from consideration of cheapness and cost efficiency of collection management. And cost efficiency is overall more important than straightforward staff efficiency because it takes into account the relative cost of staff as well as the time expended. Cost efficiency will show whether it may be more efficient to restructure a complicated task and employ more hours of cheaper time or automation to do some of the work than to persist with a craft-based approach in which a highly-paid member of staff does every part of a task such as stock editing or selection. It is suggested that Staff efficiency receives lowest priority as a performance indicator, except when detailed analysis of an operation is needed and no major system changes are contemplated.

Summary and conclusions

For the institution, the outputs of the library are simply some of the inputs (among many) to the main objectives of the institution. The library contributes via student and staff use of library services. Collection management is a capital investment which underpins the direct service operations of the library. For the individual library user, the optimum library collection is one which has all the books one is likely to want, located close together on the shelves, where one expects to find them, not obscured by too many which are not required, and available when one wants them. The problem for the librarian in such a specification is that it is loaded with contradiction, unpredictability and expense. We operate a community service with finite means. Such a service must be imperfect. But it may be more or less so.

There is no single performance indicator which adequately measures collection management performance, for the good reasons that there are several aspects to performance and that the collection contributes to a number of different library services. To focus on one easily constructed measure such as issues per volume or expenditure on collections per student is misleading and counter-productive. However, the number of indicators must not be too large (as arguably the COPOL and SCONUL statistics are) because the non-expert rapidly becomes totally lost in a sea of statistics. The performance indicators used must collectively reflect all the aspects of performance sought. They are not all quantitative because there is a qualitative dimension to library services, but scaling techniques (percentage of users satisfied, for instance) can be used to advantage.

The suggested indicators of collection management performance are defined in Table 3.9. The first and most important is the Relevance of the collection management objectives to the needs of the library and the institution (P1). Confirmation that the collection management objectives are appropriate is fundamental to using the other performance indicators correctly and to interpreting the results. The objective must be expressed in a form which allows determination of whether the collection achieves other targets as expressed in the other performance indicators: Delivery (P2) of the proposed performance; and whether the services delivered achieve Effectiveness (P3). In assessing both Delivery and Effectiveness, there is need to strike a balance between surveys to measure user satisfaction and objective (quantitative) measures of what is produced.

The other side of the performance equation is the Cheapness (P4) and Cost efficiency (P5) of the collection management operation, with Staff efficiency (P6) as a subordinate indicator. Given the long-term, capital investment nature of collection management, caution is needed in assessing Cost efficiency and Staff efficiency, and further research is needed to define satisfactory performance indicators of Cost efficiency.

Concern is frequently expressed about the amount of effort which calculating results for performance indicators may require. The solution is only to seek the level of accuracy needed to inform judgement and decision-making – and therefore using suitable methodologies. There is also no particular reason why every indicator has to be calculated every week or month or year. Some aspects of library performance change only slowly and it may be worth recalculating some data only every few years. It is nonetheless valuable to do so from time to time. In other cases – delivery targets, for example – a more constant watch is appropriate. What is needed is a sense of proportion. A sensible rule of thumb overall might be to accept the spending of 1 per cent or so of the library budget on checking that the remaining 99 per cent is well spent. Such an equation generates enough time to carry out satisfactory performance evaluation, if sensible use is made of methodologies developed elsewhere and of cooperative action.

There is no one ideal of collection management, permitting the application of a standard set of performance indicators in any academic library. The choice of indicators, and the relative weight given to each, are key matters of judgement for each library and each institution in the light of its own objectives. However, steady progress is now being made towards standardizing assessment tools and data definitions, so that reliable comparative data will be available. Without standardized tools, comparisons between libraries will be misleading and superficial. This is why it is important that collection management librarians apply their knowledge and insight to performance measurement. Without such a comparative databank, performance measurement is limited to comparison over time of the performance of a single library.

The resulting review of collection management objectives may lead to a substantial shift away from the Bodleian Grail and towards more effective and more economic academic library collections.

References

1. Lancaster, F.W. (1988), *If you want to evaluate your library...*, London: Library Association, p.14.
2. Slote, S.J. (1975), *Weeding library collections*, Littleton: Libraries Unlimited, p.20.
3. Ford, G. (1980), 'Stock relegation in some British university libraries', *Journal of Librarianship*, **12** (1), p.52.
4. Buckland, M.K. (1975), *Book availability and the library user*, London: Pergamon, p.3.
5. Winkworth, I.R. and B.J. Enright, (1986), 'Relevance and reality in academic libraries', *Library review*, **35** (2), 79-90.
6. Committee of Vice-Chancellors and Principals, (1985), *Report of the Steering Committee for Efficiency Studies in Universities*, (Jarratt Report), London: CVCP.
7. Kent, A. et al. (1979), *Use of library materials: the University of Pittsburgh study*, New York: Dekker.
8. Tables 1 and 3-8 are drawn from: Winkworth, I.R. *Performance indicators for polytechnic libraries*. (Forthcoming publication based on a discussion paper prepared for the Council of Polytechnic Libraries, October 1989.)
9. Winkworth, I.R. (1990) 'Stock management and disposal: collection building and demolition', in M.B. Line (ed.), [provisional title] *Academic library management: proceedings of a study conference, Birmingham, January 1989*. London: Library Association Publishing. (Forthcoming publication.)
10. Buckland, M.K. and A. Hindle (1976), 'Acquisitions, growth and performance control through systems analysis', in D. Gore (ed.), *Farewell to Alexandria: solutions to space, growth and performance problems of libraries*. Westport: Greenwood Press, pp.44-61.
11. Buckland, M.K., ref. 4, pp.119-131.
12. McDowell, E. (1987), *Book availability survey October/November 1986*, Newcastle upon Tyne: Newcastle upon Tyne Polytechnic Library, (Planning and Research Notes, 72).
13. Revill, D.H. (1987), '"Availability" as a performance measure for academic libraries', *Journal of Librarianship*, **19** (1), 14-30.
14. Council of Polytechnic Librarians (1989), *Output statistics, 1987/88*, Oxford: COPOL. (Obtainable from: P. Jackson, Oxford Polytechnic Library.)

15. Stockard, J. et al. (1978), 'Document exposure counts in three academic libraries: circulation and in-library use', in Ching-chih Chen (ed.) *Quantitative measurement and dynamic library service*, Phoenix, Arizona: Oryx Press, pp.136-148.
16. Peacock, P.G. (1978), 'The presentation of library accounts', *Aslib proceedings*, **30** (12), 426-430.
17. Lancaster, F.W. (1977), *The measurement and evaluation of library services*. Washington, DC: Information Resources Press.
18. Lancaster, F.W. ref. 1.
19. Goodall, D. (1988), 'Performance measurement: a historical perspective', *Journal of Librarianship*, **20** (2), 128-144.
20. Revill, D.H. (1990), 'Performance measures for academic libraries', in A. Kent (ed.) *Encyclopedia of library and information science, vol. 45, supplement 10*. (Forthcoming publication.)
21. Centre for Inter-Firm Comparison (1984), *Inter-library comparisons in academic libraries*, London: British Library. (BLR&DD Reports, 5763.)
22. Council of Polytechnic Librarians. *Statistics of polytechnic libraries*, 1977-1989, Oxford: COPOL. (Published annually.)
23. SCONUL (1986-) *Statistical database*. London: SCONUL. (Published annually.)
24. Perkins, D.L. (ed.) (1979), *Guidelines for collection development*. Chicago: American Library Association.
25. Research Libraries Group (1981), *RLG Collection development manual*. 2nd ed. Stanford: Research Libraries Group.
26. Association of College and Research Libraries (1989), 'Standards for university libraries: evaluation of performance', *College and research libraries news*, **50** (8), 679-691.
27. Lancaster, F.W., ref. 1, pp.49-50.
28. Buckland, M.K. (1972), 'An operations research study of a variable loan and duplication policy at the University of Lancaster', *Library quarterly*, **42** (1), 97-106.
29. Lunsford, E.B. and T.I. Kopkin (1971), *A basic collection for scientific and technical libraries*, New York: Special Libraries Association.
30. Voigt, H. and J. Treyz (1967), *Books for college libraries*, Chicago: American Library Association.
31. Clapp, V.W. and R.T. Jordan (1965), 'Quantitative criteria for adequacy of academic library collections', *College and research libraries*, **26** (5), 371-380.
32. Library Association (1982), *College libraries: guidelines for professional service and resource provision*, 3rd ed, London: Library Association.
33. Association of College and Research Libraries (1986), 'Standards for college libraries, 1986'. *College and research libraries news*, **47** (3), 189-200.
34. Lancaster, F.W., ref. 1, pp.90-103.
35. McDowell, E. (1983,1984,1985), *The Set Text Collection, 1981/82* (Planning and Research Notes, 45); *The Set Text Collection, 1982/83* (Planning and Research Notes, 49); *The Set Text Collection, 1983/84* (Planning and Research Notes, 56). Newcastle upon Tyne: Newcastle upon Tyne Polytechnic Library.
36. Kilgour, F.G. (1962), 'Recorded use of books in the Yale Medical Library', *Bulletin of the Medical Library Association*, **50** (3), 429-449.
37. Newcastle upon Tyne Polytechnic Library (1989), *Use of loan stock 1987/88*. Newcastle upon Tyne: Newcastle upon Tyne Polytechnic Library. (Planning and research notes, 81.)
38. Hamburg, M. et al. (1972), 'Library objectives and performance measures and their use in decision-making', *Library quarterly*, **42** (1), 107-128.
39. Lancaster, F.W., ref. 1, pp.52-70.

40. McDowell, E. (1986), *Book availability survey, October-November 1986*. Newcastle upon Tyne: Newcastle upon Tyne Polytechnic Library. (Planning and research notes, 72.)
41. COPOL, ref. 22.
42. SCONUL, ref. 23.
43. Newcastle upon Tyne Polytechnic Library (1981,1986,1990), *Allocation of staff resources, Autumn Term 1980*, (Planning and research notes, 29); *Allocation of staff 1985*, (Planning and research notes, 64); *Allocation of staff time, February 1989*, (Planning and research notes, 83). Newcastle upon Tyne: Newcastle upon Tyne Polytechnic Library.
44. Clapp, V.W. and R.T. Jordan, ref. 31.
45. Library Association, ref. 32.
46. University Grants Committee (1976), *Capital provision for university libraries: report of a working party* [Chairman: Professor R. Atkinson], London: HMSO. p. 29.
47. Brown, A.J. (1980), 'Some library costs and options', *Journal of Librarianship*, **12** (4), 211-216.
48. Stephens, A. (1989), 'Life cycle costing', *British journal of academic librarianship*, **3** (2), 82-88.
49. Enright, B. et al. (1989), *Selection for survival: a review of acquisition and retention policies*, London: British Library Board.
50. Butchart, I., Private communication.
51. Kent, A. et al., ref. 7.
52. Trueswell, R.W. (1969), 'User circulation satisfaction vs. size of holdings at three academic libraries', *College and research libraries*, **30** (3), 204-213.
53. Hardesty, L. (1981), 'Use of library materials at a small liberal arts college', *Library research*, **3** (3), 261-282.
54. Newcastle upon Tyne Polytechnic Library (1989), *Use of loan stock 1987/88*, Newcastle upon Tyne: Newcastle upon Tyne Polytechnic Library. (Planning and research notes, 81.)
55. Centre for Inter-Firm Comparison, ref. 21.

4 The impact on collection management of automated systems and services

Ian Lovecy

Library automation in the UK has had two aims: cost-cutting, in terms particularly of numbers and grades of staff, and the improvement of the visible services to readers. If that sounds cynical, there is nevertheless a good deal of truth in it. Automation of cataloguing provides both elements (records can be bought in by fewer, less-qualified staff, and an OPAC can give readers better access than before); and automated circulation clearly not only affects readers directly but can also reduce the time spent by staff filing slips. In acquisitions, the benefit to users is indirect and the main benefits would be to library staff. It is hardly surprising, therefore, that in a survey carried out in 1984 by the Marc Users' Group 73 per cent of the 70 academic libraries in the sample used automation in cataloguing, 63 per cent used it in circulation, and only 17 per cent used it in acquisitions.[1]

It is fully in keeping with this approach that the production of statistics, even from those aspects which *are* automated, lags behind the potential. Librarians have kept statistics since time immemorial, not always sure why but convinced it was a 'good thing'. When systems became computerized the statistics could be kept on disc rather than with five-barred gates on scraps of paper (or sometimes in elegant ledgers, painstakingly written in copperplate); few have questioned whether we need to keep the *same* statistics, or whether there are others which are now available. Collection management makes considerable use of statistics; whether because of the continuing paucity of these, or a lack of belief in collection management itself, it is not really surprising that little has in fact happened to that aspect of librarianship since the widespread introduction of automation.

That there is no commercial collection-management module available is equally unsurprising (it is more to be wondered at that there should be an experimental system, described at the end of this chapter). What is more worrying is that the potential of many systems to contribute to this activity is still hampered by gaps in the data collected or archived, or in the programs available for analysis. Given the close connection between collection development and acquisitions, a brief look at the state of automation in that area may prove enlightening.

Automation in acquisitions

Computerization of acquisitions has largely been driven by two aims: more efficient, quicker, and less staff-intensive ordering and accessioning procedures; and the desire to reduce keyboarding by entering a record into the system at the earliest possible moment. The aims of the Lancaster University system echo many others. It is designed to:

- record bibliographic details of all books ordered, produce printed orders to suppliers, and provide information on the progress of any order;
- process invoice information as orders arrive, and maintain up-to-date expenditure and commitment figures for numerous budget categories;
- provide a basic bibliographic record which can be enhanced to form the final catalogue entry.[2]

The automation of these processes is not by any means irrelevant to collection management; efficient management certainly requires the additional speed of ordering, and this can be brought about by using bought-in data from standard bibliographies which therefore do not (or at least should not) require checking. Library suppliers are gearing themselves for electronic ordering systems,[3] and the facility – related to specific suppliers – is offered by systems such as BLCMP. At present the facility is more used by public than by academic libraries, because of the tendency for the latter to make use of a wider range of suppliers for specialist material.[4]

Equally, insofar as ensuring that budgets are spent productively is a part of collection management, the potential of automated ordering systems for alerting staff to the existence of duplicate orders is clearly important. This may be done by checking ISBNs (with a possible problem in that a book may be ordered under two different ISBNs: hardback and paperback, or English and American), by an acronym check on author or author and title to see whether similar entries already exist in the index, or by using an authority file to call up any existing records with the same author. The use of full MARC data produced by another library assists this checking, since once the MARC record has been found it can be checked in a number of ways with the existing file; it will always match with any previous copy recalled. This obviates the danger that the same book will be ordered under two different forms of the author's name, or a variant title deriving from the recommender's lapse of memory. It would be possible (although no system currently offers it) to use a series entry in the MARC record to produce a warning for the librarian, thus catching some of those cases where an item is ordered individually which duplicates one arriving under a standing order for a series.

Another helpful feature of many automated systems is the appearance in the same file (usually an OPAC) of both order and catalogue records, with a consequent saving in time of checking and minimizing of chances of excessive purchase. Interfiling of orders and catalogue records is not, of course, only possible in automated systems – many manual catalogues contain order records also. However, given the staffing levels at which academic libraries in general currently operate, the duplication of labour-intensive tasks such as filing is not an attractive prospect, and such manual systems are very vulnerable to staff cuts.

Modern acquisitions systems do include some data for evaluative purposes, usually relating to assessing supplier performance. This is, for example, a feature of the Lancaster University system already mentioned; and the production of management information (such as vendor performance reports) appears in the list of functional criteria for the system at ICRISAT.[5] It is also an aspect of the acquisitions modules of many of the major systems suppliers. However, other important information – such as details of the recommender or the price (expected and actual) – are entered as standard into most order records. Where such information can be linked with that from other areas of library operation, either through the use of an integrated housekeeping system or by reading data from disparate sources into a microcomputer, the potential for sophisticated management of collections becomes greater.

The processes of collection management may be regarded as falling into three areas: how to acquire what; how to treat it in the library; and when to withdraw it to where. The first, in these days of financial stringency, must include the question of whether the particular item is better purchased or borrowed through some local or national form of cooperation. The second relates to the question of the number of copies and the possibility of short loan or reference as a way of making the item more available. The third, not far from heresy in university libraries at least, concerns the withdrawal of material to store, to cooperative stores, to specializing libraries, or its total discard! All these involve value judgements, and as such are still best handled by people rather than computers. It is the information needed for these judgements which is actually or potentially available from computerized housekeeping systems, or from external automated systems which have often grown up to feed housekeeping operations. It can be considered under the following headings: *Availability, Demand,* and *Balance.*

Availability covers the various aids to selection, and also what is known about the location of other copies. *Demand* covers the questions of *who* needs an item, how high a priority it has, and how urgently it is needed. *Balance* relates to the way in which the collection covers the spread of academic activity, the satisfaction and indeed the production of purchasing policies; these days it must also include questions of whether the available funding is properly spread not only between departments and subjects but also between material in different media.

The data on availability, demand and balance feed into all three areas of collection management identified above, although clearly some have closer links with certain areas than with others. Under the three headings I have chosen (which can be further sub-divided) I should like to consider both the impact of existing automation (whether or not it has yet been recognized) and, by looking at trends, the likely impact of future developments.

Availability

Book selection

In 1972 an experiment was undertaken by the Aslib Research and Development Department to examine 'the technical and economic feasibility of providing selective notifications of current books to specialized libraries by extraction from MARC tapes.'[6] Almost twenty years later, it is worth quoting from the conclusions:

> It seems that a retrieval system intended to aid book selection by special librarians could provide a list of recently published books of which about half would be of interest to the library for which the profile had been designed. As the total number of references received would be small, on average, this low precision does not seem worrying. . . Such a service . . . would provide a very useful supplement to publishers' announcements and standing orders for series known to be useful. In less central areas of interest, where complete coverage is not required, a MARC book selection service providing a list of an average of fifteen books per week could save the acquisitions librarian a lot of time scanning publishers' announcements, reviews, etc.

In 1989 a similar type of service was finally started on a commercial basis, by Book Data. Book Data uses a database of pre-publication material (which must improve its currency over the Aslib experiment) and selects records from it by broad subject category. These records are supplied to libraries either as conventional print listings or as ASCII files on floppy discs; for academic libraries consideration is being given to the production of topic lists for circulation to academic staff, and to the mounting of the entire database on a JANET host.

One indicator that this service is intended primarily for selection purposes is that records are transferred in ASCII rather than in MARC exchange format, making them unsuitable for reading into many housekeeping systems. It does, however, reduce the ease with which selections can be turned into orders. On-line services such as BLAISE-LINE and OCLC are frequently used to provide records for acquisitions systems, but are seldom used as selection aids: in the 1984 Marc Users' Group survey only two of the 154 libraries responding said they made use of on-line services for selection. In the case of OCLC some blame may attach to the search facilities, but BLAISE-LINE was designed in part as an on-line retrieval system. Other disincentives might be on-line costs, and the whole tradition of on-line searching which relies on librarians as intermediaries – and which consequently sorts ill with the tradition of selection by academic staff. Finally, it should be noted that in the academic context on-line searching has been regarded as a way of answering specific questions rather than of providing general selections; even today, on-line-based SDI services are only embryonic in the academic sector.

The appearance of CD-ROM has effected a significant change in this respect, for by transferring the charge from usage to an initial subscription, producers of CD-ROMs encourage greater use as a way of reducing the unit cost. The number, and more importantly, the nature of such products is now significant: *Books in print plus* from Bowker (who also produce *Books in print with reviews plus*), Whitaker's *BOOKBANK*, and *BNB on CD-ROM* are perhaps the most important in the current publications area, but subject-specific products such as the *GPO monthly catalog* or *Biography index*, and even major bibliographies such as the *Cumulative book index*, are also relevant.

Almost without exception the CD-ROM products are the equivalents of hard-copy services. Their advantage over the printed versions is the facility to search them in a number of ways on particular fields or combinations of fields, especially the ability to use keywords and Boolean logic. This can assist in finding specific items, as in many OPACs, particularly in the case of government departments where the exact title is not known; but searching across titles, subject headings, and perhaps even contents notes using relevant keywords can produce a selection of potentially relevant items. Although these may have to be considered individually, considerable time is saved over traditional methods such as ploughing through the relevant classified sections of *BNB*; moreover, some items are retrieved which would not be found by traditional methods because of the limitations of the classification systems used.

Because the items retrieved can be saved on disc and subsequently printed out, use of CD-ROMs makes possible the circulation of lists for perusal by other colleagues or by academic staff – the sort of service, indeed, which Book Data operates. Equally, because searching involves no additional expenditure irrespective of the time it takes, academic staff may use the system themselves. However, the CD-ROM products do not have the advantage of currency which Book Data offers. Partly because they have been seen, in practice, more as a way to get order records into a system at an early stage than as a selection tool, and partly (I suspect) because of the high storage capacity of the discs, which makes it at least *appear* uneconomic to produce a disc with only a few more extra tracks, they tend to be less current than their hard-copy equivalents. *BNB on CD-ROM* is updated quarterly, as opposed to the weekly issues of the hard copy; *Books in print plus* is another quarterly, while the CD-ROM version of the *GPO monthly catalog* is in fact updated *annually*. Interestingly, Whitaker's *BOOKBANK* has the same monthly frequency as Whitaker's *British books in print*, but because of the format of the records is a selection tool greatly superior to the hard copy, which is generally used more for confirmation of the accuracy of data.

A further disadvantage of CD-ROM services is their single-user nature. Lists derived from them can of course be circulated; but only one person can actually produce the list at any one time. Because of the storage capacity a single disc will cover a lengthy period of book publication, so that for any update of *BNB on CD-ROM* there could have been at least twelve copies of weekly *BNB* at various stages of circulation among staff. Even if publishers of the CD-ROMs ceased to make them cumulative and published a new one for each update (and the cumulation is one of their advantages, of course), the lack of equipment on which to use them would still restrict the number of staff who could access them simultaneously. Networking of CD-ROMs is still in its infancy, and the indications are, from the fact that agreements for the products stipulate that they are only for single-user systems, that networking will not be allowed without a substantial increase in cost. The cost is already high enough to make multiple subscriptions, at least in academic libraries, unattractive.

It is here that a version of the Book Data database mounted on JANET would score very heavily. Accessible from any terminal on a campus network, there would be no communications costs; and if it were charged as an annual subscription, it would have all the advantages of CD-ROM with many of the advantages of the hard-copy also. In some cases systems suppliers are able to provide suitable databases. BLCMP has mounted the Whitaker database, and has investigated the possibility of mounting the databases of major library suppliers. However, once again the rationale is the provision of full bibliographic records at an early stage, rather than facilitating book selection. Other systems, for example Geac and Bookshelf, provide potential requirements files, and some of these have searching facilities comparable to OPACs.

Given the fact that in the Marc Users' Group survey referred to, 41 per cent of academic libraries said that *BNB* was less important for book selection than publishers' announcements, and a further 21 per cent rated the two sources of equal importance,[7] potential requirements files into which data from both booksellers and ultimately publishers can be imported are likely to be quite important in the academic context. The sort of system which might be established is perhaps hinted at in public library experience. Leicestershire Libraries and Information Service has established a profile with T.C. Farries, which produces from publishers' advance information a Forthcoming Top Titles list. This list is scanned by all those in Leicestershire with responsibility for book selection; in addition to the Farries' data the list contains locations of the same ISBN which are already within the system, and also details of other editions of the same title. The latter data are currently input manually, but clearly the task could be done by computer using acronym searching techniques (this is presumably not yet felt to be worthwhile or cost-effective). In an academic library, the use of profiled lists of publications which can be considered simultaneously by a number of people (outside the library as well as within it) in the context of other data relating to the need for the item could clearly be a considerable help in book selection.

Alternative sources

Many academic institutions have library systems which cover more than one campus; with the recent wave of mergers some, such as Anglia Higher Education College, cover more than one town. It is clearly important for such institutions to know whether an item which they intend to purchase is already available at another site. It may, of course, still be necessary to buy a further copy, or it may be necessary to relocate the book to provide an optimum service; these are matters which can be decided on the basis of demand. The availability of union catalogues which are reasonably up-to-date, and which can often be created fairly rapidly following a merger, is nevertheless an example of the impact of automation on collection management.

However, it is in the context of official or unofficial cooperation with other libraries that automation has had a really significant impact. Manual catalogues, with the exception of those which were actually printed and published, are for the most part available only in the library for which they are created. The creation of a regional union catalogue is a major undertaking and it is scarcely surprising that the only means of access to locations of modern books in such systems has often been the ISBN. Moreover, such catalogues are held centrally, away from inspection by the staff of member libraries, let alone by members of the public; they are useful for location of copies to borrow, but cannot assist with the question of whether to buy in the first place.

Automation is changing all of this. The ISBN lists of the UK Regional Library Systems have been computerized and produced on microfiche for circulation; some, such as the Wales Regional Library System's listing, are being made available on-line. This enables a preliminary check to be made to see whether an item already exists in the area, although its use is limited by the delay in inputting data into the database, the failure of many libraries to submit the necessary information, and the significant lack of accurate information about withdrawals and losses.

The most sophisticated of these systems is undoubtedly VISCOUNT, run by the London and South Eastern Region (LASER).[8] Although in origin an interlibrary loan system, the LASER database has been for some time used by a number of libraries as a source of catalogue records. The networking which is the essence of the VISCOUNT project is still directed at interlending, with priority given to the transmission of requests; it nevertheless allows the inspection of the database to see who holds what in a way which can assist decisions on whether or not to purchase. As the system is extended to areas away from the South East (VISCOUNT is now being offered to many other regions) provision is being made to search the database starting with local members and widening the search subsequently. This clearly has relevance to the question of checking for alternative holdings before purchase, since the existence of a copy in a library a few hundred miles away may be irrelevant.

However, even less sophisticated systems, or completely informal systems, have benefited from automation. The ability to search some part of the British Library Document Supply Centre (BLDSC) catalogue over JANET, for example, may affect decisions on collection building – if only because an item needed urgently may come more rapidly from BLDSC than from a bookseller. The encouragement of Local Information Plans (LIPs) has given an incentive to cooperative acquisition and the sharing of resources, but this would be virtually impossible without the ability to hold up-to-date catalogues of one's partners on computer output microfiche (COM), or to access them on-line. Whether such systems have started as interlending and resource sharing initiatives, or as fully-planned cooperative acquisitions schemes, the result is the same in terms of the reduction of purchases of peripheral material which is essential to the collections of another member of the LIP.

Other schemes have been based on cooperative cataloguing – the cooperation between the three major libraries in Birmingham is an obvious British example; and if OCLC has really not gone much further than interlibrary loans, both the network of the Association of Research Libraries (ARLiN) in the United States and the Consortium of Research Libraries (CURL) database in the UK have a distinct place in collection management. In these instances the main impact may not be on collection *building* so much as on cooperative *withdrawal*; ensuring that a copy of a text remains available, extant somewhere in the system, but allowing other libraries to withdraw surplus copies. The CURL database, which makes provision for input of information about the condition of the item, is also intended to assist libraries in conservation programmes, in directing resources to the improvement of items of which there is no well-conserved copy elsewhere. A similar use could be made of ventures such as the *Eighteenth century short title catalogue.*

Such schemes of cooperative withdrawal (or retention, depending on your point of view) are perhaps more cost-effective than the cooperative stores, such as that at Egham, Surrey, used by the libraries of the University of London. However, one advantage of a cooperative store is that the copy which is retained is always that which is in the best condition; should a later withdrawal be of a higher standard it can be substituted. Unless some indication is made of the condition of the item in the catalogue record, or unless a library can indicate in its catalogue those items which it is willing to retain in perpetuity so that withdrawn copies in good condition can be sent for possible replacement, then a system may find itself retaining a copy which is falling to pieces and withdrawing a near-pristine copy.

The interavailability of catalogues has also meant that the interlibrary loans librarian is no longer the sole guardian of the knowledge of where to find material. Academic staff, researchers and even undergraduates can access catalogues on-line via JANET. A rapid glance at the *Directory of library catalogues on JANET*[9] shows that a large number of academic libraries are making their catalogues available in this way, and there is a fair amount of evidence to suggest that readers are actually using these – particularly where a locality has more than one academic library. What this does to their awareness of available resources is perhaps best considered as part of demand.

It is this ability to consult each other's catalogues which has led in some measure to the substitution of informal cooperative acquisition in place of formal schemes. These latter, such as the London Union Catalogue or the scheme covering the UK interlending regions, began to fall down as the volume of publishing increased and the budgets failed to keep step with book prices. In general, few academic libraries took part in such schemes (being at the time fairly confident about the need for self-sufficiency, at least in a university library). Purchasing a book which one might never use oneself but would instead continually lend to others is a policy which library committees have always found hard to swallow. If, however, it is easy to see whether anyone has already bought the book, it becomes much easier to leave it to the first library that really wants it to make the purchase; a library may well refrain from buying second copies of items which will be little used and which have been purchased by a neighbour, in favour of the purchase of other peripheral material which would not be available in the area at all, irrespective of any theoretical specialization. Often cooperation over withdrawal operates on the same random basis, on the assumption that over a period and a range of titles it breaks about even, apart from the potentially disastrous consequences for conservation already mentioned. Cancellation of serials titles may work on the same principle – although this does tend to cause some bitter feelings on occasion; again, it is easier to administer if one is dealing with the up-to-date details of what is subscribed to which can be found in an on-line catalogue, rather than relying on printed or photocopied lists which are frequently out-of-date. Local serials holdings lists are more easily generated by combining computerized files, and an on-line check to ensure that the latest, or some other specific, volume has arrived in the holding library can make requests, or referral of readers, less chancy.

Demand

Recommendations

Many academic libraries are reliant, wholly or in part, on the academic staff of the institution for recommendations as to book purchases. In such a pattern there are always tensions: a single member of a department may hold almost dictatorial power over the collection; or everything must go before a committee, which meets infrequently and struggles to achieve consensus; or recommendations are held up almost indefinitely because the appropriate member of staff is the newest person in the department, with lecture courses to write, no influence to persuade more senior colleagues to make recommendations, and no enthusiasm for the job whatsoever. The traditional methods of trying to overcome this, from the library side, are the feeding of relevant staff with publishers' blurbs and constant harassment in varying degrees of subtlety. One thing which can make staff reluctant to order material is the need to fill in an (often complicated) form, and to search for data with which they would not normally concern themselves, such as ISBNs (and even price!).

Clearly anything which reduces the manual labour is likely to improve the situation. Allowing lecturers access to an on-line recommendations system may well assist. If recommendations are dated, a check can be made – by the library – as to whether any effort is being made in the department to deal with them. Equally, library staff would be able to scan the list and on the basis of their expertise to convert some recommendations into orders before the departmental representative gets round to it. Depending on how access to the list is managed, it might be possible for a different department to place the actual order from that in which the recommender serves (although in the present financial climate that would probably require anonymity of requests; a more likely scenario is that Department B decides not to order because they see that someone in Department A has recommended the title).

The question of how the data get into the file is equally of relevance. If any member of the academic staff with a terminal connected to the campus network can make a recommendation, that may attract some of the reluctant form-fillers. If the data can be transferred from elsewhere, for example the catalogue of another library in which the member of staff has found the book, then the labour involved will be less still. Equally, the departmental representative who objects to looking up price and ISBN may take a different line when offered Whitaker's *BOOKBANK* and the facility to transfer all the data to the recommendation file without the need to write out a form at all. Thus the use of the various automated selection aids already mentioned may not only simplify selection but increase recommendations.

In theory, it would be possible with a system like this to make some assessment of the level of demand or support for a book, by allowing people to add their names to recommendations which already exist (rather like motions in the House of Commons – some would say, with about as much effect). In some respects this is what happens in Leicestershire, where those responsible are library staff, who can be trusted both to do the job and to give sensible thought to it. The recommendations of the several branch librarians are all recorded against a title, and the result can be looked at by a stock coordination meeting to ensure that the total balance is correct. In practice it is difficult to see how this sort of system could work in an academic setting, where only a part of the staff would bother to engage in such a process, and where (as noted above) the financial pressures militate against adding support for something which is likely to be bought from someone else's funds.

Response to use

All the aspects of automation so far mentioned have been related to acquisitions or cataloguing systems. However, the effects of automating other areas of library housekeeping operations are at least as important for collection management. Even if the recommendations system does not encourage suggestions, or allow the library to assess demand, real need which is unsatisfied by library stock (or at least by the stock of *a* local library) will surface as interlibrary loan requests. It has always been theoretically possible to analyse the interlibrary loan requests of a university by title, journal, and department, but it has to be admitted that the average university library, making perhaps over 5 000 applications a session, has not in recent years been able to spare the staff time to make the analysis. Modern automated interlibrary loan systems, such as that developed by Lancaster University,[10] can produce statistics of use for book or journal titles, and list all those which exceed a number entered by the user. Various analysis codes can be entered, usually related to a requester's subject area, and statistics are kept separately for different statuses of users – staff, postgraduates and so on. This enables specific groups making heavy use of the system to be shown up, and this may in turn be an indicator of areas of weakness within the library stock; certainly a high number of interlibrary loans for undergraduates in a particular department suggests a need for more material. The availability of resources to correct any such weakness is a different matter, of course; but highlighting potential gaps can concentrate efforts in useful directions. It also allows some assessment to be made of the relative cost benefits of purchase or interlibrary loan, particularly in the case of periodical subscriptions.

It is, however, the circulation system which is of prime importance to the collection manager. A satisfactory computerized circulation system can produce all sorts of data of relevance to the stocking of the library; the only question which such a statement begs is what is meant by satisfactory. With a system which is truly integrated all sorts of interesting data could be produced. For example, if the bibliographic record retains acquisitions information, titles could be selected according to who recommended them. The subsequent circulation history for these titles could then be looked at. Over a period of time, it might be possible to identify those members of staff – there are bound to be some – whose recommendations are rarely if ever borrowed. Future recommendations from that source may be treated with some scepticism; but equally the feedback may be of use to the person in question. The subjective and sometimes prejudiced feelings of library staff can be replaced by such evidence as 'of the twenty-four books purchased on your recommendation in the last five years, one has been issued twice and three others once'. This may to some extent reduce the political and personal problem of putting this to the member of staff in question. At Reading University an assessment of a similar sort was made of books recommended for the Short Loan Collection, where Library staff perception had long been that the books which were used were the ones transferred as the result of requests by students rather than by teaching staff. The result of the effort put into this was not only the reduction of the collection from 6 000 to about 3 500 volumes, but also considerable interest among some of the worst offenders among the academic staff as to *why* the books they thought were needed were not used. This led to the reassessment of reading lists in some cases, and can therefore be said to have affected not just stock management but the quality of teaching also.

Sophisticated, fully integrated systems are not yet the norm for academic libraries: the Reading exercise was confined to the Short Loan Collection because there were manual records of who had recommended the transfer, the stock was small enough for these to be associated with the statistics, and non-loan could be identified because a transaction record existed changing the status of the book to short loan. However, a circulation system alone can still provide a quantity of useful data for the collection manager. Analysis of use of particular areas is the prime element in this; or perhaps it should be analysis of *non*-use. To be able to divide the stock by classification, in varying degrees of detail, and to discover if parts of it are rarely borrowed, is a great help in indicating areas which perhaps need attention. The ability to change the range of classification numbers surveyed makes it relatively easy to refine down a search – to see whether the problem exists across all of British History, or whether it is the lack of interest in the Tudors which is affecting the rest of the section. Similarly 'hot spots' of high use may be drawn to the manager's attention as potential areas where additional stocking – of copies, titles or both – may be necessary.

Taking the appropriate action is, of course, still a matter for the judgement of a librarian. There is, for example, no point in increasing the stock of books on the Tudors if the reason they are not borrowed is that the topic is not taught! One advantage of automated systems is that they can present the collection manager with several aspects of the information required to make decisions: how many books there are in the area, the dates of publication, and so forth. Again, a sophisticated system would enable an area to be analysed, in terms of use, by date of publication, thus allowing the librarian to see whether it is the existence of an historic and now irrelevant collection of material which is disguising the proper level of use of more recent acquisitions.

The more information which can be drawn together from different sources the better informed will be the decisions on collection development. A subject area may have a generally aging stock, but one which is still relatively heavily used. Is this because these are still the standard works, or is it because there is nothing else for students to use and they must use *something*? Assessing the past few years' publications in that area may give some indication of whether newer material is available; again, this is hardly likely to be done if it means counting items in *BNB*, but it may be possible using either an on-line or CD-ROM database. Either of these could be searched by class number where there was a more or less exact match; the use of subject keywords could overcome problems of, for example, a library which uses Library of Congress classification searching a Dewey-based index. Some of the services, for example Bowker's *Books in print with reviews plus*, attach book reviews to their references, which would be helpful in such circumstances; alternatively citation indexes might be used to find out which of the new texts have aroused interest – and indeed, whether the existing old stock is still part of the general current research effort. Again, while this could be done manually, it would be more feasible using an on-line process (and with the recent agreement to mount ISI databases on JANET, cheaper too).

On a less general level the analysis of specific titles is obviously important both in the purchase of additional copies and in deciding on the appropriate loan regime. Sussex University developed the Geac system in its library to provide an historical record of the number of loans per copy per term for the previous six terms for any title.[11] The analysis by term is helpful also in predicting periods of high use for titles which are not constantly active. Such information allows the collection manager not only to ensure an adequate supply of copies, but also to put some or all of them into a short loan collection at the appropriate time; at Sussex the experience has been that current provision can be significantly improved without prejudicing collection building for the future.[12] Often such systems require someone to look at the record for a specific title; it is not unreasonable to expect that an automated system could itself trigger investigations into the adequacy of copy availability. This can be related to total number of loans; number of loans per copy; number of loans per copy over a specific period; or any similar figure. The last of these is the most satisfactory: the longer the period over which usage is averaged, the easier it becomes to disguise peaks. Equally, however, an analysis period must be long enough for more than one loan to take place. Hence the termly basis established at Sussex is probably the most suitable measure.

More satisfactory than simple loan analysis might be reservations analysis, which will show up actual rather than highlighting the potential failure in provision. The SWALCAP shared circulation system automatically flagged an item for transfer to the short loan collection when there was a set number of current reservations for it; such flagging both helped to solve the immediate problem of supply and acted as a warning to staff that there might be an inadequate number of copies of the title. The BLCMP Library System (BLS) automatically reduces the loan period of a heavily-reserved book. However, such a system is reliant upon the willingness of users to place reservations on books which are not currently available; this is something which many are reluctant to do, especially undergraduates whose need for a book may have a definite and short time-limit. Here again automated systems may provide at least a partial solution. It is a small step from an OPAC which gives details of whether copies are in the library or on loan to one which enables readers to make a reservation themselves for a book they need. The difficulties are not so much technical as practical: should one insist on the use of a personal identity number (PIN) to ensure that reservations are not made mischievously for others? Will students reserve large numbers of books and then fail to collect them? Will students simply reserve the recommended texts and not explore the existence of other resources in the library? Most of these questions can in fact only be answered by making a trial of the system; and whatever other resources the library may have, it has to be accepted that an unsatisfied request for a specific item represents a failure. The more information which can be obtained about what students need from the library, the better chance there is of acquiring and organizing material to satisfy the need.

Relegation

Relegation may be seen as the negative aspect of demand, and as such the statistics of use (or non-use) already discussed play a major part. So too may the existence of copies elsewhere in the locality as shown by fiche catalogues or accessible OPACs. There are, however, one or two ways in which the automation of library systems can specifically help the processes of relegation, and may prevent glaring mistakes from being made. In the context of computerized catalogues, it becomes possible to print lists of items which appear not to have been used and circulate them to academic staff for comment (a dangerous, frustrating, but frequently necessary process). It may be possible to print selected parts of the classification system together, thus producing lists relevant to the work of particular departments. In theory lists could be sorted by fund code or department of recommender to ensure that all relevant material was sent to a department irrespective of where it had been classified (and conversely that a department was not being asked to comment on the suitability for withdrawal of an item in fact used by students on another course). However, to do this would require an integrated system into which full acquisitions data had been entered; as such systems have been in existence generally for a very short time it is sincerely to be hoped that the items covered by them are not yet candidates for withdrawal!

The whole question of withdrawal is a particularly vexed one especially in university libraries (polytechnics are less worried about the macho image of big collections). The withdrawal of duplicate copies is frequently uncontroversial (unless they are incunabula!); an automated system can provide a positive warning that the copy to be withdrawn is the last in the system. When withdrawal *is* contemplated, one method frequently adopted to lessen the trauma is the creation of a closed-access half-way house in which the use made of volumes can be monitored carefully, in-library use as well as borrowing. Two difficulties of such a procedure are the time taken to alter catalogue records and the potential distortion of use which results from the unwillingness of users to ask for a closed-access item. This latter point is often over-emphasized: in the first place, if the user can manage without the item, who is to say that it really *should* have been used, and is therefore essential to the collection? Secondly, readers show no great reluctance to face the far greater delays and form-filling associated with interlibrary loans for an item not in stock at all; why should they be reluctant to fill in a form for a book which will be available within the hour? Finally, there is always the point that if this were truly a deterrent to research no significant work would ever have been done in the closed-access Bodleian Library.

However, it is obviously important that the location of the book is clearly indicated to the reader, and that the process of retrieving it is made as simple as possible. In this automated systems can assist, although not all are capable of the necessary procedures. In Reading University it became necessary to weed the Science Floor of little-used books. It would have needed far more resources than the Library had to inspect every book, or even every book with a history of non-loan. (That statistic was in any case difficult to use, since for half the books the only identifier held in the circulation system was the accession number.) Nor would the resulting list of books to be moved have had a common characteristic by which the location in the catalogue could have been altered as an automated batch process; indeed, although for about half the items there were brief bibliographic records on the circulation file, about three-quarters at least, being in general the older stock, would have had no MARC record at all on the computer system. Instead, the decision was taken to use the issue system, which was based on the barcoded accession number, and all books more than fifteen years old were issued to the closed-access collection. In Reading this still meant that a reader would have to be sufficiently interested in a book to check it in the catalogue, to look for and then fail to find it on the shelves, and finally to attempt to see if it was on loan by looking it up by accession number on the public circulation terminal.

Had there been at the time an on-line catalogue which gave the circulation status of the books, it could have displayed 'closed access' as such a status. In an ideal system there would be a printer attached to such a catalogue terminal so that the reader could print out the record to take to the library staff, thus obviating the need for any form-filling. The book when retrieved would have its issue to closed access cancelled, and would then – whether borrowed or used in the library – be returned to the normal collection. In this way the books for the relegated collection would be self-selecting, rather than requiring professional guesswork to decide what was to go where. At the end of a finite period of time all the items still in the closed-access collection would have been there, unused, for however many years had elapsed; a case could be made out for their removal from the library, or alternatively a list of books issued to the 'closed access' number could be printed and circulated if it was felt necessary to consult the academic staff. Such a list could, of course, also be used to circulate possibly interested recipients of the books to be discarded.

Balance

Balance of funding

As the money available to libraries reduces, in real terms for almost all libraries and in absolute terms for some, it becomes important to ensure that the funding is spread fairly not only between departments but also between types of resource. Bangor cannot be alone in having watched the serials budget eat up the bookfund! This chapter is not the proper place to go into all the arguments for and against funding by formula, let alone into the myriad formulae which have been used (mostly in attempts to justify the librarian's professional guess). Nevertheless the automation of accounts systems, particularly those under the library's own control, does affect the sort of data available to be fed into formulae, whether of the formal type (these days almost certainly themselves run on a spreadsheet package) or the informal type which exist in the librarian's head and allow him or her to make what are regarded as fair allocations.

To take one example, average book prices may be thought relevant. These are available from the Library and Information Statistics Unit (LISU),[13] broken down into UK and US averages, and within each into subject groupings. Few university departments fit wholly within a single group; as departments are amalgamated into Schools they almost certainly cover a range of subjects, and even Faculties may not be easy to place (Psychology in Bangor is an Arts subject!). Equally, the figures in question give no help to places which consistently buy paperbacks, or which concentrate on a small area of a topic which may be the most expensive. The proportion of spending on particular aspects may be difficult to assign: with averages for language of £24.00, literature of £10.45, and criticism of £21.02 it is hard to be sure of the likely average cost for a School of English and Linguistics. Nor are all books purchased by academic libraries published in the UK or the USA. However, from a library's own accounts data it is possible to work out the actual average cost of books bought from a specific fund, and therefore to use a justifiable figure in any estimates or calculations. It also becomes possible to give an average price for, say, foreign publications; since sometimes it is difficult to find accurate prices for these, a sensible figure to put into commitment accounting is very important.

Because serials tend now to account for a high proportion of library spending, and because inflation of serials prices seems at present to be exceptionally (excessively?) high, reviews of serials subscriptions are becoming frequent, often annual, exercises. For good or ill, they are easier to organize and cope with in the context of an automated system than of a manual one. For a start, the printing of a list requires no major keyboarding, with its consequences for staff time and costs; moreover, it should be possible to print lists which are specific as to subject or as to the fund which pays for the titles; a useful feature when attempting to prevent engineers listing all the Italian journals for cancellation, or vice versa. Suitable databases may be set up on microcomputers at the expense of some initial keyboarding, and spreadsheets used to calculate the likely effects of inflation; but it is better if they come from a serials receipt and payment system containing up-to-date records of prices paid, which is also likely to be more accurate in respect of whether a title has ceased publication.

Some systems, for instance the review program in the Geac system, use complex algorithms which take into account the payment history over the previous two or three years when applying an estimated rate of inflation to each individual title; moreover, in this system as in many others current conversion rates for foreign currency are also used – a necessary feature as the pound plummets! Taken in conjunction with the estimates of inflation provided by serials subscription agents such a system can reduce the inaccuracy of estimates of serials costs in the next financial year (although such systems need to have been running for some years to have accumulated the necessary data on payments).

Because of the need to work strictly within budgets, it is important to keep the expenditure on serials under review throughout the year. If inflation is on average running higher than allowed for, money has to be put in rapidly from elsewhere; but equally if inflation appears to be lower (a quite common occurrence, as librarians make pessimistic predictions to be sure of keeping within budget) it may be possible to transfer money to book purchase before it is too late for departments to spend it profitably. The main difficulty in reviewing year-on-year inflation in mid-session is that comparing the total paid by a certain date in year A with that paid by the same date in year B is not sufficiently accurate. Invoices come at slightly different times, and a particular title may therefore be included one year and not the other; and because of the now frequent cutting exercises titles paid for on one invoice may have been cancelled subsequently and therefore not appear on the next. An automated system could output the inflation on each individual title, which could then be averaged; or it could be made to compare the payments against the same order numbers in two successive years. In the latter case, it might also be able to indicate whether in the first of these two years any of the orders had been subject to supplementary payments later than the date of review, and therefore as to whether the inflation predicted is likely to be revised upward later. None of this is being petty: even in the case of a small library like Bangor a 0.5 per cent difference in the serials budget in either direction is a matter of over £1 000.

Balance of stock

Ensuring a balanced stock involves more than just giving appropriate sums of money to various groups of academic staff; the library needs to keep some track of how that money is spent, and whether all areas of teaching are being covered. To some extent, the library may also need to be looking at future needs – acquiring the contemporary materials which will be the raw materials of future history courses, or the contemporary literature which no one will start to study until the authors are dead. Although in this sort of work the use analysis described above clearly plays a part, it cannot entirely answer the questions, particularly when it comes to collecting for the future.

One advantage which might be gained from allowing all book recommcndations to be entered into an on-line system is that the library would be able to see those which any departmental filter would otherwise stop. Like the review of interlibrary loans, this could indicate areas of inadequate coverage where interest existed, and in particular minority interests within a department. Equally useful would be the ability to review what has been published in specific areas. This becomes a more feasible possibility with the existence of CD-ROM databases with sophisticated searching capabilities, but in reality the time which would be involved would still be more than most libraries could devote to it. Even if such a selection could be checked by ISBN against books actually added to stock, so that one was only looking at items which had *not* been bought, it would still be a very large undertaking.

However, another approach is to make use of the pooling of acquisitions policies across a number of libraries. On the assumption that between a number of academics and librarians working on a specific subject most of the relevant material will have been bought, checking one's holdings against those in, say, the BLCMP database and printing out the list of what in a particular class range has been acquired elsewhere but not in one's own library could give a reasonable selected list from which to work.

At some stage, unless funds are unlimited, a library needs to produce a collection development policy which sets the parameters within which the collection manager works. This may do little more than state the subjects, or the topics within subjects, to which the library gives priority; it may, however, seek to build on particular strengths which have been built up over a number of years, and in effect to guide the teaching and research of the institution into those areas for which suitable resources are available. In recent years a system of grading both existing holdings (based on comparisons with other libraries) and acquisitions policies (relating to the proportion and language of published items acquired) has been evolved, known as Conspectus.[11] It has been widely used in the USA, and more recently has been applied to the British Library, the National Library of Wales, and to the Scottish university libraries.

Automated collection analysis

Although the knowledge acquired from Conspectus may be applied more widely using computers,[15] it is in itself a manual approach, and as such relies to a considerable extent upon subjective assessment. The sort of comparison within a cooperative database mentioned above could be automated, but for general application two problems emerge. The first is that not all libraries are members of cooperatives; the second and more significant is that not all libraries in a cooperative represent a proper peer group. For example, the large number of public libraries within BLCMP would mean that any analysis of modern British literature would (if one were using selections based on Dewey) include a large amount of popular fiction, and perhaps even junior fiction, which would not be of interest to most academic libraries. Equally a database such as the former BLAISE-LOCAS database would be hopelessly distorted by the British Library holdings; and the holdings of others of the really major libraries (Manchester, Edinburgh, Leeds) could equally have the same effect.

Recently a considerable amount of work on automated collection analysis has been done by staff of OCLC, related not only to their extensive database but also to the concepts involved in Conspectus.[16] It differs from Conspectus in being title rather than number based, and in being quantitative rather than qualitative – a logical concomitant of the automated nature of the system. The software can be used to show how the level of holdings in a particular library compares with that of peer-group libraries; whether the holdings are the same as those of most of the peer group or are different; how many titles held by particular ranges of peer libraries are not held by the individual library; what the effect would be on the overall pattern of holdings if those titles were purchased; and to some extent what this would cost.

Clearly a system which can indicate that there are a small number of commonly held titles missing from a particular library would be a considerable help in collection management: considering the purchase of fifty titles is a different matter from looking at several hundred published in a year. Obviously the identification of such titles could not mean their automatic purchase: they might be in areas of the subject common elsewhere but not represented in the institution; they might represent different presentations of information already available in other books in the library; or they might, of course, be out-of-date stock collected ten years ago. The data have to be interpreted in accordance with the collection development policy of the specific institution; but they can also contribute towards the production or evolution of such a policy by indicating clearly where the library stands in comparison with its peer group.

Conclusions

It can be seen that automation has had a slight impact on collection management to date. The systems which currently exist could in many instances be used more to assist collection management; within the present capabilities of integrated library housekeeping systems more relevant information could be obtained, and thought should be given in systems design to building in some of these possibilities and identifying the relevant categories of book or reader for statistical purposes; and new technology is opening up the possibility of systems designed specifically for collection management. What has also emerged, I hope, is that all the automated systems in the world are only able to *assist* the job of the collection manager, and that in the end the job involves the application of professional knowledge, judgement and experience to the computerized data produced.

References

1. Marc Users' Group (1985), *Subject access and the Marc record: report of a questionnaire conducted by the Marc Users' Group*. Reading: Marc Users' Group.
2. Harrison, K., and D. Summers (1988), 'Development of an automated acquisitions system at the University of Lancaster Library', *Program*, **22** (2), 146.
3. Boss, R.W., and J. McQueen (1989), 'The uses of automation and related technologies by domestic book and serials jobbers', *Library technology reports*, **25** (2), 127-251.
4. Harrison, K. and D. Summers, ref. 2, p.145.
5. Haravu, J.L. et al. (1987), 'A microcomputer-based book acquisitions system in India using dBASE II', *Program*, **21** (1), p.39.
6. Wainwright, J. and J. Hills (1973), 'Book selection from MARC tapes: a feasibility study', *Program*, **7** (3), 123-144.
7. Marc Users' Group, ref. 1, Appendix 2 table 8.
8. 'The VISCOUNT project at LASER', *Vine*, 1987, **68** (November), 11-18.
9. *Directory of library catalogues on JANET*, Brighton: University of Sussex Library, 1986; *Supplement*, 1987.
    JANET User Group for Libraries (1989), *Catalogs: JANET addresses of ... OPACs ...*, Brighton, University of Sussex Library.
10. 'A multi-user inter-library loans system from the University of Lancaster Library' *Vine*, 1987, **68** (November), 3-10.
11. Young, R.C. (1985), 'Integration and feedback: some features of the Geac-based system at the University of Sussex Library', *Marc Users' Group newsletter*, **84** (1), pp.46-7.
12. Peasgood, A.N. (1986), 'Towards demand-led book acquisitions? Experience in the University of Sussex Library', *Journal of librarianship*, **18** (4), 242-256.
13. *Average prices of British academic books, 1974-* Loughborough: Library and Information Statistics Unit. Published successively by LMRU, CLAIM and LISU.

14. Stam, D.H. (1986), 'Collaborative collection development: programs, problems and potential', *Collection building*, **7** (3), 3-8.
Hanger, S. (1987), 'Collection development in the British Library: the role of the RLG Conspectus', *Journal of Librarianship*, **19** (2), 89-107.
Pringle, R.V. (1988), 'Conspectus in Scotland – report to SCONUL', *LIBER news sheet*, (**2**), 5-17.
15. Ferguson, A.W. et al. (1987), 'Internal uses of the RLG Conspectus', *Journal of library administration*, **8** (2), 35-40.
16. Dillon, M. et al. (1988), 'Design issues for a microcomputer-based collection analysis system', *Microcomputers for information management*, **5** (4), 263-273.

5   The role of suppliers: a North American perspective

Douglas Duchin*

The role of the vendor in library collection management has changed dramatically over the past 15 years. As library staff sizes have plateaued, while the volume of publishing has continued to increase, libraries have turned more and more to vendors to supply services that once were produced in-house. The emergence of automated vendor inventory systems and automated library acquisitions systems has provided a fertile ground for the proliferation of automation-related services. Competition between vendors for a piece of a static market has forced them into jockeying for position, while development of new systems has provided the library with tools rarely seen two decades ago. On-line ordering, approval plans, retrospective collection development, bibliographic and invoice data transmitted with book, and access to vendor inventories are all relatively recent developments in the struggle to survive in a small market.

* The author was Vice President, Approval Services at Blackwell North America from 1987 to 1989, and previously held the position of Vice President, Approval Services at Yankee Book Peddler, from 1976 to 1987.

Competition

Competition is the mother of invention – along with being the mother of marketing, consumer analysis, and bargain-basement pricing. The truly positive aspect of competition in an industry closely aligned with both the manufacturer and the end consumer, however, is in the number of value-added services that develop. The vendor, or jobber/book supplier, in order to meet the most basic needs of the library, must develop an extremely sophisticated in-house system that mimics and expands upon the library acquisitions department. The value-added services have always existed in that the vendor was always more flexible than the publisher and has often had a broader view since he was dealing with anywhere from 15 000 to 30 000 publishers. With the technical advances that marked the end of the 1960s – OCLC, MARC formats, automated acquisitions and circulation systems, and so forth – the vendor really came into his own. In America, the growth patterns predicted for research libraries in the middle 1960s failed to materialize. 'Before 1971, regular and rapid increases in all library statistics are apparent, but just after that, acquisitions plateaued, then declined by one-fourth; staff size plateaued and remained virtually unchanged for a decade or more, and expenditures were briefly slowed before resuming rapid growth.'[1] It was at this point that many of the vendors who still dominate the American scene either opened shop or expanded their services to libraries.

Vending is a service, and like many service functions, is dependent on both the buyer and the manufacturer for direction. The simple services of the 1960s – customized invoicing, special handling and blanket orders – gave way in the 1970s to much more sophisticated services. Among them were approval plans, automated databases, retrospective searches, binding and shelf preparation, collection development including opening day collections, full bibliographic data, instant credit memos and serial standing orders. In the 1980s the services have blossomed even further. Data conversion, automated authority files, direct access to vendor databases, bibliographic records in full MARC format, integrated approval/firm order/serial/periodical plans, deposit accounts, collection assessment against specific data bases, out-of-print search services and statistical management reports are all on the newest menus.

Many of these services were by-products of the vendor's own internal systems and most required computer enhancement to be practical.

When the vendor automated his inventory control, he often created customized invoicing and management reports as a by-product. Automated authority files required massive databases that resulted in making bibliographic records available in MARC or MARC-like formats on a regular basis.

Competition has given an added impetus. Once one vendor can offer a service, the other vendors must choose to either join in the fray, or niche themselves in some area where service overwhelms the mechanical furbelows. The financial drain on any organization that is being *forced* into retooling is tremendous. In some cases the cost of the value-added services provided on the sale of a single title can far outstrip the vendor's profit to the point where it would make more sense to sell the services and throw in the book for free.

Services

Vendors can now supply libraries with a wide variety of services – many of them at or near cost, many of them free with the purchase of the book. Some services, such as retrospective searches, are supplied at no charge at all. The simple expectation is that the library will purchase at least some, if not all, the books cited on the bibliography from the vendor providing the list. Most vendors feel that the goodwill generated by their giveaways will result in sales that will far outstrip the immediate costs.

Until the advent of automation, probably the key reason for using a vendor was summed up in one word: batching. While the value-added services now rank very high, it is still important to remember the initial reason for using a vendor rather than going direct.

At the 1989 Charleston Conference, Doug Phelps, Director of General Technical Services at Vanderbilt University Library delivered a paper on 'Publisher discounts – but at what price?'[2] In his study of the cost of acquisition, Phelps discovered that it cost his library $1.15 per order to place an order directly with a publisher while it cost only $0.56, half as much, to place the same order with a vendor. Some of the savings were obviously in the mechanical processing. The order staff were familiar with the acquisitions code for most vendors, but had to pause to look up many publisher codes. Vendor orders could be batched – up to twenty orders per envelope – while most direct orders were single orders and required additional work, not to mention postage. On the receiving end there were also major savings. Vendor orders could be received in 1.82 minutes per order, while direct orders took 3.92 minutes. The difference here lay in the simplicity and familiarity of the vendor invoice. All were the same, all were in title order; whereas publisher invoices were in a wide variety of formats. For this library, the differences in cost and time between vendor orders and publisher orders were dramatic.

Batching is still a prime reason for using a vendor in the acquisitions process, but the added services have even more far reaching consequences and value within the library. The vendor operates on at least three different levels in the library. He is an integral part of the daily function of ordering and receiving books, but he is also involved in the longer range budget planning and collection management. With his help in collection management, the library can definitely cut costs and improve planning. The vendor can help with estimates and management reports that can plot past activity and help plan budgets for the coming year. In a more competitive mode, the vendors can bid against each other to provide a wider range of services at a lower rate. To take the relationship even further, the vendor today is capable of being involved in book selection and collection development with approval plans, standing orders, retrospective or comparative searches, and out-of-print services. Most of these services have been the results of library needs, although a few have been the by-product of vendor in-house computerization. In the next few pages, I will review, historically, the development that led up to the current state of the art – and some possibilities for future library/vendor relationships.

The acquisition process

The relationship between the vendor and the library functions most commonly at the acquisitions process level. That is, the ordering and receiving of books. Over the past few years, however, that relatively simple transaction has become much more sophisticated. Within those brackets exist possibilities for tremendous customization in everything from invoices to shelf preparation.

In invoicing, the advantage with the vendor, of course, is in consistency. Vendors are capable of rearranging and reporting data on invoices in ways publishers cannot. Competition has increased the original author or title option to include listings by purchase order number, fund codes, subject classification, or date of order. Where the publisher often offers a short title and a list/net price, the vendor can, on the paper invoice, display limited author and title, volume or edition statement, series information, the ISBN or ISSN, list price, service fees, discounts, and net price. In addition, the library may choose to have its purchase order number and fund codes or account names printed on the invoice. The invoice can be further customized to the point where the library may opt for a single invoice per title (although this is hardly cost effective for either the library or the vendor) or invoices and shipment split by subject, size, dollar value, and so on. Because the vendor is in competition, most are willing to follow very complex processes. This, of course, is only the paper format and only for basic firm orders. Many vendors, because of outside pressure and because they have become so automated in-house, also have the option of transmitting invoice data directly from their system to the library acquisition system, or providing the invoice data on disc or reel-to-reel tape.

In the initial agreement with the vendor, the library often spells out shipping methods. Vendors normally offer the option of postal service or private carrier, and, in some cases, their own shipping service which can not only deliver, but also pick up returns of rejected titles as well. This is a major competitive point in approval plan services. Some libraries, because of staffing problems, have stipulated that shipment must arrive on the same day each week, at the same time. Others have indicated that shipments for certain materials must be delivered to different points within the library and that no box may weigh more than 20 lb. Most vendors are willing to accommodate these variations as a part of their service.

In addition to customizing the invoice, the vendor can usually allow the client to customize the credit request. With most publishers, credits and returns require telephone calls, letters of permission, credit memos and special shipping labels to specific returns addresses. With most vendors, the library has the option of writing its own credit memo on blanks supplied by the vendor, or simply striking through a title on the invoice and returning a copy of it with the book. No prior permission or special processing is required by most vendors. The fact that one is able to return unwanted merchandise is one of the curiosities of the publishing industry: it seems that a very large percentage of the materials seen by most vendors can be returned to the manufacturer. Return rates are built into most vendor budgets and, with the exception of approval plans, a return rate of 2 to 3 per cent from the library is not considered unusual. With approval plans, return rates may go as high as 15 per cent without raising a vendor's eyebrow.

Another option available with most vendors is choice of binding format. Some libraries have found it practical, in times of budget constraints, to order paper bindings and have the vendor bind in cloth for them before shipping and billing. Regardless of the practicality or ease of use of a rebound paperback, almost any vendor should be able to substitute paper for cloth for the library on a regular basis.

At the heart of the order process is the order form, and almost every library's form is unique. No two seem to be alike. While libraries spell out in great detail exactly how the invoice is to appear, they are more creative in establishing the format of their own purchase orders. I have seen everything from handwritten lists on napkins to crisp, machine-generated forms lacking only the name of the ordering institution, unfortunately. Every vendor needs a minimal amount of information, beginning with the name of the ordering library, and including author, title, publisher (and address if available especially if it is obscure), edition or volume, format, expected price, imprint year and the library's cancellation date. Usually, as a part of the setting up of the account, the library will create some general parameters. For example, orders are usually left open for a year and the library will generally indicate if and under what circumstances the alternate binding is acceptable; which substitutions may be made; if alternate editions are acceptable; and if the library will allow the vendor to instigate an automatic out-of-print search. Naturally, not all vendors have all these capabilities, but they are far from uncommon – competition being what it is.

Benefits of automation

Most vendors have computerized some or all of their internal processes and, consequently, are able to offer a variety of computer-related services. The personal computer explosion has resulted in a PC on many library desks. It is very interesting that libraries were among the first groups to take automation to heart while the rest of the population was still playing video games. The consequent familiarity with PCs on the part of both the vendor and the library has resulted in some extraordinary packages available for book ordering. Periodical vendors were among the first to use the PC order/claim/search systems. By now, however, a

124

number of book vendors offer PC ordering systems, which include claiming ability. Some systems also provide access to the vendor's database. In some cases this is merely a listing of their approval plan titles published in the last year or two; in others, the library has access to the vendor's inventory system and is able to see what is in stock and the list price. The library can use the system for comparative shopping, since it will have already established an account with the vendor. At this point it becomes a question of timeliness versus discount. As a part of the customer's master record or profile, the vendor may also be able to provide an automatic out-of-print search service. While most vendors do not perform the search themselves, they may have a link to a national computerized search service. Naturally, titles obtained as a result of out-of-print searches will be more expensive than if they were still in print, as well as being non-returnable.

Some vendor PC systems also provide for a claiming process; others print out monthly status reports on all outstanding library orders and mail them to the libraries. For those libraries whose systems provide complex search capabilities, there is the option, or at least the temptation, to download a portion of the vendor's database into their own systems to assist in retrospective searches for collection development.

The size of databases is often cited as a competitive point between vendors. Vendor A claims to have an approval plan that reviews 25 000 titles a year; Vendor B counters with a database that cites 40 000 new titles a year, and Vendor C jumps in with 55 000 titles a year. Depending on the library's needs and focus, the smaller database may prove just as adequate as the larger. As the data accumulate, and many databases have been accumulating on-line for many years, the size of their publisher lists grows proportionately. Publisher address lists of over 50 000 are no longer considered excessive and some vendors continue to add new publisher addresses at the rate of 300 or more a month. One problem with the larger database is pinpointing the specific publisher when there are several with similar names and the library cites only the key word of the publisher's name. Luckily, the vendor has other clues to work from, such as the ISBN prefix, but the more specific the citation is, the less chance of misfires. One large advantage of the vendor's publisher address file over the library's own is the listing of idiosyncracies, return policies, proforma requirements, and special ordering instructions. Few libraries can afford to maintain such detail, always up to date, on tens of thousands of publishers. On the other hand, few vendors can afford not to. While we are looking at the advantages of using vendors, another major advantage to keep in mind is the single customer service number, usually toll-free, for these thousands of publishers through one vendor.

The part of the order/sale process that has probably benefited the most from competition and automation is the data-with-book. At one point, most libraries were content to receive a brief bibliographic description, consisting of short title and author's last name, with the book. Now the vendor is capable of supplying a full MARC-formatted record along with the book, not only on paper, but often in a machine-readable format, transmitted or supplied on a disc. The actual content of that record has been the subject of recent competitive forays. The completeness of the record, the format of the record, the source of the record and the method of transmission are all bargaining points in the current battle. While not every library has a fully automated system, those that have often also have the book budgets with clout. To hold on to existing customers or to attract potential customers, a vendor can now offer full bibliographic records, not only in MARC format, but with full Library of Congress MARC data. The in-house vendor description in MARC format will no longer suffice for some libraries and the full Library of Congress record is now required. In addition to the full record, the library also wants, and often gets, the invoice data included with the Library of Congress data, or supplied separately in machine-readable format.

Customer service

When all else is equal in the press for library attention, the customer service department can often make the definitive difference. While no vendor wants to fail the client, errors occasionally happen. Many vendors have tried to establish a one-to-one relationship between the customer-service representative and the library – usually by linking a single customer-service representative to a single sales representative. This means that the library staff can develop a relationship with a single representative in-house – the library's personal representative. The relationship works both ways. The customer-service representative is familiar with the library account, and when the weekly shipment doesn't arrive on time the representative is probably already aware of the storm or strike that blocked the delivery and may have already made alternative provision for the shipment. The representative will more than likely also be aware of whether or not the delay will affect the institution. Familiarity is also helpful when the library has unusual requirements in shipping or billing. By having a single representative, the ground rules do not have to be re-established with each telephone call. As a part of their one-to-one programme, some vendors have supplied the library with photographs and brief biographies of their team members to increase familiarity. While the error rate with most vendors is under 1 per cent (compared to the up to 10 per cent error rate vendors experience with publishers), that 1 per cent looms much larger than the 99 per cent rate of correct fulfilment – which is why vendors strive for the most knowledgeable and personable customer-service representatives possible.

The largest proportion of customer-service work is in the area of claiming. Unless the vendor supplies reports on outstanding orders on a regular basis, and the library feeds the information into its acquisitions system, there will be a steady stream of claims and queries for outstanding orders. On the whole, manual acquisitions systems tend to claim too infrequently and automated systems claim too often and too blindly. At least with a vendor, the library avoids the most common responses from publishers: 1) a double shipment against both the order and the claim; or 2) no shipment at all, but a polite note rubber stamped onto the claim that reads 'This title is available, please order'.

The competitive vendor responds promptly to claims with an intelligent answer. The non-competitive vendor responds promptly with a standard note that the claim has been noted. The stronger the competition, the better the claim responses. Claiming for some vendors is now part of the PC order package, and responses to machine-generated claims may soon be downloaded into library PC systems for continuous and timely updates.

One further point that should be made about the vendors' acquisitions services is that there are a number of services available that can be tagged on to the library book sales. Physically, books can be prepared in different ways and to different degrees by many vendors. Dust jackets, checkout cards and pockets, and stamps or plates can be added to the books. In some cases, different services can be provided for juvenile books than for adult books. Mylar and other covering materials can be added to paperbacks to prolong their shelf life. Many vendors provide a rebinding service for paperbacks, in a variety of strengths, fabrics and colours, sometimes through an outside bindery. The cost of rebinding or reinforcing can be included in the book invoice or invoiced separately.

Vendors can also supply bibliographic data in a number of formats. Some offer catalogue cards, either created in-house and checked against standardized main entries and subject headings, or through an outside agency. As discussed earlier, bibliographic data may also be provided in machine-readable formats, allowing the library to create its own cards, or add them to its automated acquisitions system or on-line catalogue.

Evaluating suppliers

Establishing the parameters of the library/vendor relationship, including financial terms, estimates and projections for future expenditure, and evaluating past performance are integral parts of collection management planning. It is these parameters that allow libraries to step back from the day-to-day relationship and evaluate service – both quantitatively and qualitatively – and do a little comparative shopping. One of my greatest regrets, professionally, was that there was no class in library school on the business end of library services.

Automation has made many of the evaluative processes simpler and more standard. Bids, quotes and estimates are far more accurate and timely. Projections based on past performance by a library, combined with current publishing output information, allow vendors to make more practical offers to libraries for services and discounts.

In America, the entire bid/quote/estimate system has long been a matter of sharp pencils and long memories. With computerization, many vendors can now instantly review the library's past expenditure, both in terms of volume and mix, and discount accordingly. A library with no exotic requirements as to shipping or billing, and which purchases from the top 500 presses with a tendency for trade-discounted titles, is going to receive a better proposal than the library that sends a vendor only orders for small press or proforma press materials, and requires separate billing for each title, along with free airfreight. All this can be run through a computer and the vendor can know in a matter of minutes just how good an offer he can make for this library.

Bids are becoming popular in America. Certain states, such as Texas, have had bid/contract situations for years. Others, such as Virginia, have just begun. Again, with automation, the vendor can review potential sales against publishing output and come up with a discount on book sales, or additional services, that just clears the margin for profitable sales. Past decisions based on 'guesstimates' have often resulted in just as many unexpected large losses as in unexpected large profits. In approval plans in particular, and to a lesser degree in serial standing orders, predictions from computer analysis have benefited both the library and the vendor. The library knows just what it will get for its money, and has data to present to the parent organization, while the vendor can predict sales, impact on staff, and profitability. In 1988, for example, American vendors saw an overall increase in book prices for academic libraries of about 8 per cent. The largest increase was in imported scientific books, while the average university press titles went up only 6.8 per cent. It is this type of machine-generated data that makes next year's budget planning more accurate and predictable.

Collection management focus on the financial aspects of acquisitions has resulted in other benefits as well. When an account is first set up with a vendor, the parameters of discounts, service fees and shipping and handling fees are set up based on projected sales. It is to the library's advantage to review this at least once a year and put it on a competitive basis. From my experience, the quality of service from one vendor to another varies only fractionally. Most vendors know how large their sales are with their clients, and how profitable. In some cases the library is already way ahead in the discount and services area; in other cases there is room for negotiation. Libraries should request that their discounts be reviewed each year, and check with competitors to see if the same service can be provided at a better price.

One method of financial control often overlooked is the deposit or proforma account. The library and vendor agree to a certain volume and type of sale for an extended period and the library deposits a sum against that sale. (As an aside, do not ask for a deposit account of less than $10 000: it is not worth the effort.) In return for the deposit, the vendor makes an interest payment – either in a lump sum or over the life of the deposit. Or the vendor may offer a higher discount or free services in lieu of the interest.

At the other end of the collection management spectrum is the retrospective view of performance. Many management reports are available from vendors. Some indicate the volume of sales by type of sales – firm orders, approval orders, periodical or serial standing orders, and non-book sales. Others have become increasingly sophisticated in their data. The library can request a report, by subject or by press, or even a listing of every book supplied during the year. Reports are also available showing what the library spent by fund account, by purchase order prefixes, and even by price. For approval plans, reports are available that show rejection rates, claim rates, and sales by subject or publisher, including average prices. The entire range of management reports is a direct result of automation and competition. In order to maintain internal control over sales and provide full bibliographic data, massive files have been constructed with multiple access points. Once the data are created, it is a relatively simple process to massage that data into usable formats. Competitive pressures create new formats continually. The reports themselves are of great value to the library as measures of performance and as tools in developing and defending budgets.

Collection development

So far I have reviewed the day-to-day activities of acquisitions and the fiscally oriented aspects of collection management in the library/vendor relationship. Automation and competition have had their impact on almost every aspect of that relationship since automation became a factor in the 1970s, and reductions in budgets resulted in plateaued staffing and book buying. At the time that this was happening, a buzz word was being heard in the halls of academic and public libraries – collection development. Libraries focused more closely on their own development, independent of faculty or off-campus recommendations as to what was appropriate for the collection. This transfer of responsibility for the selection of library materials that began in the 1960s continues today.[3] While few libraries have developed a new collection development staff of trained subject specialists, many did introduce the position of collection development officer, or placed a new emphasis on this function as distinctly separate from acquisitions. For the vendor this was a major and dramatic change. Where there had been requests for books on a title-by-title basis, or at most, series of titles, there were now requests for large chunks of publishing output. At first these were fairly simply expressed in the concept of standing order plans or blanket order plans for the publications of a single press or a clearly related group of presses. Staffs had been reduced, but book budgets remained steady. There was still money to be spent, but fewer librarians to select books and far fewer staff members to process the orders and receipts. With the requests for simple gathering plans came also requests for simple cataloguing – temporary descriptions of books on 3x5 slips that could act as temporary records in the card catalogues. That was only 15 years ago: what a revolution there has been!

Approval plans

The approval plan, in all its variety and ubiquity, probably best demonstrates the new relationship between collection development and automated, highly competitive vendors. Although we can probably trace acquisitions plans back to Thomas Jefferson's shopping for Americana in Paris, most of the existing approval plans in the US date back to the days of the late 1960s. The plans began with a simple agreement to 'shop' for the library, based upon a few basic rules – no textbooks, no reprints, no law or medical books and no fiction. Most libraries preferred simple lists of the presses to be covered, and set a few other limitations on price, imprint year and books in series. The vendor, with book in hand, compared his description of the book with various library profiles and decided whether or not to send the book. If the book was almost, but not quite right for the library, a slip would be sent. If the library did not want the book, it was fully returnable with a library-generated credit memo. In some cases, the library would accept books from any press, but the more common view seems to have been to limit the press list to specific groups of presses, such as the university presses, or to even smaller groups. Budgets were broad enough to encompass the occasional wild card and the staff was too small to do much deselection.

Within ten years, the fish was out of the water and walking on two feet carrying a shopping bag. Instant evolution. The approval plan had come of age and the competition was hot. As soon as one vendor added a selling point, the second vendor matched it and added one of his own. The rules changed so fast that much of it turned into a personality game. Competitive advertisements were run in journals as each vendor touted his product. And the library community took firm positions for and against approval plans. Today half of all US college and university libraries 'participate in some form of approval plan and together they purchase approximately 30 per cent of their books that way.'[1] In its ideal setting, the approval plan provides the mainstream of publishing, appropriate to the collection, on a fully returnable basis, in a timely manner. In its worst guise, the approval plan becomes a browsing collection for professors and results in exorbitant return rates. Or, in an equally undesirable scenario, takes the place of librarian-based book selection and all shipments are accepted without review. The average approval plan falls somewhere in between. Most have moved away from the blanket order concept – that is, a simple instruction to send all publications of XYZ press. In its place have appeared library profiles, or parameters that limit approval plans by subject and non-subject parameters, and by publisher. Whether the profile is handled by the vendor as a fill-in-the-box selection or it is based on an extensive interview between the vendor representative and library staff and faculty, most vendors have a thesaurus or classification scheme of some sort. Two of the most common subject classification schemes are based on the Library of Congress Classification Schedule or the vendor's own in-house scheme. Both cover all subject areas, both have their pluses and minuses. On the one side, the faculty and library staff may be more familiar with the Library of Congress Classification Schedule; on the other side, the in-house classification scheme may be more in tune with publishing vagaries and more suited to book buying than the shelving device of the Library of Congress scheme. Additionally, some vendors offer alternative, but nationally known schemes for classification – Dewey Decimal Classification, the National Library of Medicine Classification or the National Agriculture Library Classification.

The second part of the profile usually deals with non-subject parameters such as designators for textbooks, reprints, foreign languages, and higher priced books. Many are common between vendors, but, in a competitive mode and responsive to their own clientele, some vendors have added fillips to their non-subject parameters (NSPs). For example, one vendor may simply indicate that a book is a reprint (and even here definitions of reprint may vary wildly) while another acknowledges that a book is a reprint, but can then sub-select by date of original publication, allowing the vendor to send reprinted books when the original title is over ten years old, but send slips when the original is less than ten years old.

Museum or gallery exhibition catalogues are another competitive area. One vendor simply makes the distinction that a title is a museum catalogue and the originating publisher was the Fine Arts Museum of XYZ. The second vendor may include that information, plus all data on the travelling exhibition, including dates and places, and the fact that the cloth edition was published by ABC Publishing Co. This information allows the library to make the decision as to whether to accept the timely paperback from the museum or wait for the cloth edition to be published.

Each NSP, from the number of pages in the book to the homeland of the author, varies from vendor to vendor. Each vendor, usually in response to a single library's request, modifies and further delineates his subject and non-subject parameters. The trap here is that the more refined these become, the more pitfalls there are in interpretation. At the receiving end, the library is trying to anticipate what will come on its approval shipments. The more detail there is, the harder it actually becomes to anticipate shipments. And the more approval plans the library sets up with competing vendors – ordering science books from one and social sciences books from another – the more chances there are for duplication in shipments, or worse yet, unknown gaps in the collection. Rarely does a book 'slip through the cracks' with a vendor. More often, the profile has been made so narrow by the library that the book is excluded on a small technicality. Vendor coverage is usually measurable. If the vendor reviews 25 000 titles for general approval plans in one year, chances are likely that he looked at every title reviewed and thousands that were not. Even the most prolific review media in America rarely exceed 5 000 titles a year.

The third area covered on most approval plans is the publisher list. Here competition truly flourishes. Vendors tout the 'most complete publisher list', 'over 154 university presses,' 'over 200 university presses', '800 presses with guaranteed coverage', 'every press covered', and 'over 17 000 publishers on our press list'. Again, wording is vital, interpretation even more so. Most vendors could do 60 per cent of their business with a stable of 20 publishers – the rest is service. Beyond a core list of 300 publishers, the vendor may make very little profit or actually lose money, which is why the mix of publishers is vital to the relationship between the vendor and the library. When vendors claim to have 17 000 publishers on their lists, does that mean that they are truly in touch with all 17 000 on an annual basis and review every book they publish? I think not. What should be of more concern is a guaranteed list of perhaps 800 publishers from whom the vendor reviews *every* title for consideration on its approval plans. For the library wanting a comprehensive plan, I still recommend a core guaranteed list, leaving the vendor to flesh it out with as many other appropriate titles as he can locate.

The size of the publisher list is meaningless unless every publisher is in constant contact with the vendor. The guaranteed list is meaningless unless the library constantly spot checks on coverage. One should be able to pick up a publisher's catalogue at random, select a single title, and, if the publisher is on the guaranteed list, find the title in the vendor's database. Whether the vendor allows direct access to the database, or provides hard copy of the database in the form of fiche or printed copy, the library should have some access point to the approval-plan data.

Those are just some of the basic competitive points in the ongoing approval plan. The preliminary presentation, bids, and requests for proposals leave even more room for negotiation and competition, as they do in any library/vendor relationship. To take best advantage of the competitive spirit, the library should draw up an initial Request for Proposal or Request for Information which specifically spells out the 'musts' and the 'shalls' of the relationship. The library should also be totally honest with the vendor in setting up the presentations. It costs a vendor at least $1 000 to make a presentation and, depending on how many people are brought in to the presentation to make the proper impression, the costs to a vendor can be staggering. If a vendor does not have a chance of getting the account, the library should not invite him to make a presentation.

At vendor presentations, librarians should be ready with questions, and should also limit the presentation to the library's decision-makers. The vendor should already have provided preliminary material, which library staff should have read before the presentation, making notes on areas needing clarification. When the presentation is over, the decision makers should meet alone with the vendor representatives to discuss negotiations. It is often helpful to the library to arrange vendor presentations as closely together as possible, and helpful to the vendors if response is made promptly. Every vendor thinks he has a good chance of getting the account, and every vendor making a presentation wants the account. The approval plan, once in place, should be monitored regularly to be sure the vendor is living up to the agreement. The vendors who did not get the account will still want it, and both the library and the incumbent vendor should keep that in mind.

Approval plans generate data, and that data can form the basis for retrospective searches. *Books in print*[5] and similar services have been in place for some time already, offering access to bibliographic data at any number of points for use in acquisitions or collection development. Using such a tool, and its search capabilities, the library can draw up listings of books derived from complex searches limited by such parameters as author, title, keyword, and so on. Several vendors now offer similar services based on their approval-plan databases. Searches can be kept simple – all publications from a single press, for example – or can be extremely complex and matched against every nuance of a full blown approval plan profile. Not only can this type of search provide the library with a bibliography of desirable titles, it can act as the basis for budgeting information and allocation. A few months ago, the third edition of *Books for college libraries*[6] was published. This listing of approximately 50 000 titles appropriate to a college library is available in both hard copy and in machine-readable format. Some vendors are now offering tape matches against this listing. Tapes may also be used for matchings against the vendor's own database. In both cases the library provides a listing of its current holdings in a standardized format, and the vendor runs this tape against his files to produce a listing of titles missing from the library's collection. The cost? Again, a competitive product. The appearance of *Books for college libraries*, because it does not distinguish between titles in and out of print, may give a boost to one of the less visible services of some vendors: the out-of-print search. The vendor who offers out-of-print services may find himself doing a land office business, since many of the titles in *Books for college libraries* are pre-1970 imprints.

Standing orders

Serials standing orders, or continuations, also are a door to collection development and are certainly a target for automation and competition. Too often, serials standing orders have been a stepchild of the acquisitions business, particularly in relation to automation. With the now rapid proliferation of automated acquisitions systems with serials modules, more and more booksellers are being forced to make the decision to automate their serials departments, if for no other reason than simple communication between buyer and seller. The results will, of course, provide better access to information and better system management. Claiming will become an automated part of the system, and schedules will be set up to provide for binding. Costs can be projected and collection weeding will be simplified when the addition, revision or deletion of records becomes push-button managed. This is an area where vendors will be looking to the libraries for leadership. But, just as surely as library needs dictated the advent of the invoice on disc, library needs will dictate an automated linkup between monographic serial services and library serial acquisitions that may move beyond those services already being offered by periodical vendors.

Publishers and publishing

Vendors tend to be very *au courant* with publishers. Many have publisher-relations departments that maintain daily contact. The results of those contacts, combined with data retrieved from their in-house systems, make it possible for vendors to issue periodic reports on the state of publisher pricing. These reports can often be broken down by subject areas and types of publishers. Trends, which are watched closely by vendors for internal purposes, can be translated easily by the library into budget projections. While fortune telling is a fading art, trends and cycles can often present worthwhile information. For example, I completed a recent study covering several years which shows that book list prices tend to follow the same rhythm each year in their steady upward climb. In American academic publishing, there is a steady rise from December to April, a plunge in May-June, a return to average by August, a small dip just before Christmas, and then the cycle begins again. This is the sort of information available from vendors that can help the library in monthly budget planning.

In addition to such data, many vendors publish newsletters, announcement services, pre-publication announcements and review publications. Naturally, the intent of such publishing is to create sales, or at least goodwill. The result of this competitive venture is to provide the library with a great deal of data at no charge. Newsletters often cover such areas as publisher mergers and new publishing ventures. Whether the library orders through the vendor or not, such data can improve the library's own order information. The newsletters often herald new services as well, and almost every service is another point of competition.

Review media published by vendors serve two purposes. They present valuable reviews to the library, albeit highly selective, but they also have an influence on how the publisher sees the vendor. The review media help present the vendor to the publisher in a better light, which may result in improved relations – both fiscally and informationally. Some vendors also offer pre-publication announcement services to libraries. Often available as 3 x 5 forms, these slips announce forthcoming or newly published titles for library selection. Automation has made some of the services available in machine-readable formats and, linked to PC ordering, they become on-line catalogues for library shopping. Many of these services are still in developmental stages, but in the highly competitive market, clones and copy-cats cannot be too far behind.

Conclusion

Why all the competition? There are about 55 000 new titles published each year, about 31 000 libraries in the United States to buy them, and about two dozen large, nationally recognized wholesale vendors. (Although there are 927 listed in the *American book trade directory, 1989-90.*)[7] 'Overall, books are bought more frequently through wholesalers than direct from the publishers. About 80 per cent of all libraries spend between 50 and 100 per cent of their budgets with wholesalers.'[8] Looking at the numbers, it is easy to see why the vendors are competitive. While it is unlikely that any one vendor will get all of the six million dollar book budget from one large university library, it is not inconceivable that he may have at least one million of it, and that is a plum devoutly to be desired. To pluck that, or any other portion of the market, the vendor must be competitive. They all offer approximately the same services, close to the same prices, and the difference often lies in those almost unquantifiable subtleties of personality and image and responsiveness. When a new product appears on the market, the gloves really come off and the battle does not let up until all players in the same marketplace have similar products.

Vendors distribute a lot more than books these days. If any trend is obvious, it is the emphasis on the electronic 'aura' of the book, more than the book itself. Libraries can now acquire full bibliographic descriptions of the book, in machine-readable format, on tape or via direct transmission, with annotations. They can pick up a bibliography from the vendor on similar books or books by the same person. They can establish an authority control for the main entry and subject headings, and glean statistics on the book and where it fits into the whole of the book world. At the same time, libraries can pick up a table of contents and a review of the book from some vendors. If it is in a series, the vendor can indicate where that volume belongs bibliographically, and who else bought it geographically. The book itself almost begins to look like a by-product of the industry it supports.

Automation and competition have resulted in an increasingly wide range of services being offered to libraries by vendors. Most are free or below cost and are of tremendous value to the library. Most vendors are still seeing these value-added items as just that, and are still pricing with the book as the main sale item. At the present moment, libraries are in a very positive position. Virtually every vendor is gearing up to meet existing services or retooling for new ones. The changes over the next 15 years will be even more exciting and beneficial to both libraries and vendors than those of the past 15 years have been.

References

1. Seibert, W.F. et al. *Partial update of the 'Purdue studies' preliminary results on growth in the seventies.* Paper presented at the meeting of the Association of Research Libraries, Minneapolis, MN.
2. Phelps, D. (1990), 'Publisher discounts – but at what price?', *Library acquisitions, practice and theory.* (Forthcoming publication.)
3. Atkinson, R. (1989), 'Old forms, new forms: the challenge of collection development', *College and research libraries,* **50** (5), 507-520.
4. *The Bowker annual of library and book trade information, 1988,* New York: R.R. Bowker, p.397.
5. *Books in print,* New York: R.R. Bowker. Annual.
6. Clar, V. (ed.) (1988), *Books for college libraries,* 3rd ed., Chicago: American Library Association.
7. *American book trade directory, 1989-90,* New York: R.R. Bowker.
8. *Ibid.,* p.399.

6   The influence of the library user on collection management

Helen M. Workman

> For some time, collection management has been gravitating away from the technical services sphere, where it historically grew out of the library's role as a processor of faculty book requests, into the public services sphere, in a conscious effort to be more responsive to changing user needs.[1]

Before discussing the influence of the library user on collection management, it is necessary to define the term 'collection management' as it is used in this chapter, and also to outline the various categories of library user. In particular, the term 'collection management' needs to be distinguished from the more widely used term 'collection development'. A recent on-line search of the Library and Information Science Abstracts (LISA) file retrieved over 990 references published since 1969 containing the term 'collection development' but fewer than 160 on 'collection management'. Brindley[2] distinguishes collection development and collection management in hierarchical terms with collection development at the highest level as 'a planning function for the systematic and rational building of a collection'. This is very much broader than the common use of the term to denote the selection and acquisition of material. From collection development plans, she argues, 'flow decisions on selection, acquisition, weeding, preservation and evaluation, all embraced and often quantified in collection management'. Thus collection management can be seen as the day-to-day implementation of collection development policies, extending to cover those aspects of library operations and services concerned with making the collections available to the library's users. The term 'collection management' begs the question 'management for whom?', which can only be answered with reference to the needs of the users.

Library users have different needs relating to the library, its services and collections, and it is useful at this stage to present a broad grouping of library users according to those needs. As reflected in many mission statements, academic libraries are charged with supporting the teaching and research of their institutions, and undoubtedly the most fundamental division of academic library users is into staff and students. However, it is important that user groups are defined more closely according to special needs. Obviously students undertaking research are likely to require access to more extensive collections than course students. For the latter the timely availability of a limited range of material is likely to be the key to a good library service. Part-time students and overseas students can have additional needs for library services, and in particular collection management policies should endeavour to cater for these needs. Academic staff make use of the library and its collections at a variety of levels. The library's collections must be selected and managed to support their teaching and they should also be capable of supporting their research interests, supplemented where necessary by the interlending service.

The influence of the library user on collection management occurs at various stages of the collection management process, three of which I wish to study in detail in this chapter. Firstly, what items should be selected for the library's collections and how can the library user influence the selection decision? Secondly, once material is in the library, how can its availability be maximized? Questions to be considered here include the provision of multiple copies, variable loan periods and the needs of special categories of users. A related topic is the removal from collections of little-used materials, and collection management for the self-renewing library is briefly discussed. The third stage of collection management discussed in this chapter is concerned with helping the user to exploit the collections and includes such topics as catalogues, classification, guiding, enquiry services and user education. The final section of the chapter comprises a brief summary of techniques for the assessment of user needs in relation to collection management.

The influence of the library user on selection decisions

The decision to acquire an individual title for the library's collections is influenced by the library user either directly, through recommendations for purchase, or indirectly, through the librarian's knowledge of the teaching and research interests of the institution. According to Thompson and Carr[3] 'it seems universally agreed that responsibility for selection is best shared between library staff and academic staff.' Spiller discusses two extremes, firstly where the administration gives almost total control of the bookfund to the librarian, with suggestions from departments and faculties permitted, but not particularly encouraged, and secondly where the bookfund is divided on a departmental basis leaving the librarian with only a minimal allocation to balance up departmental orders. He argues that neither of these extremes is satisfactory:

> Not to make full use of the subject expertise of the university lecturing and research staff for selection is obviously absurd. At the same time, a system which relies entirely upon departmental selection is bound to result in lack of balance . . . However effective the departmental ordering, some central control is needed to balance up inequality of treatment between subjects, order interdisciplinary material, and fill in titles which for one reason or another have been missed.[4]

Even in those academic libraries where library staff are largely responsible for selection (Spiller's first extreme situation), decisions as to which titles to purchase are taken in the knowledge of the teaching and research needs of the institution and are thus indirectly influenced by the library user. Such libraries may have an acquisitions policy which has been formally approved by the library committee and which enables selection decisions to be made in accordance with priorities set out in the policy. In most academic libraries in the UK, however, selection work is based primarily on recommendations made by academic staff and the common policy of allocating book grants down to the departmental level encourages the purchase of material at the behest of departmental library representatives. The weight attached to the role of the departmental library representative, and one must suppose by extension to the library itself, can vary enormously between departments within one academic institution; from the head of department or a long-serving staff member to the most recent junior recruit. However, whether this difference in seniority has any discernible effect on the material purchased for each department is open to question. As a result of the departmental library representative scheme it is often only a few members of the academic staff who are involved in selection work and 'if a department uses its allocation to purchase highly specialized materials, the general stock in that subject can be neglected entirely'.[5] At the other extreme, in one department in a UK university the available bookfund is notionally divided equally between all members of the academic staff in that department. Whilst having the advantage of involving all staff in selection decisions for the library, such a situation can lead only to the building of piecemeal collections.

Funding

Many academic libraries have investigated the use of a formula in an attempt to arrive at an equitable and justifiable division of available funds between departments, a topic covered in more detail in Chapter 2. Most often formula funding is simply applied to bookfunds, although logically the concept can and should be applied to the allocation of funds for all library services, including interlibrary loans, on-line and other information services and periodicals, as well as to books. One of the most basic criteria incorporated in formula funding is the number of staff and students in each department, the latter often being weighted according to status (undergraduate, postgraduate course student or research student) on the premise that the level of library support required by each type of student is different. Thus, at a most basic level, the library user has an impact on selection decisions merely through being registered with a department.

The influence of the library user on the level of funding available for book purchases between each subject area has been taken a stage further at the University of Sussex. Peasgood[6] describes the introduction of a demand-led book acquisitions programme. From an investigation of loans data of recently acquired material it appeared that users of different subject areas were getting very different access to new books. In some subjects over 90 per cent of loanable stock had been lent in the first two years of shelf life, in others less than 40 per cent. Beginning in 1982/

83 a rebalancing of funds was undertaken, concentrating initially on those subjects at the extremes of the loans analysis. As a result of further monitoring, Peasgood was able to conclude that 'current book selection policies are apparently satisfying borrowing demand more adequately than did earlier ones.'

Subject specialization

A scheme of subject specialization is employed in many academic libraries in the UK; a survey of 61 academic libraries by Woodhead and Martin[7] showed that 48 libraries had subject specialists to varying degrees. Subject specialists ideally have qualifications in their appropriate subjects as well as in librarianship and they are responsible for reference and information work, as well as book selection. They are thus well positioned to be aware of the needs of library users in their subject and to respond to these needs, for as Spiller[8] states, 'such staff usually have a close relationship with the academic departments'. The importance of subject specialization with regard to book selection is stressed by Thompson and Carr[9] who argue that 'the subject specialist will bring his expertise to bear on book selection duties, thereby making that process a more sure and informed one.'

Regardless of who is responsible for book selection, whether it be library staff or academic staff, appropriate members of the library staff should ideally be members of the institution's faculty boards and other relevant committees in order that they are aware of, and can have input into, future academic developments which will have an impact on the collection requirements of the library.

Most academic libraries allow individual users to suggest titles that they would like to see added to the library's stock. Whether such titles are acquired depends not only on the availability of appropriate funds, but also on whether library staff view the title as properly belonging within the scope of the library's collections. A further source of information on which to base individual selection decisions is interlibrary loan requests. The feasibility of monitoring these requests should be improved with the introduction of automated packages with interlibrary lending modules and a single mode of request for titles currently not available within the library.

Serials

Whilst library users, particularly members of the academic staff, have a major influence on the selection of individual monograph titles for the library's collections, the situation with serial titles is somewhat different because of the ongoing commitment of a new subscription. In many libraries there is no shortage of library users making requests, indeed even pleading desperately, for new journals, but the funding is just not available to allow the library to respond positively to these requests. Thompson and Carr[10] summarize the present situation as follows:

> In truth, such is now the outlay on periodicals in every university library that the selection – or cancellation – of periodicals subscriptions is the major selection exercise. Because of the very nature and variety of periodicals, the exercise is always a collaborative and consultative one between library and teaching staff. A usual pattern is to divide the titles to be selected – or cancelled – into subject, departmental or Faculty groups, and judgements made on the basis of peer-group evaluation. The librarian's role is often no more than to present information as to subscription cost, and as to the level of funding available or as to the level of savings required.

The influence of the library user on serial collection management has in some instances been very great, for example with the voting procedure used to evaluate the holdings (and non-holdings) of the University of Sussex Library.[11] Such a zero-based budgeting approach to the evaluation of the serials collection has been used in other academic libraries, such as the University of Surrey, where a recent exercise resulted in the cancellation of 285 titles and the ordering of 215 new titles, the net loss of 70 titles yielding a cash saving of the order of £18 000 per year.[12]

Reading lists

If the library is to offer a good service to students, it is essential that material on reading lists, and otherwise recommended to students by lecturers and tutors, is available when required. Part of the challenge relates to the management of the number of copies of particular titles and of loan periods in order to provide adequate title availability. The key to ensuring that a copy (or copies) of material on reading lists is selected and acquired for the library's collections is good communication with the teaching staff. Ideally the library should receive a copy of all reading lists together with an indication of the numbers of students likely to be taking each course several months before the start of a session. This lead time will enable orders to be placed and the majority of books to be supplied, catalogued, classified and otherwise processed, and to be available on the shelves for the start of the first term. As well as trying to obtain copies of reading lists in good time, special forms may be available for completion by teaching staff, requesting details such as basic bibliographic information, the course number, number of readers expected, and inviting suggestions as to the number of copies required and loan period requirements. Such stationery is available at the reference desk of the British Library of Political and Economic Science (BLPES) – the library of the London School of Economics (LSE) – and a display containing the forms, together with a container for the completed forms, has been mounted in the Senior Common Room of the LSE in an attempt to increase the academics' awareness of the need to inform the Library of the material required in support of teaching and also to make it easier for them to do so. However, it is the information that is important, rather than the form in which it is received; a colleague who is responsible for ordering material for the Teaching Collection at the BLPES tells the new lecturers during the library session of their induction course that phone calls and backs of envelopes are also acceptable, just so long as the information reaches him!

At the University of Sheffield a 'bookshop correspondent' scheme is in operation. Departmental representatives compile a list of textbooks being recommended for purchase by students in the department and forward this list to the library. The library coordinator then circulates copies of the lists to local bookshops and, of course, ensures that the library's holdings of these titles are adequate.[13] This raises an interesting dilemma: should the library be responsible for the provision of core textbooks, or can it reasonably be assumed that students will purchase their own copies? Again it is important that good communication exists between the teaching staff and the library staff, so that the latter are aware of the intensity with which the library's copies of reading list items are likely to be used.

Often reading lists change very little from year to year, and the acquisitions department needs to know only of new material being added to reading lists. (Ideally appropriate action should be taken to check that all items on a reading list are still available on the library shelves, but the task of checking every item each year is clearly enormous.

Also multiple copies of titles no longer on reading lists will need to be withdrawn from stock, although care must be taken that such titles do not appear on the reading lists of other lecturers.) The development of on-line public access catalogues (OPACs) and integrated library systems provides scope for alerting the appropriate library staff to changes in reading lists, whilst at the same time enabling the bibliographical accuracy of reading lists to be improved and classmarks to be incorporated once the material has been acquired and processed. These improvements should ensure that not only is the request to purchase reading list material received and acted upon more quickly but also that students can find this material more easily.

Maximizing availability of the collections

The introduction of automated circulation systems has provided librarians with a powerful tool to improve the management of their collections, and in particular to improve the availability of specific titles. The management information packages of such systems are capable of ranking titles according to the number of times they have been issued or reserved over a specified time period. The loan period of titles thus shown as being in heavy demand can be shortened to increase availability and consideration can be given to the purchase of additional copies. At the other end, the highlighting of titles which have been issued relatively infrequently can be used as a basis for decisions concerning relegation, for example from a short loan collection to the main collection. Thus, through the use or non-use that is made of specific items in the library's stock, the user is influencing the management of the collections. It must be said that in spite of the fact that 'the promoters of automated circulation systems have been quick to point out the facility offered for a closer analysis of issues within detailed subject areas and other parameters',[14] with many such systems, high priority does not appear to have been given to the provision of the information required for the optimal management of collections.

Reserve collections

In reserve and short loan collections which are on closed access (or where there is no seating provided within the collection) loan statistics provide an accurate picture of the use of individual items. As Peasgood[15] points out:

> Academic librarians have for many years selected from the main stock items to be placed in the Reserve and Short Loan Collections, and have acquired stock specifically for such collections. The justification for both transfers and purchases has been the ability to satisfy demand which would otherwise have been frustrated. Given the costs involved, both of staff time and of direct expenditure, librarians have recorded and analysed the use of such collections quite intensively in order to monitor the return on these outlays.

The following description of the method of operation of the Reserve Services collection in the library of the University of Calgary, Canada, serves to illustrate Peasgood's points. Books from this collection are issued for a minimum period of one hour by a manual system so that items can be retrieved from the borrower as soon as requested by another reader after the initial hour. (Borrowers have to indicate on the issue slip the number of the table at which they will be working and the library staff can then demand the return of a requested item.) At the start of each day the records of the previous day's issues are input into the automated circulation system so that statistics on usage can be produced with the ultimate aim of identifying the most heavily used titles. In this way a staff-intensive collection can be restricted in size and titles no longer in heavy demand cease to have their availability unnecessarily decreased by a very short loan period. (Restrictions are also placed on the number of titles and the number of copies of each title that any one member of the teaching staff can recommend for this collection.) This method of operation demonstrates firstly the use of very short loan periods in an attempt to maximize access to material and secondly the importance of issue statistics in managing the collection.

Part-time students

In order to manage the library's collections effectively it is necessary to have a knowledge of the needs of different groups of library users; ways of determining the needs of different user groups are described below. From the results of such studies, consideration must be given to maximizing the availability of collections for user groups with special needs. One particular group which has caused librarians to think carefully about the ways in which collections are managed are part-time students. Because such students can only use the library for limited times, for example on the day that they are in the institution and at the weekend, they will be disadvantaged if they are expected to compete for library materials with full-time students. At BLPES we have recently started telephoning part-time students to inform them when books they have reserved are available for collection. The normal method of notification, via pigeon holes in the library and via messages on the OPACs, meant that books were often no longer available when the part-time student next used the library. We were reluctant to increase the number of days reserved books are kept on the 'held shelf', as this would mean decreasing the availability of material to all users. Access to material is also improved for part-time students at the LSE by allowing this category of user to borrow books with a normal loan period of one day for a week.

A useful summary of possible modifications to library services to benefit part-time students is provided by Heery and Barr.[16] They outline a total of 71 ways to help part-time students, and of particular interest to those responsible for collection management in academic libraries are the following suggestions:

- create special collections for part-time students;
- loan more materials to part-time students;
- weekend loans of reference copies;
- create variable short loan periods;
- buy extra copies of books on part-time reading lists;
- give part-timers priority in your reservations system;
- have a closed access collection.

At a 1989 seminar on the subject of library services for non-traditional students[17] Quiney emphasized that the part-time student is time-starved and may be willing to pay extra for added-value services, such as the facility to order photocopies by telephone. Evening staff have an important role to play in terms of communicating complaints back to management for action. Certainly one of the most important points raised was that the librarian needs to ensure that there is feedback from part-time students, and needs to be willing to review stock and services in the light of such feedback.

Access students

At the same seminar, Stockton discussed library services in relation to the needs of access students (students without traditionally accepted qualifications for enrolment on a degree-level course). She commented that while such students typically have a background of negative experiences about education and a lack of confidence in their academic ability, they are mature, articulate and highly motivated. The priorities for library services to this group of students must be to provide a friendly, supportive atmosphere, to provide practical help in the form of library tours and printed guides and to provide a good collection of materials on study skills so that the student will be encouraged to progress towards becoming an independent learner.

As the size of the population of school leavers decreases, academic institutions will, in line with government policy, be recruiting students from a much more varied population in terms of age, educational qualifications, and time available for study. This will have important implications for librarians, as the numbers of part-time students, access students, short-course students and distance-learning students increase substantially. In particular collection management policies will have to be reassessed to make sure that the library needs of all students are being met adequately.

Collection management for the self-renewing library

The concept of the self-renewing library was put forward in the report of a working party set up by the University Grants Committee in 1976 (the Atkinson report).[18] The working party felt bound

> to question the concept of providing for the whole of a library's existing stock and anticipated accessions, since it rests on the assumption of indefinite accumulation, possibly at a high rate of growth, which would lead in a comparatively short time span to financial and reorganizational problems of such magnitude as to pose a threat to the university library system, even if substantial funds were available to sustain it.

It developed as an alternative, the concept of a self-renewing library in which 'new accessions would be relieved by the withdrawal of obsolete or unconsulted material to other stores'.[19]

Material in a library's collections may no longer be in use for a variety of reasons. The wrong material may have been selected in the first place. Reading lists for courses may have been updated or the courses themselves may have been altered. Research interests of a department change over time with new appointments and resignations and retirements of academic and research staff. In recent years significant parts of academic library collections may have fallen into comparative disuse through restructuring exercises and the closure of whole university departments.

Use of stock

In order to determine the material to be moved to other collections or stores the librarian must endeavour to define that portion of the stock which is not being used. As mentioned earlier, the data collected by automated circulation systems can be used to highlight material which has not been issued, or only issued infrequently, thus providing one possible quantitative criterion for relegation. This is often used in combination with other criteria such as date of publication. However, it must be acknowledged that loan statistics do not adequately represent usage of open-access collections where in-library use of materials may be significant, and this is particularly true for journals. The weeding of back runs of journals is sometimes based on citation analyses, in which case the use made of the journals is assessed at a global level, and not related to the use they receive in a particular library. To collect data about use of material in the library, a re-shelving survey can be undertaken, where readers are requested not to return to the shelves material they have consulted, so that library staff can analyse the material (for example, by journal title and year) before re-shelving it. Another option for assessing in-library use of specific material is to ask readers to initial a slip on the cover of each journal volume or issue every time they use it. The effectiveness of these methods is, of course, dependent on the cooperation of the readers. Nevertheless, efforts must be made to determine in-library use in any stock relegation exercise, otherwise readers will be inconvenienced and unnecessary costs will be incurred, if titles which are being consulted in the library are removed to a store.

Weeding

According to the Atkinson report, 'selection for withdrawal can be done either by category, or by individual judgement applied to each item. The former method is rough and ready but relatively cheap, the latter is academically preferable but may require many hours of work by highly qualified staff.'[20] Incidentally, weeding by the application of 'individual judgement' is frequently recognizable by the activity being referred to as 'stock editing'. Thompson and Carr[21] outline the difficulties of using qualitative criteria for weeding collections. They claim that 'it is virtually impossible to mount a systematic, comprehensive and consistent weeding programme based on departmental cooperation' and, because library staff will always carry the main burden, 'the preference for quantitative criteria is understandable'. Thus the influence of the user on weeding decisions is mainly indirect, through the level of use of material over past years.

Library services in support of collection management

An important aspect of collection management concerns the accessibility of the material in the collections. Not only do appropriate selection decisions have to be made (collection development in its narrower sense) and loan periods allocated and monitored, but library users must be able to find material they require. Lancaster[22] summarizes the stages the user has to go through to find a particular bibliographic item. Is the item owned? Is it catalogued? Can the user find the entry? Is it on the shelf? Can the user find the item on the shelf? By looking at the process as a series of probabilities, the probability that the user will leave the library with the required item is the product of the five component probabilities. Taking Lancaster's example, suppose that the library owns 90 per cent of the items sought by its users, that 80 per cent of owned items can be located in the catalogue, that 75 per cent of these are on the shelf when the users look for them, and that users succeed in finding items on the shelf (when actually present there) 90 per cent of the time, then the probability that the user will leave the library with the required item is only 48 per cent!

Many of the operations performed by library staff are designed to increase the probability that the users will find the material they require. Whilst these operations are listed below, few are discussed in detail. Cataloguing and classification are well covered in the literature and, within the confines of this chapter, it is inappropriate to do more than indicate the role that these operations play in the collection management process. The librarian should not lose sight of the fact that no operation should be seen as an end in itself, but should be undertaken as a means of assisting the user to exploit the library's collections.

Impact of OPACs

The catalogue is the main tool enabling the user to ascertain whether a required item is held in the library and if so where, and, increasingly, whether it is available for use or not. Its other function is to enable the user to determine what material the library holds on a particular subject. The introduction of OPACs in recent years has offered users a more effective and sophisticated means of searching the catalogue than was possible with earlier catalogues on cards or microfiche. Subject access is much easier, with many systems providing options to search by subject keywords or using Boolean logic. While not all library users may be aware of the full capabilities of the OPAC, it is a very useful tool for staff on the enquiry desk who are using the catalogue to exploit the collections on behalf of individual users.

The easy-to-use yet powerful searching capabilities of many OPAC systems call into question many of the earlier theories and professional attitudes relating to cataloguing and classification. As pressure mounts to streamline library operations because of budgetary constraints, the value of all library processes to the user must be assessed and priorities assigned. There is a growing trend for libraries to rely, wherever possible, on derived catalogue records which have been bought in from one of the bibliographic utilities. It is not then unusual to find that cataloguing or technical services departments contain a higher proportion of non-professional (or non academic-related) staff to carry out the more routine descriptive cataloguing procedures, leaving professional staff free to concentrate on areas of the library service which are both more beneficial to the users and appropriate to their qualifications.

The level of sophistication which OPACs offer for subject searching also has implications for classification and subject cataloguing. OPACs allow users to browse the catalogue using a subject approach in a way that was never possible with the earlier kinds of catalogue, and in a way that more closely resembles browsing the open shelves. Indeed, in some cases, for example in an institution with a multi-site library, browsing the OPAC may well provide a better overview of the library's holdings in a specific subject area. Given the presence of an OPAC in the library, the classification scheme serves primarily to provide adequate shelf order, with its function as an aid to subject searching being replaced by the OPAC's alternative and more effective subject approaches. Almost universally, browsing the classified index is the least used subject option on an OPAC. If the library uses one of the standard classification schemes, the more adventurous collection management librarian may choose to accept the classification number assigned by the British Library or the Library of Congress, whether from the bought-in catalogue record or from the Cataloguing in Publication (CIP) data found in the book, thereby streamlining the process of cataloguing and classification even further.

Another important advantage to the library user which has occurred with the introduction of OPACs and integrated library systems is that records are created for items at the ordering stage and such records are retrieved during catalogue searches. Thus a user can reserve a book before it actually arrives in the library, or, if the user requires a book urgently it can (at least in theory) be taken from the cataloguers' shelves and be made available more quickly. In summary, the introduction of integrated on-line library systems has improved the availability of the collections, both through improved searching facilities and through improved timeliness of records. In the Strategic Plan for BLPES the principal objective for transferring records to LIBERTAS is stated as 'to make the Library's collections far more accessible to users than manual records are able to do'. (The secondary objective is stated as 'to reduce the cost of cataloguing and other forms of processing', but that is another story!)

Arrangement of the collections

It must be acknowledged that browsing in the relevant sections of the open access shelves is a popular and often fruitful method of exploiting the collections, so that to have the material arranged in a logical order on the shelves is essential. An important issue for the arrangement of a library's collections is whether all material dealing with a particular topic should be kept in close proximity, regardless of its format. In some academic libraries, shelves of books in a particular classmark range are placed adjacent to shelves of periodicals in the same classmark range. In other libraries, periodicals are shelved on different floors from books. In many libraries a separate collection of current periodicals is maintained, often with a variety of seating. The philosophy behind this arrangement is that users wish to have easy access to recent periodicals for current awareness purposes. Other forms of material are often placed in close proximity to the equipment needed to view them, such as microfilm readers and video players. Although this arrangement can be to the benefit of both library users and staff, at the Applied Science Library of the University of Sheffield use of the video collection (mainly Open University programmes and videos made by the University's Computer Services Department) increased significantly when the videos were shelved among the bookstock at the appropriate classmark, which reinforces the notion of the importance of browsing for many library users. Most academic libraries operate short-loan collections, where material deemed to be in heavy demand is held in a different location from the rest of the library stock.

Undergraduate library

The idea of a separate undergraduate library has not gained wide acceptance, at least in the UK context. One of the main reasons for this, according to Thompson and Carr, is 'the almost universal feeling that an undergraduate, even though he apparently may need basically to use only a certain limited number of texts, should be exposed and have ready and convenient access to everything else the library has to offer.' An important advantage to the student of having a separate undergraduate collection within the main library building is that 'the student is thereby largely spared the quite genuinely overwhelming and confusing effects of an unavoidable and premature confrontation with a very large, research-orientated library.'[23]

Reference collections

Another important collection to be found in most academic libraries is the reference collection. While it is relatively easy to define the core of reference material to be located in a central and easily accessible reference collection, it is often difficult to define where the boundaries of this type of collection lie. Should bibliographies be located there, or should they be located with the material on the subjects which they cover? Should foreign language dictionaries be located in the reference collection, or should they be available on the appropriate subject floors? Such questions should be addressed with the needs of the users of the individual library in mind.

Signing and guiding

Whatever the layout of the collections in a particular library, it is essential that the building and its collections are well signed. As soon as users enter the library building it should be possible for them to find the facilities and services required. Where is the catalogue? Where is the short-loan collection? Where are recent journal issues? Where are books with classmark beginning 532 located? (And, of course, where are the toilets?) The library building must be as well signed as the best department store, and in matters of visual identity and customer care, libraries can learn much from the retail business.

Reader services

The reference desk or enquiry service enables the library staff to help the user to exploit the collections on a one-to-one basis. Thus a first rate enquiry service facilitates the exploitation of the collections and it also provides library staff with information relevant to the management of the collections. It is perhaps one of the most important services performed by professional staff in academic libraries.

The one-to-one reference desk service is inevitably expensive in library staff time, and what many users require is basic information about the library's collections and services. Such information can be made readily available through a series of guides. These can range from the simple bookmark displaying opening hours through to the more comprehensive guide to library services or the more in-depth description of the library's holdings on a particular subject. There may sometimes be opportunities for these guides to carry an advertisement for the local bookshop, thereby helping to offset the cost of their production.

User education

It is difficult, and perhaps unnecessary, to draw the line between library guides and user education, and in any case this line is becoming further blurred with the employment of techniques other than print on paper.

Tape-slides and videos are often used to provide students with an early introduction to the library and its collections and services. As in a number of National Trust properties, some academic libraries now use personal cassette players, such as the ubiquitous Walkman, to guide visitors round the building and to draw attention to its contents. Some librarians have experimented with the use of interactive computer learning to instruct students in the use of the library. One particularly useful tool increasingly available to the librarian is the OPAC. The help facility of such systems enables users to obtain instructions related to the activity they are currently undertaking, whilst the information facility available on some OPAC systems provides the librarian with the opportunity of giving information about the library and its services.

However, user education certainly extends beyond ensuring that the user is aware of the services offered by a particular library. It is also concerned with informing the user about literature searching and information retrieval techniques in particular subject areas. Here the librarian is likely to be involved in giving lectures, seminars and workshops. Close collaboration with the academic staff is desirable and the timing of such sessions is a vital factor in their success. A very useful summary of recent issues in the field of user education is the *British Library research review* by Cowley and Hammond.[24]

Assessing user needs

If library collections are to be managed for the benefit of their users, it is necessary for those responsible for collection management to be aware of, and responsive to, the needs of the users. Of course, it is not easy to define the needs of the users, as Line has made clear: 'an information need is a basic requirement for information that is of value . . . A person may not – and this is a crucial point – always be aware of his needs. A want is a felt need; a demand is an expressed want; and a use is what it says it is.'[25]

However, attempts have been made to assess users' needs in relation to information for research. One of the earliest studies was in fact undertaken by Line and colleagues at the University of Bath and published as the *INFROSS (Information Requirements in the Social Sciences) report* in 1971.[26] A more recent study was carried out by Slater and was designed not only to update the *INFROSS report* and subsequent studies but also to discover if any needs uncovered by such studies still remained unmet. Slater concludes that while

> academic social scientists still seemed to be relatively well-served, although provision may compare unfavourably with that enjoyed in former years . . . information problems experienced in the 1980s were compounded by a harsh external environment, a difficult economic climate, with consequent lack of resources (funds, staff, time) amongst both users and information providers in the social science community.[27]

Studies of this type, although not directly applicable to collection management within a single academic library, nevertheless provide valuable background information for those responsible for collection management.

A recent study of particular interest to academic librarians is that carried out by Pocklington and Finch in 1987.[28] Their aim was to assess the impact on the process of research in universities and polytechnics of budgetary constraint in research libraries, by seeking qualitative data from academic staff engaged in research in four institutions (University of Leicester, University of St Andrews, University College London and Sheffield Polytechnic). They found that the attitudes and behaviour of some academics had changed as a result of the decline in funding for libraries. For example:

> Academics widely reported having to spend more of their own money in order to obtain items of literature relevant to their research interests, and more generally in order to remain abreast of the rapidly expanding knowledge base. The decrease in the purchasing power of the acquisitions budget of each library and the consequences this was having were seen as the main reasons behind the need to spend their own money.[29]

Pocklington and Finch suggest that if current trends are allowed to continue, academic libraries 'will have become a less central feature in the working lives of academic researchers'.[30] It will be interesting to see if the more detailed research currently being undertaken by Pocklington and Finch, based on four subject groups, will be able to provide positive suggestions as to how academic library collections should be managed under conditions of financial restraint to avoid such predictions becoming reality.

More specific studies can be undertaken to assess the extent to which actual collections are satisfying user needs. A useful document in this context is *Guide to the evaluation of library collections* published in 1989 by the American Library Association. The purpose of the document is 'to provide librarians and others with a statement of principles and methods to guide them in determining the extent to which their library acquires the books, journals or other materials needed in order to satisfy users and fulfil the library's stated mission'[31] and it considers measures under two categories: collection-centred and user-centred. The latter covers circulation studies, in-house studies, surveys of user opinions, shelf-availability studies, analysis of interlibrary loan statistics, and simulated use studies. The advantages and disadvantages of each measure are outlined and a useful bibliography is included.

Many of the user-centred measures have been touched on in this chapter; for example, the use of loan statistics, particularly for the management of short-loan collections and for highlighting possible candidates for relegation, and the measurement of in-house use of library materials. Obviously such measures are of value in the management of library collections, but they reveal nothing of the extent to which the needs of library users are not being met. If librarians can investigate these unmet needs and the reasons for their existence then they will be in a position to manage the collections more effectively. Thus a survey of user opinions can be a valuable tool for the effective management of library collections. In the ALA *Guide to the evaluation of library collections*, the goal of user surveys is stated as 'to determine how well the library's collections meet the user's information needs by gathering written or oral responses to specific questions.' The uses to which information from user surveys can be put are listed as:

- Evaluate quantitatively and qualitatively the effectiveness of the collections in meeting users' needs;
- Provide information to help solve specific problems;
- Define the make-up of the actual community of library users;
- Identify user groups that need to be better served;
- Provide feedback on successes as well as on deficiencies;
- Improve public relations and assist in the education of the user community;
- Identify changing trends and interests.

The advantages of a user survey are given as:

- It is not limited to existing data, such as circulation statistics;
- Permits direct feedback from users;
- Can be as simple or as complex as desired.

The list of disadvantages is rather forbidding:

- Designing a sophisticated survey is difficult; that is, it is difficult to frame unambiguous questions that will yield quantifiable results;
- Analysing and interpreting data from an opinion survey to get usable information is difficult and imprecise;
- Most users are likely to be passive about collections and so must be approached individually and polled one at a time, increasing the costs of conducting the survey;
- Some users may not cooperate in the survey and thus results may be skewed;
- Many users are not aware of what their library should reasonably be expected to do for them and therefore have difficulty in judging what is adequate;
- User surveys may record perceptions, intentions, and recollections which do not always reflect actual experiences or patterns of user behaviour;
- User interests may be focused more narrowly than collection development policies. This may introduce a negative bias in the survey results;
- By definition, surveys of user opinions will miss valuable statements from and about the nonuser.[32]

However, if carefully designed, and if taken in conjunction with other user-centred measures, surveys of user opinions can provide useful information for librarians responsible for collection management. Not only can the results of such surveys be used to improve collection management policies on a day-to-day level, but they can also be employed to good effect in the library's bid to its institution for funding.

Conclusion

The subject content of this chapter is very wide ranging; many library operations have been touched on and some have been discussed in more detail than others. The wide brief of the chapter is indicative firstly of the nature of collection management, which is concerned not only with the acquisition of material for the library's collections, but with all library operations designed to make that material available to the library's users. The second reason for the wide ranging nature of this chapter is related to the differing needs of the various categories of library user. The librarian responsible for collection management must be aware of these needs so that library policies can be designed and modified to satisfy as many of them as possible.

The collection management function crosses the traditional technical services/reader services divide. The role of the library user, particularly the academic staff member, in the selection of material for the collections is clearly important, but such selection decisions require coordination with a view to the overall development of the library's collections. Acquisition of the required material falls in the province of the technical services section, as does the cataloguing of such material. However, with the advent of OPACs, reader services staff have become much more aware of the importance of the presentation of the catalogue to the users. Many of the traditional functions undertaken by the staff of the reader services section are designed to enable the library user to exploit the library's collections and thus form an important element in the collection management process. The subject specialist staff structure adopted in many academic libraries allows professional staff to operate within both the reader services and the technical services areas. One of the main advantages of this cross-divisional responsibility is that it places high priority on the needs of the library user.

Because the library user is the *raison d'être* of any library, library collections and services must be designed to fulfil the user's needs. The five laws of library science put forward by Ranganathan[33] as long ago as 1931 have not been bettered. In particular the first law, 'books are for use', the second law, 'every person his book', and the third law, 'every book its reader', are of value in the context of the influence of the library user on collection management. If academic libraries are to retain a central role in supporting the teaching and research of their institutions, it is essential that the library user has a substantial influence on many stages of the collection management process.

References

1. Cogswell, J.A. (1987), 'The organization of collection management functions in academic research libraries', *Journal of academic librarianship*, **13**, p.270.
2. Brindley, L. (1988), Summing up in: S. Corrall (ed.) *Collection development: options for effective management*, London: Taylor Graham, p.142.
3. Thompson, J. and R. Carr (1987), *An introduction to university library administration*, 4th ed., London: Bingley, p.80.
4. Spiller, D. (1986), *Book selection: an introduction to principles and practice*, 4th ed., London: Bingley, p.40.
5. Thompson, J. and R. Carr, ref. 3, p.29.
6. Peasgood, A.N. (1986), 'Towards demand-led book acquisitions? Experiences in the University of Sussex Library', *Journal of librarianship*, **18**, 242-256.
7. Woodhead, P.A. and J.V. Martin (1982), 'Subject specialisation in British university libraries: a survey', *Journal of librarianship*, **14**, 93-108.
8. Spiller, D. ref. 4, p.42.
9. Thompson, J. and R. Carr, ref. 3, p.173.
10. Ibid., p.86.
11. Horwill, C. and P.J. Lambert (1987), '1 man – 100 votes: a new approach to reviewing periodical subscriptions at the University of Sussex', *Aslib proceedings*, **39**, 7-16.
12. University of Surrey, George Edwards Library, *Annual report of the Librarian, 1988/89*.
13. Mann, P.H. (1974), *Students and books*, London: Routledge and Kegan Paul, pp.79-82.
14. Spiller, D. ref. 4, p.50.
15. Peasgood, A.N. ref. 6, p.243.
16. Heery, M. and H. Barr (1989), *71 ways to help your part-time students*, Bristol: Library Association University, College and Research Section Southwestern Group. (Discussion Paper 3).
17. SCONUL (1989), Advisory Committee on Information Services seminar, London, 15 November. (Unpublished proceedings.)
18. University Grants Committee (1976), *Capital provision for university libraries: report of a working party* [Chairman: Professor R. Atkinson], London: HMSO.
19. Ibid., p.6.
20. Ibid., p.10.
21. Thompson, J. and R. Carr, ref. 3, p.110.
22. Lancaster, F.W. (1988), *If you want to evaluate your library...* London: Library Association, p.14.
23. Thompson, J. and R. Carr, ref. 3, p.88.
24. Cowley, J.A. and N. Hammond (1987), *Educating information users in universities, polytechnics and colleges*, London: British Library. (British Library Research Review, 12.)
25. Line, M.B. (1981), 'Ignoring the user: how, when and why', in *The nationwide provision and use of information. Aslib-IIS-LA joint conference, September 1980*, London: Library Association, p.80.
26. Line, M.B., et al. (1971), *Investigation into the information requirements of the social sciences, research reports 1-5*, Bath: Bath University Library. (OSTI reports 5096, 5097, 5099, 5106.)
27. Slater, M. (1989), *Information needs of social scientists: a study by desk research and interview*, London: British Library, p.iii. (British Library research paper, 60.)

28. Pocklington, K. and H. Finch (1987), *Research collections under constraint*, London: British Library. (British Library research paper, 36.)
29. Ibid., p.19.
30. Ibid., p.30.
31. Lockett, B.A. (ed.) (1989), *Guide to the evaluation of library collections*, Chicago: American Library Association, p.1. (Collection management and development guides, 2.)
32. Ibid., p.11.
33. Ranganathan, S.R. (1931), *The five laws of library science*, Madras: Madras Library Association.

7   The management of serials collections

Hazel Woodward*

Serial literature constitutes a major part of all academic libraries' collections, and typically accounts for more than half of their expenditure on library materials – often a great deal more than half. For many academic and research staff, the serials to which the library subscribes are the most important and useful elements of its stock; for librarians they represent material which is expensive to acquire and difficult to manage. Serial literature thus merits separate attention in a study of academic library collection management.

In many ways managing a serials collection differs little from managing a bank, a soccer team, or any other organization. The fundamentals of a shared mission, commonly defined objectives, open two-way communication and clearly perceived tasks and responsibilities drive any organization to its level of appropriate success. Essential to the successful management of serials collections in libraries is an understanding of the nature of the collection being managed, and of the managerial forces at play over the collection. The type of library in which the collection

*The author gratefully acknowledges the help received from John F. Riddick, Associate Professor and Head of the Acquisitions Services Department, Central Michigan University, in providing ideas and information on US serials collection development issues.

resides will call forth varying managerial responses – but while styles and methods of organizing staff may differ among various academic libraries, the principles of management remain the same whether in London, Los Angeles or Lagos.

The nature of the collection

Terminology associated with serials can be confusing, as a variety of words are used to describe similar material. ISO Standard 3297 defines a serial as 'a publication, in printed form or not, issued in successive parts usually having numerical or chronological designations and intended to be continued indefinitely'. Thus the term serial encompasses an extremely wide range of material including journals, newsletters, newspapers, technical and research reports, yearbooks and annuals, and national and international government publications. In current usage the terms 'journal' and 'periodical' are synonymous. Harrod[1] describes a periodical as 'a publication with a distinctive title which appears at stated or regular intervals, without prior decision as to when the last issue shall appear. It contains articles, stories or other writings, by several contributors.' In the UK, the term 'magazine' is normally reserved for popular, mass circulation titles, but this is not the case in the US, where it is synonymous with the word 'journal'. In reality, each academic library will make its own decision about what is to be regarded as a serial, thus defining the scope of its serials collection, in a manner best suited to the needs of its users.

The collection manager in an academic library must be prepared to deal with serial literature published in a variety of physical formats in addition to the traditional print on paper. Microfilm and microfiche have, for many years, been popular serials formats. Serials are usually acquired in microform either to save shelf space, or because older or rarer material is unavailable in printed format. An important development in recent years is the increasing number of serials available in electronic formats, either as full text on-line databases or on CD-ROM. However, on-line databases can be expensive to use, and many of the full text journals available on-line are targeted towards the business and financial sectors, rather than academic libraries.

CD-ROM is the current major growth area in serials publishing. Although few individual serial titles are currently available on CD-ROM, due to the high cost of mastering a disc, the trend is for publishers to bring together a number of titles in a specific subject area. This is well illustrated by University Microfilm's *Business periodicals on disc*, which contains the full text of 300 business and management journals, updated every two months. CD-ROM is a particularly useful format for indexing and abstracting services, and the number of indexing and abstracting journals on CD-ROM is increasing almost on a weekly basis. Core titles such as *Biological abstracts, Index medicus, Science citation index* and the US Educational Resources Information Centre (ERIC) databases are widely available, sometimes from several different publishers. Keeping up to date with new titles published on CD-ROM can be difficult in such fast moving times. One solution for the collection manager is to scan the professional literature on a regular basis: there are a large number of journals covering the broad area of information technology, including such titles as *CD-ROM librarian* and *Electronic library*. Titles such as *Serials* and *Serials librarian* also provide a wealth of serials-specific information in this area.

Bibliographical control

Because of the disparate nature of serials, satisfactory bibliographical control has proved to be difficult. The serials manager will need to be familiar with a wide range of bibliographical tools to assist in the successful management and development of the collection. The most comprehensive general attempts at serials listings are *Ulrich's international periodicals directory* and the *Serials directory*. The latest edition of *Ulrich* (1989), lists over 111 950 titles in a classified sequence, which may be accessed by a title and ISSN index. Detailed information about individual titles, which can assist the collection manager, includes year first published, ISSN, publisher and address, price, language, editor, title changes, format, and information about which abstracting and indexing services cover that particular title. *Ulrich* is updated on a quarterly basis with annual cumulations; it is also available on-line and on CD-ROM as *Ulrich's plus*. The *Serials directory* is based upon the Ebsco subscription agents' internal database and the Library of Congress CONSER file. (CONSER – Co-operative Conversion of Serials – is a North American project to develop an on-line database of serial titles held in libraries in the US and Canada.) Published as an annual volume, the *Serials directory* is also arranged by subject category with a title and ISSN index, and provides a similar range of information about each title to *Ulrich*. It, too, is available on CD-ROM.

The British Library, particularly the Document Supply Centre (DSC) at Boston Spa, is an important source of material and information relating to serial publications. The list of *Current serials received*, is an especially useful tool for interlibrary loan librarians. *Serials in the British Library* is a more detailed publication, containing data from BNBMARC back to 1950. In addition, a new CD-ROM product has been launched by the British Library: entitled *Boston Spa serials*, it contains over 366 000 serial records from the collections of the British Library, Cambridge University Library and the Science Museum Library.

More specialized information sources include *Current British journals* which is a classified listing of British journals with a title and subject index, and *Magazines for libraries*. Famous for its citation indexes, the Institute for Scientific Information publishes an annual volume entitled *Journal citation reports*, which provides ranked lists of journal titles in broad subject areas. There is considerable controversy within the profession as to whether these lists of titles, ranked by number of citations, are applicable in the general library context, but many librarians believe that they give some indication of core titles within a particular subject area. For the collection manager they may be one of a number of tools which can assist the selection and deselection processes. A further application of citation counting of interest to the collection manager is reported by Devin and Kellogg.[2] The authors attempted to determine guidelines for developing a serial/monograph ratio for research library budgeting, by analysing citation studies to establish serial/monograph usage for each subject.

An additional source of bibliographical information is the serials agent's database. Many agents such as Blackwells, Swets, Dawsons, Faxon and Ebsco provide printed catalogues of serials to their library customers. Such catalogues normally represent only a proportion of the total number of titles available in the complete database. More recently, agents have begun to offer customers on-line access to their complete databases through, for example, such services as Data Swets and Ebsconet. In addition to providing bibliographic information, such services may also offer facilities to the serials manager for on-line ordering and claims, and financial data relating to local holdings.

Turning to the bibliographical control of local serial holdings, the collection manager may, or may not, be responsible for the serials cataloguing function. Many librarians believe that library staff should be organized by function, with the cataloguers, not the serials staff, responsible for the bibliographical record. This record is, after all, the keystone of modern systems for the retrieval of books and journals and its production should be the province of specialized staff, who are able to exercise their knowledge of MARC fields, proper subject headings, holdings formats, and classification schemes. Whether or not serials cataloguing falls within the remit of the collection manager, it is important that he/she develops a sound knowledge and understanding of local bibliographical practices, as these underpin a large proportion of serials-related activities.

The role of the serials collection manager

Just as the nature of the serials collection varies from library to library, so does the role of the collection manager. The organization of staff within a library will have a significant impact upon the way in which collection management decisions are made and implemented. In a small college library, a single library assistant handling check-in and claiming might comprise the entire serials staff, with all collection management decisions being made by the college librarian. In larger academic libraries, the staffing pattern may range from a senior library assistant in charge of day-to-day housekeeping activities, overseen by the collection management librarian, to a professional serials librarian with responsibility for all aspects of serials collection management.

Managing a serials collection differs in significant respects from managing a monographs collection. The nature of the material is diverse; receipt and claiming missing issues is complex; vast amounts of shelf space are consumed on a continuing basis; decisions regarding retention and weeding need to be made on a regular basis; detailed and accurate financial control and budgeting are difficult and time-consuming. If a serials collection is to be managed efficiently and effectively, clear objectives for the collection, and therefore for its management, should be established. One such set of objectives for a serials department, identified by Woodward,[3] is paraphrased as follows:

- To ensure that the serials collection is, and remains, relevant to the needs of the user community. This can imply liaison with users over selection and deselection decisions, collection analysis and production of management information; use and user studies; and the formulation of a written collection development policy.
- To ensure prompt and uninterrupted receipt of serial issues by careful budgeting, regular updating and maintenance of the financial control systems, timely payment of invoices, claiming parts not received and close liaison with suppliers.
- To conserve and preserve material within the collection as appropriate, by binding and other conservation procedures.
- To facilitate access to up-to-date information about the range, scope and location of material within the serials collection. This covers the importance of clear and consistent cataloguing and classification practice, including ongoing catalogue record maintenance and updating.
- To facilitate access to current and back issues of serials held in the collection – in other words, ensuring the efficiency of processes and arrangements for checking-in, shelving and tidying.
- To exploit the collection by alerting users to the range of serial acquisitions, and by assisting users seeking information. Methods of exploitation include the organization and maintenance of displays of serial material; current awareness and selective dissemination of information (SDI) services; and answering users' enquiries.
- To supervise serials staff and oversee the processes by which serial material is acquired, to ensure an efficient and effective service to library users. This involves the application of such management techniques as the setting of objectives, staff training, appraisal and motivation.

Particularly in larger academic libraries, collection development – including liaison with users, selection of new titles, cancellation and weeding decisions – may not fall within the responsibility of the serials collection manager. Where collection development decisions and functions are separated from those of collection management, however, it could still be argued that the collection manager executes a significant, if oblique, influence on the development of the serials collection. Even if the subject specialist or subject bibliographer holds the primary decision-making power over which journal titles will be subscribed to and which will be cancelled, it is almost invariably the collection manager who guides the subject specialist through the thickets of retention, binding, location and cataloguing decisions.

For example, how long should the library maintain a title in its holdings? Newsletters, bulletins, newspapers and associated materials need only a short six to twelve month retention period, before being discarded or possibly replaced in microform. In other cases the subject specialist may need to be reminded that a particular title's quarterly issues are cumulated or superseded by an annual volume and should therefore be discarded in a timely manner. In many other cases all issues of a title should be kept in perpetuity.

Yet how should they be kept? Binding may be the standard response, until closer inspection reveals margins which are too narrow, paper which is too brittle, or usage too heavy for issues to be worth binding. Once again the collection manager may have to lead the subject specialist through the steps of electing fan gluing, oversewing or placing in tie-binders. Or, rather than binding at all, the suggestion might be to throw out the tattered issues and purchase the title in microform as its permanently held format.

Where should the new journal be placed? In some cases the special subject collection in law or medicine may be self-evident. However, does the *Financial times* go to the newspaper collection or the business library? Does the Dun and Bradstreet publication go to the reference collection, the information department or the stacks? In some cases the subject specialist will provide the accompanying detail; in others, the question is left unanswered for the collection manager to resolve.

The professionalism of the serials collection manager will be considerably enhanced by involvement in professional affairs outside the local library. It might even be suggested that there is an inherent responsibility to attend (if not vigorously participate in) the available serials seminars, workshops and conferences. Excellent continuing education programmes are offered by such organizations as the UK Serials Group (UKSG), the North American Serials Interest Group (NASIG) and the Australian Serials Interest Group (ASIG). Such programmes offer a valuable opportunity to discuss matters of mutual interest and concern, and new trends and developments in the serials industry, with publishers, subscription agents and colleagues.

169

Serials automation

The application of automation to serials control dramatically changes the work of the serials manager. Putting aside the immediate impulse to accept automation as better, at the very least it presents the collection manager with a mixture of advantages and new problems. The automation of a serials department initially consists of the selection of a system, its installation, and the training of staff in its use. Once in place, automation can materially advance the manager's control of the serials collection through superior public access to information, improved claiming for missing issues, enhanced binding control, and a far wider range of financial and management reports. The serials collection manager will become to some degree an expert in automation. The initial selection of an automated serials system, whether operating on a single stand-alone microcomputer or on the largest mainframe, implies some awareness of, or learning about, the types of systems in existence and how the local serials system may be supported or enhanced by each. Consideration should be given to the local applicability of the following automated serials functions:

- check-in
- claiming
- routing
- binding
- ordering and subscription renewal
- financial control
- management reports
- union lists
- on-line user access
- circulation.

A wide range of literature on the subject of serials automation is available, and this might be consulted in the early planning stages. Of particular note are works by Rush[4] and Boss,[5] which provide detailed advice on the writing of an operational specification; and works by Leeves[6] and Dyer[7] describing individual systems. A major trap to be avoided at all costs in this initial stage is the attempt merely to replicate the existing manual system, or the first generation automated system. Such restrictive thinking usually fails to engender enhancement to the serials programme and often fails to exploit the full potential of the new system.

Once a short list of potential systems has been selected, it is important to gain hands-on experience of each system, and to take the opportunity to discuss the details of the systems with their suppliers. At this stage an appreciation is needed of the capabilities of each package's operating system; its file structure; estimated storage needs; need for various files; growth capacities; security capabilities; networking possibilities; and the compatibility of various peripherals such as hard discs, printers, wands and scanners, telephone modems and backup tape drives.

A degree of basic understanding of how the operating system interrelates with the data files operated, input or generated by the system is also necessary. The smaller the system – and especially with a microcomputer driven system – the more software knowledge the manager must have. At a minimum there should be an appreciation of how to load new software and files, analyse file sizes, fix floating clusters, configure software linking peripherals such as printers and discs to the system, and of how to run tape or floppy disc backups to the system.

In the environment of a mini- or mainframe operated system, the serials module is likely to be a segment of a total integrated library system, probably supported by a systems librarian. Even in this situation, however, some basic knowledge is useful of how the software works, and how it might be applied to achieve the objectives of the serials department. Experience seems to indicate that a better final product will emerge in circumstances where the librarian knows a little about computers, than in those where the systems specialist knows a little about serials librarianship!

A few cautions are in order at this point. Firstly, the serials collection manager should consult with staff handling serials on a daily basis, right from the early planning stages. Their knowledge and expertise of routine procedures and processes may help to avoid expensive and time consuming problems at a later stage of implementation. Secondly, if the new system provides an OPAC screen display of full, or partial, serials records, sample records should be shown to public services staff to ensure that the format is clear to library users and that records can be accurately interpreted. Some of the more abstruse technical services terminology may have to be abandoned. Finally, as previously mentioned, it is important to become familiar with the standards to be used for the bibliographic expression of the title and its holdings statement. A tendency exists to express the title as it appears on the journal's cover for ease of identification at the time of checking in, and to shape the holdings statement in a manner unintelligible to users. Use of formal MARC standards will certainly bring about greater long term clarity. And, as Boss has observed, 'If properly constructed, the bibliographic database may prove to be the most lasting component of an automated serials system'.[8]

Once installed, serials automation of almost any type should enhance the management of a serials collection. This will be particularly true when operating in a network environment, where on-line public access to serial titles and their holdings is available. Library users generally find that OPACs are a considerable improvement over manually produced serials lists, which become out of date so quickly. Depending on the flexibility of the system's software and display screens, and on the expertise of the serials and systems staff, information may also be displayed regarding missing and claimed issues; special locations for certain issues or titles; details of which issues are routed; and which volumes have entered the binding processes.

Serials acquisition

The acquisition of both current and back issues of serials is a major responsibility of the serials collection manager. Despite the forecasts of some librarians that automated serials control systems would make the task of ordering serial subscriptions direct from the publisher much easier, most collection managers continue to use subscription agents for the bulk of their serials orders. Traditionally, agents have assisted librarians by providing a range of services, such as: a minimum number of invoices in one currency; invoices tailored to special requirements; pre-payment plans; assistance in budgeting and financial management; and monthly update bulletins. More recently, many of the major national and international vendors have offered various automated options to their clients – ranging from PC-based serials control systems to electronic transmission of orders and claims. Given current staffing and financial considerations in academic libraries, if the agent were to be by-passed in favour of direct ordering, it is unlikely that any money saved would compensate for the increased workload which would fall upon the serials department.

An important task for the collection manager is to determine which agent, or agents, will supply journals at the best price with the most appropriate supporting services. The value of costs versus service has been argued about for many years. The only changing factor has been the transition from selecting the lowest agent's discount, to eliciting the lowest service charge. The reduction in the amount of discount publishers offer to subscription agents is a matter of serious concern, not only to agents, but also to librarians. Most agents would hope to achieve an overall profit of about 11 per cent, but the worldwide publishers' discount averages out at 8 per cent; therefore, to maintain profitability, the agent needs to make a service charge to the librarian. Indeed, if the steady erosion of discounts were to continue to its logical conclusion, libraries would be faced with a minimum service charge of 10-11 per cent.[9] It is imperative that the collection manager gains a thorough understanding of each agent's charging policy, and ensures that all relevant details are clearly displayed on invoices. Net price, service charge and total for each individual title should be the norm on every invoice.

The most suitable method of payment also needs to be discussed in detail with the vendor. Some librarians opt for a one-line invoice which may be issued in June or July of one year, to cover the following year's subscriptions. One-line invoices frequently attract a discount for early settlement, and in addition they ensure that no extra charges are incurred during the financial year, as credits or debts are adjusted in the next year's one-line invoice. A disadvantage is that exact subscription prices of titles are not known until relatively late in the financial year, when the full definitive invoice is received. Thus, libraries with local serials financial control systems are unable to enter data and generate reports. Other types of pre-payment plans also need careful consideration. In some circumstances, a library may arrange with a vendor to pay an agreed sum of money (usually at the beginning of the library's financial year) which is then invested by the vendor and accrues interest at an agreed rate until such time as an invoice is raised for the following year's subscriptions. The collection manager must ensure that such a deal is in accordance with institutional regulations: many organizations will not allow such a transaction, arguing that higher interest rates can be obtained by the institution itself investing the money. Such investment, of course, rarely benefits the library directly.

An attractive cost package may make a vendor, but nothing will break the relationship faster than bad service. At what point does the manager decide to change subscription agents, bearing in mind that any change involves a significant amount of extra work and inconvenience? If the agent's fiscal, service or communication patterns fall below the highest standards of honesty and integrity, it should be axed immediately. Other service matters can often be corrected after discussion with the appropriate people in the company. Service of claims, rapid initiation of new subscriptions, and various financial and management reports can often be obtained, or improved, if needs are clearly articulated and some patience exercised. If, however, matters cannot be sorted out to mutual satisfaction and the agent's service must be terminated, the prudent collection manager must consider in advance the selection of a new agent, preferred time of transfer, and the ways in which local records will be updated to reflect the change in source.

If faced with selecting a new subscription agent, what factors might the collection manager consider? In an increasingly competitive and shrinking market, all agents offer a price quotation service, and librarians are encouraged to submit lists of titles to which the agent responds with the relevant price information. This can be a useful starting point, but must be viewed with caution. Unscrupulous agents can, and do, undercut prices for the first year in order to obtain business, and then proceed to increase prices once subscriptions are established. Managers should view with suspicion any agent who makes extravagant discount offers which vary substantially from the norm; they must also resist pressure from institutional finance departments to accept the lowest quotation. In addition to the previously mentioned questions of ethics, charges and services, there are a number of holistic elements to examine when selecting an agent. These include the company's history and reputation, the opinion of other librarians using the firm, its vision of future developments within the trade, and the level of professionalism displayed by all members of the company.

Discussion so far has concentrated upon the acquisition of journals where a subscription charge is levied by the publisher. However, all serials collections also contain a proportion of material which is received free of charge, either by exchange or donation. When offered to the library, such 'free' material should not automatically be accepted by the serials manager; it is just as important to apply selection criteria to this material as it is to purchased titles. Research by MacDougall,[10] calculates the cost of zero subscription ('free') material in terms of processing, collection maintenance, storage and binding, demonstrating that significant resources are often committed to such material.

Housekeeping

A major part of the serials collection manager's function is the establishment and maintenance of effective and efficient housekeeping routines. This aspect of collection management is of fundamental importance: if basic housekeeping activities are not carried out well, then the collection will not meet the needs of library users to maximum effect. Thus, procedures for accurate and timely ordering and checking-in of serial parts must be devised, introduced and supervised, together with routines for claiming missing issues, binding completed volumes, and reshelving and tidying the collection.

If the library has not automated its housekeeping processes, this will entail optimum deployment of staff time to ensure that parts received are recorded on a Kardex, Kalamazoo, or other manual system as soon as they arrive in the library, and that missing parts are claimed as soon as their due date has passed. Such operations (particularly claiming) are performed more quickly and efficiently in an automated environment, but staff time still needs to be organized to ensure that all published serial issues are made available to users with minimum delay.

Claiming

It is essential to exert well-organized and consistent effort to locate missing issues quickly and effectively, and chase those titles whose receipt has ceased entirely. As publishers print fewer and fewer issues in their print runs, the expeditious identification of missing issues is critical. An automated system can be of great assistance in locating claims, preparing the printed claim, or creating a file for electronic transmission directly to a subscription agent. A great mistake, however, is to assume that the claim identified from either a manual or automated system is valid; whenever possible, a check of the shelves should be made before the claim is despatched. The validity of claims is likely to be enhanced by several per cent if this is done.

Claiming for missing issues may, indeed, be an art rather than a science, and many factors surrounding a journal's publication and distribution must be taken into account. For example, has the journal established a trend of running late in its publications schedule? Were the publisher, the postal system, or the dock workers on strike? Are there a varying number of issues per volume and volumes per year? Does the supplier have the correct mailing address? Was the title properly renewed and payment made? It may be necessary to claim for an invoice in addition to the missing issues. Many automated systems set a default claim period for different serial frequencies; for example, the system might allow twelve days to elapse before generating a claim for a monthly title, and thirty days for a quarterly publication. Clearly it is important that this default period may be overridden manually, to allow for the idiosyncrasies of individual titles. If no action is forthcoming after two routine claims, then a personal telephone call is often highly effective. Many US agents provide a nationwide toll-free telephone service to libraries for this purpose.

Binding

In many libraries the preservation, or binding, programme falls within the administrative responsibility of the serials collection manager. In small and medium sized colleges and universities, the serials manager frequently assumes this responsibility simply because the bulk of material to be bound comprises journal or serial volumes. Supervising the binding programme implies a knowledge of budgets, the application of automation, when available, and the technical characteristics of the bound volume. It also implies the ability to decide between the various possibilities of binding, rebinding, or permanent acquisition in microform.

Although many of the day-to-day binding processes will be handled by library assistants, the serials manager usually has the responsibility and authority for the establishment of a contract between the library and the commercial binder. In both the US and the UK, a few of the largest academic and research institutions have highly skilled departments for conservation and preservation within the institution. More usually, however, a library will enter into a contract with a commercial binder. In such cases, it is the task of the collection manager to negotiate appropriate levels of service, such as the length of time material will be held by the binder; quality of materials; price; quality control guarantees; and special services. Extensive binding programmes consume a significant portion of the library budget and it is important to recognize that the same patterns of decision making and ethics apply in the selection of a binder, as in the selection of a subscription agent.

Many automated serials systems now offer binding modules which have eliminated much of the drudgery of journals binding. The provision of system-generated pick-up slips, notifying when a completed volume is ready to be bound, is a particularly useful feature: such slips can be annotated to include information about the provision of contents and title pages, and indexes. The preparation of the 'rub' (a sample of the spine lettering and numbering), and any special instructions, can be reduced to a few bytes of information and stored away until either printed out on a bindery instruction form or loaded onto a floppy disc for transfer to the binder. On-line records provide both users and reader services staff with up-to-date information about the progress of individual titles as they undergo the various stages of binding; here the serials manager must cooperate with public services staff to ensure that on-line binding data are clear and unambiguous. Commercial library binders have also taken advantage of automation with stamping machines using locally stored data, or data supplied by the library, as well as automated invoicing procedures.

For centuries the decision to bind a completed journal volume has been almost automatic. With the emergence of new types of sewing and glues, new binding techniques, and sophisticated methods of treatment for acid paper, the serials manager possesses a greater array of possible means for preserving the library's journal collection in some form of appropriate binding. For example, in US libraries, a movement towards the flat-back bound volume, and away from the rounded-and-backed volume, seems to provide a more durable product in the face of the photocopier's punishment. Even cheaply and poorly produced serials with narrow margins, or on low quality paper can now be preserved if required. Today, however, new forces are playing upon the decision to bind. With the democratization of university education and the proliferation of the photocopy machine, what has not been stolen, mutilated, or battered through heavy use, will not be automatically despatched to the binders. A variety of alternative forms of access to journal literature is now available, and the collection manager may decide to discard the printed format entirely and provide access via replacement microform, or on-line or CD-ROM full text databases. Alternatively, in the case of low use material, a decision may be made to provide an on-demand service through interlibrary loan or other document delivery services. There is no correct solution to the problem of ownership versus access, and the debate within the profession is likely to continue unabated.

Financial control and budgeting

The serials collection manager needs little reminder of the complexities surrounding serials budgeting and financial control. Serial prices have risen alarmingly in the last ten years, a fact which is well illustrated by examining Blackwell's annual survey of periodical prices published in the *Library Association record*. For example, the survey shows that in 1979 the average price of a periodical was £44.18; by 1989 this figure had risen to £136.99. Similar reports, such as Faxon's many-faceted report appearing in the *Serials librarian*, and the *Library journal's* periodicals prices survey, provide useful broad studies of national and worldwide prices from which valuable data may be extracted and manipulated for local use.

Such price rises, combined with static and decreasing library budgets, have meant that libraries are spending more money to acquire fewer titles. This in itself is an area of extreme concern for all librarians, but unfortunately the problems do not stop there. Unlike books, which are paid for as and when published, serials are paid for well in advance of publication. As discussed previously, a library will typically pay for one year's issues in the September or October of the preceding year. Budget formulation takes place even earlier – certainly well before publishers' official prices are announced. Thus, most serials budgets in the past have been derived from the previous year's figures, with an amount (achieved by guesswork) added on for inflation. Such formulation of next year's budget has all the logic of 'looking back to the future'. In recent years this dilemma has eased somewhat with more data being made available on forthcoming prices – data employed by the major subscription agents to forecast remarkably accurate future price trends. The cooperative efforts and understandings sought by UKSG and NASIG are facilitating the sharing of such information.

A major factor affecting budget preparation and allocation is the effect of exchange rates on journal prices, as many libraries, particularly in the UK, acquire a high proportion of US and European titles. American publishers normally set one price in US dollars; thus the price paid by British librarians depends upon the prevailing strength or weakness of the pound sterling at the time of purchase. Some British publishers have in the past acutely annoyed American librarians by applying an inflated US dollar rate to American libraries (commonly known as 'price gouging'), claiming that the extra charge is made to cover risk of losses from currency conversion, air freight, and the additional cost of postage and claims. A new twist to the exchange rate saga for British publishers and librarians alike is the rapid approach of the single European market in 1992. It would appear that the European Commission is beginning to demand that European publishers set one single European price for all their titles. Such a move, while simplifying financial transactions will almost certainly increase the price paid by UK libraries.

Although libraries, like all organizations, are subject to worldwide economic forces, the collection manager can assist the budget formulation by producing foreign currency exchange-rate reports and forecasts related to local holdings, and ensure that these are distributed to all library staff involved in collection development. In addition, close liaison with subscription agents will reveal which agencies are working the system to best effect by buying in foreign currency at appropriate times to provide a cushion against the worst effects of currency fluctuations.

A variety of regularly produced financial reports will benefit both the collection manager and collection development staff. Financial reports are clearly easier to produce in an automated environment, and most serials control systems will generate basic reports relating to fund accounting and total expenditure, and lists and totals of outstanding bills. More sophisticated reports required by individual libraries may be available through the system's programming language, and, once again, the collection manager may be required to demonstrate programming skills. In libraries which operate manual serials systems, financial reports may be more difficult to produce. Access to PC-based spreadsheet and database packages can help considerably in this respect. Data from the national and international surveys previously mentioned may be utilized, and increasingly subscription agents will provide reports relating to local financial data in printed format on disc.

Access and exploitation

Management of serials collections implies decisions about the way in which a library's serials holdings are arranged, in order to offer maximum convenience and benefit to library users. Should, for example, serials be shelved as a separate collection from monographs and other library material? Should the arrangement of stock be on a subject basis, with all types of material on a particular subject kept together? Should current issues of serials be shelved separately from backruns? What about indexing and abstracting journals? The answers to these questions will vary from library to library, and be dependent in part on the nature of the space available to house the collection. For example, multi-site libraries are far more difficult to manage than single-site libraries; purpose-built libraries far easier than old converted buildings. Space constraints apart, librarians should be concerned to arrange their stock in a manner best suited to the majority of the library's users – which in an academic library usually means shelving serials and books on the same subject in separate sequences, but in close proximity to each other. It is also necessary to decide whether serials holdings are best shelved in one sequence, or several sequences divided by subject groups, and whether there should be separate sequences for different types and formats of serial material. Within each sequence, the arrangement of titles might be alphabetical by title or by class number – this too needs to be considered.

The physical housing, storage and preservation of serials also raises different problems from those encountered with monographs. Long runs of bound journals, large numbers of flimsy unbound issues, deteriorating copies of newspapers, and the nature of microforms, all present particular difficulties for the collection manager. Guidelines need to be established for the maintenance of the serials collection which take into account shelving, tidying, retention, conservation, and deselection. Shelving and maintaining order in a serials collection is a major staff-intensive activity in academic libraries, aggravated by the size of the collection and the constant flow of material onto and off the shelves. Even if overall use of the serials collection is perceived to be low (and in most libraries it is rarely quantified), a library subscribing to thousands of current daily, weekly, monthly and quarterly titles has a significant management task in ensuring that new material is shelved, and existing material is reshelved, as quickly as possible. Library users, after all, expect to find serial parts in their correct places on the shelves, not in the serials office or on a distant table. A further point which should be emphasized is that the signing and guiding of the serials collection must be of a high standard to enable users to locate material quickly and easily.

Many academic libraries, both in the US and the UK, provide a current periodicals area, or reading room, which may be physically adjacent to the serials department and administered by the serials collection manager. It may be argued that a reading room offers a better service to users by providing centralization of current, heavily-used issues, improved security, and provision of staff assistance. The manager must ensure that serials records accurately reflect the location of current issues: while the library user may believe that all current journal issues are placed in the reading room, this is rarely true, except in the smallest of libraries. A major problem in current periodicals reading rooms is created by newspapers. Their vigorous use and subsequent untidy mess mean that special care must be taken in displaying and tidying these titles on a frequent and regular basis. Once again, records control is an imperative, to give accurate information on whether newspapers are discarded or stored until a microform replacement is received.

A further decision required of the collection manager is whether to provide periodical listings or OPAC terminals within the current periodicals area. Reference staff are frequently chary of the reading room staff's ability to provide substantive guidance to the user. Reading room staff, in turn, find it awkward to have to direct users to another part of the library to consult serials catalogues. Once again the diplomatic manager must be capable of establishing appropriate policy and procedure with the other departments of the library, in determining what level of public services will be offered in the reading room.

Reader services activities are a vital element in the process of making serials collections, and the information they contain, available to library users. A carefully selected and well-maintained collection is not fulfilling its purpose if it is not exploited to maximum advantage. Users need to be aware of how they can find out what is included in the collection, and how to locate specific titles and information. The introduction of the OPAC has made the retrieval of information about the serials collection much easier and more effective, although it must be pointed out that at the time of writing many UK academic libraries have not completed the necessary conversion of serials bibliographical and holdings data. For library users accustomed to separate book and serials catalogues, it is a considerable step forward to find details of all library material held on one database. OPAC subject and keyword searching can retrieve records for any type of material, and the user seeking a specific item does not need to know whether the library treats it as a monograph or a serial.

Other aspects of reader services to which the serials collection manager needs to give attention are the provision (or not) of current awareness services; the routing of newly-received serial parts to interested users; and circulation policy. Manual current awareness services, such as the distribution of photocopies of contents pages, are not undertaken to any great extent in most academic libraries, for the familiar reasons of economic constraint and staff shortages. There is, however, increasing demand for externally generated on-line current awareness services. Normally these will not be undertaken by serials staff, but the provision of such services does generate further demands for access to serial literature. Routing of serial parts to users is also usually done sparingly: any such operation denies access to current serial issues to the rest of their potential readership, often for unacceptably lengthy periods.

Most academic libraries restrict at least their current serial holdings, and sometimes the whole collection, to use in the library only. The reasons for this are twofold: firstly to ensure that current issues are accessible, and secondly for security reasons. Serials go out of print very rapidly and it can be extremely difficult, very often impossible, to replace missing current issues or older volumes. When available, the cost of second-hand volumes of serials from dealers is high. (It is unfortunate that the reverse situation does not hold true. Libraries wishing to sell back runs of journals frequently experience difficulty in finding a buyer, and where one is found, the price offered is generally low.)

Exploitation of the information contained within serials is normally undertaken by reference or information staff assisting users in manual, on-line or CD-ROM searching. Abstracting and indexing services are the main tools for this activity, and the acquisition of both printed abstracts and CD-ROM databases will almost certainly be a task for the serials department. Once again, decisions regarding, for example, the classification, location and binding schedules of printed abstracts must be made in close liaison with subject specialists and information staff. Provision of public-access CD-ROM workstations, and the issuing of CD-ROM discs, manuals and instructions will also need careful consideration. US librarians have introduced such services well in advance of their British colleagues, and UK librarians would be well advised to consult the literature (articles by Stewart[11] and Crane,[12] for example) to avoid pitfalls which have already been encountered.

Conclusion

Serials present a range of problems to the collection manager. New titles are constantly being published in printed format, and the range and scope of electronic formats continue to increase. Spiralling serial prices force many libraries into unwelcome cancellation exercises, which in turn deny users access to serial literature and reduce subscriptions to unacceptable levels for publishers. Concern about the low use of many journal titles within library collections has also prompted many managers to question the cost effectiveness of current provision.

In terms of academic library collection management, it is likely – for all the above reasons – that there will continue to be some shift of emphasis from acquisition and collection building to the provision of access to information. Nevertheless, the basic commodities, the journal articles and research reports, will still be required by library users. Electronic publishing may alter the storage medium, but at the end of the day users normally require a convenient printed output. The British Library is currently conducting research in this area – the Adonis project – with a sample of 219 biomedical journals stored on CD-ROM. Findings from this research have been reported by Braid.[13] Another detailed study of journal acquisition versus article delivery has been conducted at Loughborough University. This research involved detailed use studies and costing exercises of four different models of journal provision within an academic library. These models ranged from current provision, through the establishing of a 'core' collection of titles, to no hard copy journal provision at all. It concluded that 'a complete switch to electronic journal article transmission in the present state of technological development and financial provision would leave the librarian and the reader at a severe disadvantage'.[14] It would therefore appear that the serials manager will continue to have a collection to manage and nurture for some years to come.

Management and financial expertise, knowledge of automation and policy development skills are all expected of the serials manager. Each of these characteristics has its own validity, but the most important and most forgotten is humanity. Without a basic commitment to staff and library users, the serials manager will fail, whatever the size of the library's budget or computer. Moving the electrical outlet, shifting a desk closer to the window, encouraging personal development and the participation of staff in the process of policy formulation, all strengthen morale and teamwork within the serials department and contribute to successful collection management.

References

1. Prytherch, R. comp. (1987), *Harrod's librarians' glossary*, 6th ed., Aldershot: Gower, p.596; and also 1990, 7th ed., p.472.
2. Devin, R.B. and M. Kellogg (1990), 'The serial/monograph ratio in research libraries: budgeting in light of citation studies', *College and research libraries*, **51** (1), 46-54.
3. Woodward, H. (1990), 'Training for serials', in R. Prytherch (ed.), *Handbook of library training practice volume II*, Aldershot: Gower.
4. Rush, J.E. (ed.) (1983), *Library systems evaluation guide. Volume 1: Serials control*, Powell: James E. Rush Associates Inc.
5. Boss, R.W. (1986/1987), 'Developing requirements for automated serials control systems', *Serials librarian*, **11** (3/4), 37-70.
6. Leeves, J. (1989), *Library systems: a buyer's guide*, 2nd ed., Aldershot: Gower.
7. Dyer, H. and A. Gunson, (1988), *A directory of library and information retrieval software for microcomputers*, 3rd ed., Aldershot: Gower.
8. Boss, R.W., ref. 5, p.39.
9. Merriman, J. (1988), 'The work of the periodicals agent', *Serials librarian*, **14** (3/4), 17-36.
10. MacDougall, A. and H. Woodward (1988), *Optimization of serial holdings: a study of the chemistry and economics serials holdings in a university library*, (BLR&D report, 5979), London: British Library.
11. Stewart, L. (1987), 'Picking CD-ROMs for public use', *American libraries*, **18** (9), 738-740.
12. Crane, N. and T. Durfee (1987), 'Entering uncharted territory: putting CD-ROM in place', *Wilson library bulletin*, **62** (4), 28-30.
13. Braid, J.A. (1989), 'The Adonis experience', *Serials*, **2** (3), 49-54.
14. MacDougall, A., et al (1986), *Modelling of journal versus article acquisition by libraries*, (BNBRF report, 23), London: British Library.

8 Management of collections of non-book materials

Ian Butchart

The term 'non-book materials' (NBM) is chosen as a convenient term to categorize the range of information sources other than books and periodicals that many academic libraries collect. It is not feasible within the limits of this chapter to comment on the full range of formats now available. However, general principles for the collection management of NBM will be identified and then illustrated by a commentary on a limited range of formats. These will include the following categories drawn from the second edition of the *Anglo-American cataloguing rules (AACR)*:

- sound recordings;
- video recordings, including interactive video discs;
- graphic materials – photographs, illustrations, postcards and slides;
- microcomputer software, including CD-ROMs.

There are many other forms that are covered by the term NBM such as microforms, models, wallcharts and cinefilm, but the four categories identified above will suffice to illustrate the collection management of NBM by libraries.

It is also necessary to discuss a number of issues that differ markedly from those for books and journals, including the question 'Do we actually need to collect them?' After all, it is only in recent years that the librarians' bible, *AACR*, formally recognized such forms as worthy of attention. It was the publication of *AACRII* in 1978 that brought all NBM within a common cataloguing framework and 'the tremendous step forward that this code represents in the cataloguing of audio-visual materials for the general library collection'.[1]

The first section considers this general question within the context of the academic library. A general philosophy is offered that should inform a collection management policy for academic libraries. It considers how NBM fit into the overall mission of the parent institution and their value to particular groups of clients. General problems in acquiring NBM are then considered, followed by a section that concentrates on the four categories of NBM previously identified. The chapter concludes with a discussion of the physical attributes of NBM and their implications for collection management, and a consideration of some aspects of the in-house production of NBM.

Why collect non-book materials in academic libraries?

NBM are not uncommon in academic libraries. Individual forms such as 16 mm film were collected by USA college libraries as early as the 1930s. The University Grants Committee in its 1965 report *Audio-visual aids in higher scientific education*[2] stressed the need for good teaching practice and research which recognized the value of NBM. In 1971 Leslie Gilbert and Jan Wright wrote:

> Non-book materials (NBM) have increased the range and means of obtaining and exploiting information for teaching, learning and research purposes, but to separate books from NBM is to divide information into false compartments. Hence, it is essential that books and non-books can be jointly identified and located to meet particular needs.[3]

Similarly professional library bodies have long recognized that librarians have a part to play in this area. For example, in February 1972, when the Aslib Audio-visual Group, the Library Association and the National Council for Educational Technology held their first joint conference, the subject discussed was the education of librarians in the techniques of non-book materials. Also in 1972 the British Library Act established a National Library for the UK to consist of 'a comprehensive collection of books, manuscripts, periodicals, films, and other recorded matter, whether printed or otherwise'.[4]

However, such pious hopes have not been fulfilled in all our academic libraries and it is on the university side of the binary divide that this is most obvious. Anthony Hugh Thompson in a 1988 article exploring the links between academic libraries and audio-visual production services concluded that

> 53.5 per cent of universities in England and Wales still have predominantly print-based libraries defined as libraries which have print including microforms, but no policy of purchasing audio-visual materials. Less than half have multimedia libraries and only ten per cent have any form of formalized relationship between the library and the audio-visual production service. This suggests that the universities are out of step with colleges and Institutes of Higher Education and polytechnics which, with only a few exceptions, now have some form of relationship with the audio-visual production service in the institution.[5]

Various reasons may be forwarded for this divide:

- A lack of understanding or only recent concern with the learning processes by university academics. This differs from many of the Institutes of Higher Education who had their origins in the colleges of education with their natural interest in educational theory and practice and were early pioneers of the learning resources centre concept in the UK. Similarly a number of the polytechnics merged with colleges of education and as a result benefited from their extensive teaching practice collections. These were then available to students and academics in other disciplines.
- The university's strong belief in the primacy of the printed word for research collections. This is illustrated in Neil Postman's diverting work *Amusing ourselves to death* in which he described how the oral examiners of his doctoral thesis criticized his use of a footnote. 'Told to the investigator at the Roosevelt Hotel on January 18th, 1981, in the presence of Arthur Lingeman and Jerrold Gross'. This brought forth the charge that 'You are mistaken in believing that the form in which an idea is conveyed is irrelevant to its truth. In the academic world, the published word is invested with greater prestige and authenticity than the spoken word. What people say is assumed to be more casually uttered than what they write. The written word is assumed to have been reflected upon and revised by its author and reviewed by authorities and editors. The written word endures, the spoken word disappears; and that is why writing is closer to the truth than speaking.'[6]
- There may be little demand from eighteen year old full-time students who may have come through a school system that was similarly dominated by teacher input and the reading of lecture notes and the required textbook.

- With little motivation from lecturers there may be little pressure for change and, indeed, they may have no reason for access to NBM for assignments. This again may contrast with polytechnics which draw upon a wider age range and a large percentage of part-time students.
- The issue may also lie at the library organizational level. There may be a lack of funds to build up NBM collections, library staff with little interest in such materials, and no apparent requirement by the library committee to change. It takes a major policy shift to begin a change of this kind when there is no history of such provision.

However, it is apparent that there is now a greater urgency within higher education for changes in teaching and learning styles, brought about by employers' priorities and by educational considerations. Such developments as the government funded Enterprise Initiative in Higher Education stress the need for transferability of skills and autonomy in learning and problem solving. These result in an increasing variety of learning styles and involve a greater degree of independent and resource-based learning. Such developments, if they are to be effective, demand active and informed management of library services and the recognition of the value of all information sources for this new mission for academic libraries.

A collection policy statement for NBM is therefore based on

- a clear mission statement;
- an understanding of the clients' needs;
- library services that will facilitate its implementation.

These elements can be illustrated by examples from a polytechnic library.

Figure 8.1 gives the mission and aims for the library services as agreed by one academic board. Thus it has been accepted by the parent institution that as regards information resources the library aims:

C.1 To select and acquire information, in whatever form, to support teaching, learning, research, management and administration.

John Lindsay, in a research proposal in 1977, noted that children 'were largely unaware that information exists which can broaden their perspectives and help them to make informed decisions.'[7] The Carnegie Foundation's report *College* identified that 'colleges can be no stronger than the nation's schools'[8] and there was great value for the college in

Figure 8.1: Teesside Polytechnic Library: mission and aims

A. *Mission*

1. The mission of the Polytechnic Library is to make available and aid the exploitation of information for the benefit of the Polytechnic's agreed corporate character and purpose. Thus it enhances access to the information resources and services required to meet the immediate and long-term needs of:

   1.1 Staff and students in their teaching, learning and research work.
   1.2 Management and administrative staff in their duties.
   1.3 Agreed local and regional community clients.

2. The Polytechnic Library seeks to match this mission by:

   2.1 Identifying client needs.
   2.2 Providing appropriate resources and services.
   2.3 Supporting these efficiently and effectively.
   2.4 Systematically planning, organising, staffing and controlling its provision of resources and services

B. *Information services*

The Polytechnic Library aims:

1. To provide a range of services to include:

   1.1 Document supply service (providing specific documents and materials on request).
   1.2 Reference service

      a) seeking documents and other material on specific topics.
      b) providing specific answers, information, or data in response to client requests.

   1.3 Work-space service (providing a variety of client accommodation and associated hardware). This to include:

      i) work involving library materials.
      ii) other work.

   1.4 Instruction service (client education in the use of libraries and their resources).

2. To make these services as simple to understand, easy to use and economical of client time as possible.

3. To match these services to the specific needs of groups of clients.

C. *Information resources*

The Polytechnic Library aims:

1. To select and acquire information, in whatever form, to support teaching, learning, research, management and administration.

2. To provide access to other information resources as appropriate.

3. To ensure that the library collections are properly balanced, edited and maintained.

4. To provide appropriate equipment for accessing information resources.

D. Library management

The Polytechnic Library aims:

1. To plan an organisation and systems based on identified client needs, both expressed and unexpressed.

2. To implement staff structures, procedures and physical arrangements which will best serve its clients. Where possible these should reflect the academic character of the Polytechnic.

3. To systematically research and keep under control its operations with regard to their efficiency and effectiveness.

4. To review its aims and objectives regularly.

E. Promotion of information resources and services

The Polytechnic Library aims:

1. To publicise its resources and services and promote their exploitation by its clients.

2. To play an effective role in the Polytechnic's formal academic process.

3. To encourage its clients to express their information needs and to regard the Library as their major source of published information.

F. External relations and cooperation

The Polytechnic Library aims:

1. To develop and engage in external arrangements which will benefit the Polytechnic.

2. To facilitate appropriate access to its resources and services by the local community.

G. Library staff

The Polytechnic Library aims:

1. To develop an organisational environment which will attract, retain, develop and motivate high calibre staff dedicated to implementing the Polytechnic Library mission.

Figure 8.1 concluded

building on the undergraduate's previous experiences. There was a need for the library to become a central learning resource on the campus for 'we need liberally educated librarians – professionals who understand and are interested in undergraduate education who themselves are involved in educational matters, and who can build connections between the classroom and the rest of campus life'.[9] Central to this must be a collection policy based on the simple statement that 'individuals today have an increasing need to be able to find things out'.[10] Thus the report from the Schools' Council on *Information skills in the secondary curriculum* argues that

> schools, which are concerned with learning above all else, find great difficulty in teaching pupils *how* to learn. Although some pupils are able to use the full range of learning resources which the school can offer, most are not, and it is a central responsibility of the school to help its pupils to cope with learning.[11]

Figure 8.2 forms part of one polytechnic's consideration of how it could inform its 'Enterprise' programmes with such information issues. It lists 'nine question steps for an assignment as a practical model for delivering this central responsibility.' Each question step is further sub-divided, and under the fourth question 'Which resources shall I use?' is the question 'What kinds of resources are there?'

- pictorial resources (photographs, maps, films, videotapes);
- sound recordings on disc or tape;
- textbooks, reference books, individual monographs;
- periodicals and newspapers;
- models, specimens, museum items;
- people with specialist knowledge or experience.[12]

Such issues are now very slowly becoming part of the school process with the added incentive of the new curriculum required for GCSE. They are also used to guide the provision in higher education to meet the demands of BTEC and degree courses. Similarly for research there has been a growing demand from academics to provide collections of NBM for specific research programmes. Examples include consideration of the political use of the media, local film, archives, and oral history tape collections that provide evidence from classes which previously left very little behind them in the way of formal or written evidence.

The library services to support the mission statement and client needs are shown in Figure 8.3. All the categories of services include NBM formats such as collections of CD-ROMs, transmission of video programmes on the Cable TV system, an electronic news bulletin, Apple Macintosh microcomputers, a course on computer-mediated instruction run on an electronic conferencing system, and finally, production services for a wide range of NBM.

Figure 8.2: Enterprise in an information context

Unfortunately many children are sent out into this world with little or no knowledge of sources of information, little skill in obtaining and processing information for their own use and most important of all, largely unaware that information exists which can broaden their perspectives and help them make informed decisions. (Lindsay, J. (1977) *The right to know.*)

How can we ensure that Polytechnic students gain the following skills?

What do I need to do?
(formulate and analyse need)

Where could I go?
(identify and appraise likely sources)

How do I get to the information?
(trace and locate individual resources)

What resources shall I use?
(examine, select and reject individual resources)

How shall I use the resources?
(interrogate resources)

What should I make a record of?
(record and store information)

Have I got the information I need?
(interpret, analyse, synthesize, evaluate)

How should I present it?
(present, communicate)

What have I achieved?
(evaluate)

(Based on Marland, M. (1981) *Information skills in the secondary curriculum,* London: Methuen.)

Figure 8.3: Polytechnic library services

Collections of materials

Organised for general access by all Polytechnic students and staff

1. Books
2. Periodicals
3. Photographic slides
4. Video recordings
5. Video Discs
6. CD Roms
7. Microforms
8. Computer software
9. Sound cassettes
10. North East Television & Film Archive

Document service

Providing specific documents, equipment and materials on request.

1. Issue systems
2. Reference facilities
3. Inter-library loans
4. Audio-visual equipment
5. Transmission of programmes on cable TV system
6. Satellite television

Information service

Information retrieval, seeking documents and other material on specific topics. Providing specific answers, information, or data in response to client requests.

1. On-line retrieval from local & remote databases
2. Library electronic newsbulletin
3. Selective dissemination of information
4. Enquiry services
5. Bibliographies
6. Guides to information services
7. Electronic mail
8. Fax
9. Telex

Work-space service

Providing a variety of client accommodation and associated hardware

1. Library individual study space
2. Library group study space
3. Video viewings
4. Microform viewing
5. Sound cassette listening
6. Apple Macintosh service
7. Main lecture theatre
8. Main hall
9. Clarendon lecture theatres
10. General purpose teaching rooms (92)
11. TV studio
12. Video editing suites
13. Photocopying

Instruction and consultation service

Client education in bibliography and the use of the library, media services and resources.

1. Induction programmes
2. Information modules for specific Polytechnic courses
3. Equipment instruction
4. CAPE initiative
5. Clients' personal information systems
6. Individual student projects

Publication & production service

Facilities, techniques, equipment and advice for making and distributing a wide range of media productions.

1. Off-air recording, television and radio
2. Video publications, including recording of conference proceedings
3. Graphic production of administrative material e.g. course brochures, business cards, etc.
4. Graphic production of teaching and learning materials
5. Photographic production and processing
6. Writing and editing of publications
7. Distribution of Polytechnic publications
8. Film to video transfer
9. Exhibition stands
10. Microform prints

While the polytechnics and Institutes of Higher Education have led the way in providing an all-embracing learning support structure, ironically they have not been as generously funded as the universities. Indeed, in some cases the financial imperative to cut costs has resulted in the mergers of libraries and audio-visual production units, particularly in order to reduce staffing costs at senior management level. This latter demand may help to explain why, in more recent years, there has begun a similar movement in the university sector to merge computer centres and libraries. Academic accountants are anxious to cut down on the overheads on both sides of the binary divide! There has also been a growing academic belief that those theories that informed the development of the learning resource centre are just as relevant for the newer computerized forms. Thus, in arguing for the merger of the library and computer centre at Carnegie Mellon University in 1985, it was stated that:

> The library of the future will provide access to books, journals, manuscripts, visual images, computers, machine-readable databases, service and people. Faculty and students will come to the library, but much library information will also be available through the campus computing network. People will use books and they will use machine-readable text files. Demand for all types of information will undoubtedly increase.[13]

Acquisition of non-book materials: general

Once a collection policy involving NBM has been accepted, the librarian has to acquire the materials. Any professional librarian should have the general expertise to be able to create a collection of materials that will satisfy the diverse requirements of most clients. However, as with specific subject acquisition, there are some aspects that are peculiar to NBM and require a knowledge of the current bibliographical organization of non-book materials. They include identifying various sources of supply and a familiarity with the problems hampering acquisition. These may be traced to those deriving from publishers and distributors, and problems due to lack of bibliographical control.

Publishers

The production of NBM is complex and each form has its own characteristics. It is also extremely difficult to obtain statistics about the number of companies producing NBM for sale or hire. Producers of NBM are perhaps most prolific within the educational sector; the largest in the UK is probably the Open University, where NBM devised originally for its own students have roused such interest from other institutions that its sound tapes and films have now been made available to any purchaser. Open University Educational Enterprises has been established as a publishing firm to market Open University publications and other relevant educational materials.

Sound recordings

The production of sound recordings can be divided into two main parts: the commercial record and cassette industry, and semi-commercial institutions. The former is extremely well organized by large companies such as EMI and CBS. Current output is controlled, in a pattern similar to that of book publishing, by trade publications such as the Music Master catalogue. The semi-commercial side is less well organized and includes professional bodies such as the Institute of Welding, industrial companies such as Shell, and academic concerns like the North East Biotechnology Centre.

Videos

Video production includes feature films, cartoons, documentaries, training and educational recordings. These are usually distributed for hire or sale through video libraries. They may be produced by the film giants, such as Warner Brothers, industrial companies such as ICI, broadcasting institutions like Tyne Tees Television, and organizations such as embassies and professional associations. There may be limitations on who can use them and where they may be shown; some of these are a result of local booking conditions, copyright, company policies and medical restrictions. Their distribution pattern is also diverse, involving many smaller outlets, for example, garages and local bookshops as well as high-street video shops.

Graphic materials

The publishing pattern of graphic materials is more diverse. It is impossible to impose a coherent structure in this area. Several commercial companies, such as the Slide Centre, produce NBM and have established large lists; industrial companies, including British Gas, the National Coal Board, and ICI have also produced materials. There has often been close cooperation with the commercial companies to produce an item. For instance, the Engineering Industry Training Board produced Open University packages on engineering design, employing the combined skills of the BBC and various universities, and case studies provided by leading engineering companies. Professional associations have also contributed in this area, among them the Institute of Supervisory Management and PIRA. Book publishers, too, have become involved – Longman Group, Macmillan, Routledge.

Art galleries and museums are also major producers of slides, postcards and posters of their exhibits. Again, some of these have realized the potential value of a wider market and arranged a national distribution. The National Portrait Gallery (London) slide sets, for example, are distributed through the Slide Centre.

Some commercial producers have concentrated on their local market, such as slides of local views, and a great many valuable publications in the local history field have been produced by public libraries.

Microcomputer software

The publishing of microcomputer software is similarly diverse. Commercial provision includes book publishers such as Longman and Thomas Nelson; traditional computer companies such as Microsoft and Logica; and specialist companies such as Eyetech. Colleges and schools have also produced software that has gained national recognition, for example Lancaster University, Teesside Polytechnic, and Jordanhill College of Education.

Software may be bought direct or through local specialist distributors. Retail outlets include high-street computer shops and bookshops. However, materials are also distributed through telecommunications. Public domain software can be accessed via bulletin board systems such as Compulink.

Distributors

Many NBM producers also distribute their own materials, and this can cause problems for the librarian used to dealing with one or two library book suppliers. There is no equivalent to the bookshops in this field, although some NBM, such as portfolios or those published by book firms, may be obtained from them. The major supplier offering a comprehensive service is T.C. Farries of Dumfries. There are well-established library suppliers for sound recordings, such as the Long Playing Record Library which will provide discs, CDs and cassettes, while the Slide Centre has established its position as a distributor of filmstrip and slides for a number of other companies as well as its own productions.

Chivers, the library book supplier, also provides video recordings to libraries. Video recordings and motion pictures can be obtained from film libraries; there are over 150 such libraries and each has its own catalogue and distribution system. The Video Gallery offers a comprehensive collection of educational, sporting and entertainment videos for libraries: it has a catalogue of 1 200 videos, a facility for tracing videos and an update service.

The librarian used to obtaining books on approval will find more difficulty with NBM. The fragility of such material has caused a few publishers to insist on the library paying for any material which is damaged during preview. The dishonesty of some librarians, who have copied the material and returned the original, has resulted in some distributors refusing to supply material on approval. Indeed, some small publishers will only supply material after payment and not to an order alone. The problems associated with piracy of computer programs have resulted in many commercial providers refusing to supply this category of material on approval. They will, however, often allow the library to make one copy for security purposes, but the individual licences should be very carefully studied.

Bibliographic control

The diversity of production and distribution agencies creates problems for the librarian in identifying available materials, and this is further aggravated by the absence of any one bibliographical tool to cater for all the current output. It is well to remember that there are many more book publishers and book publications than exist in the field of NBM, but books enjoy an established and comprehensive distribution network. For example, a single work, Whitaker's *British books in print*, enables the librarian to identify a majority of the book publishers' output in the UK.

The equivalent of such bibliographic tools does not exist for NBM, with the result that information about these materials is usually dependent upon the publishers' own publicity systems. Video recordings are perhaps the best organized, with the *British national film and video catalogue*, although even this does not include the complete film output of the UK.

In summary, there is no coherent bibliographical system for NBM, merely hundreds of separate publishers' catalogues and lists. Librarians setting out to build or manage a collection of NBM will find that contact with other librarians, attendance at exhibitions and visits to suppliers are crucial. Also useful are the case studies of libraries in NBM, regularly presented in the periodical *Audiovisual librarian*.[14]

Suppliers

T.C. Farries offers the major NBM service in the UK. It has produced an *AV catalogue* which is arranged in Dewey classified order. Items are supplied in publishers' packaging and library servicing is available.

However, just as the library relies on small bookshops as well as on library suppliers, so the librarian must be aware of the smaller firms supplying specialist services for the various forms of NBM. For example, Tavistock Videotapes provide a range suitable for current approaches in counselling and effective communication and interaction. Library video recording suppliers include Chivers and Wynd-up Video. Many general suppliers of computer materials regularly advertize in computer periodicals such as *Personal computer world*.

The librarian involved in this area must be prepared to search through lists of distributors and advertisements in periodicals to obtain up-to-date details of the suppliers of specialist aspects of NBM.

Exhibitions

New developments in equipment, and the opportunity to see a wide range of NBM, make it essential to attend exhibitions. These are held regularly both at national level and by local equipment suppliers. Details of these exhibitions may be found in periodicals such as *Audiovisual librarian*, *Audio visual* and *Personal computer world*.

Personal contact

Close contact should be established with other librarians and specialists in this field, with experts from local radio and television stations, and local film and photographic societies. Area resource organizations enable libraries to share the problems of selection, and further details may be obtained through the National Council for Educational Technology (NCET) and its information officer. In certain areas local self-help groups such as the North East Media Resources Organising Committee (NEMROC) have produced directories which provide details of local experts and organizations in various non-book materials; *Personal computer world* has a regular feature on computer clubs. However, it is to the professional associations that librarians will turn most readily for help and advice. In the UK the Aslib Audiovisual Group, the Library Association Audiovisual Group, and the Library Association Information Technology Group have been most prominent in establishing workshops and conferences.

Acquisition of non-book materials: specific

It is inappropriate in this chapter to attempt to describe all the tools that are available. The aim here is to indicate a starting point for obtaining research and undergraduate materials.

Sound recordings

The three formats of vinyl disc, sound cassette and compact disc are all collected by academic libraries but vinyl discs are now more likely only to be found in research collections. Sound cassette is the major sound format for undergraduate collections, with students having ready access to equipment. Compact discs are becoming increasingly important but the equipment is still not generally available to students and this limits their immediate value.

As with NBM in general, bibliographic control of sound recordings is not comprehensive. Of particular value among the listings available is the National Sound Archive's *Directory of recorded sound resources in the United Kingdom,*[15] which lists 480 holdings including libraries, museums, archives, county record offices, local radio stations, learned societies, recording groups and private individuals. It has a regional and subject approach.

The British Library has actively encouraged the development of the National Sound Archive and, in particular, the creation of a database of its acquisitions. In partnership with the Mechanical Copyright Protection Society it has established the National Discography with the brief to 'create a database of very detailed information on all recordings that are or have been commercially available in the UK, theoretically going back to the very beginning of recorded sound'.[16] It has become available as an external service during 1990. For research into radio programmes a current microfiche publishing programme of great value is that of Chadwyck-Healey.

The bibliographic sources for musical recordings are relatively well organized compared with other non-book materials, with the non-musical recordings perhaps presenting the greatest problem. There is no comprehensive listing for non-musical recordings, although a useful source is *Spoken word and miscellaneous catalogue* published annually by *Gramophone*. A wide range of publishers' catalogues is available, some describing only tapes or records or CD audio, while other firms are now publishing all these forms.

Video recordings

The place of the 16 mm film, which used to be the staple diet of the well-established academic NBM collection, is now increasingly in archival collections. In the UK most commercial film hire collections have switched to video recordings only; video recordings are widely available, user friendly and usually less expensive than 16 mm film. The great advantage of film for the large lecture group is also being eroded with the development of video projection facilities.

However, expense is still a problem with this format, and careful analysis of the likely use is essential. The excellent hiring facilities offer the librarian the chance to preview material and judge potential demand. Where hiring is centrally organized it is possible to analyse use patterns and determine when it is appropriate to purchase a particular title. Wherever possible, academic staff should be closely involved in the development of the collection. There is, alas, often a suspicion that such material should not be generally available to students or other departments. Typical complaints are that a lecturer's teaching programme has been distorted because the students have already seen the video, or that a servicing teaching department has used the video incorrectly or merely to fill in for an absent lecturer. These are not the usual complaints about books.

The selection tools below identify sources for purchasing video recordings. The off-air recording of television programmes will be considered in the Production section.

The major national collection for research is the British Film Institute (BFI). It is the major source of information concerning film and television in the UK and corporate membership is available to educational establishments and film societies. The BFI is also responsible for the National Film Archive which aims to collect all films shown and television programmes transmitted in Great Britain. The archive is developing a computer-based record-keeping system which will allow the production of computer-typeset catalogues. BFI publishes the *British national film and video catalogue* (BNFVC), a quarterly record of British and foreign films available in Great Britain. Coverage of video recordings began in the mid 1970s, and since 1987 interactive video titles have also been included.

The British Universities Film and Video Council (BUFVC) exists to encourage the use, production and study of audiovisual media, materials and techniques for teaching and research in higher education. Its publications include the *BUFVC catalogue* which is published annually in microfiche form. The *Catalogue* includes documentary and non-fiction films, videotapes, sound tapes, computer software, videodiscs and tape-slide programmes currently available in the UK. They have been appraised for use in degree level teaching or research. The BUFVC database is also available through BLAISE-LINE.

The catalogues of the video hire libraries are important sources of information. Major video libraries include CFL Vision, Concord Video and Film Council, Glenbuck Films, and Guild Sound and Vision.

Companies which market their own videos include BBC Enterprises, Video Arts, educational institutions such as City of London Polytechnic Media Services Department and a number of industrial concerns including the Shell Film Library and British Telecom Education Service.

Comprehensive guides to video recordings are available, but many deal only with the entertainment aspect of the format. A more general source is *The Video Gallery*, which lists new releases and back issues under detailed subject headings and includes fiction and non-fiction videos. Educational Media International produces detailed catalogues on a number of subjects. The *Educational film/video locator* lists more than 50 000 films and videos and provides a subject and audience level index. Several periodicals are now available on video, for example *Newsbrief* from 1988 and *Library video magazine* from 1986. Berger and Tims produce a catalogue of non-fiction videos available for purchase that have been cleared for home viewing rights.

Equipment for video recordings is evaluated in the general equipment sources and the specialist periodicals. The loose-leaf handbook *Video production techniques* is an important updating service for the video producer.

Videodiscs

Videodisc is a newer format and there are few current bibliographical tools. The first general guide is *Internationale Bildplatten Katalog* which lists some 1000 titles. However, it is important to note that particular tools are not available to trace discs for use in an interactive manner, although a recently published catalogue, *the Videodisc monitor*, is available. A limited range of publishers' catalogues is also available: one notable higher education publisher of training videodiscs is the Open University.

The major source of information on videodiscs is the National Interactive Video Centre (NIVC). It publishes *Interactive update*, a bimonthly journal covering all aspects of interactive technology in Britain and Europe. A register of research is also available for a contact and referral service. The most important UK guide to equipment and authoring is *An introduction to interactive video*. Information concerning equipment is available from many of the above services.

Graphics

The term graphics covers a wide range of NBM. Particularly common in UK and US academic libraries are photographs, photographic slides, illustrations and postcards, which have a wide range of subject applications. There is no comprehensive bibliographic source in the quest for this material. The series *Illustrations index 1982-86*, does not have an equivalent in the UK. National collections, however, are extensive, and museums and art galleries in particular are prolific publishers. Most of the general guides to art reproductions are dated, but a comprehensive source is *Art index*, which includes listings of reproductions in art periodicals and museum publications.

One of the most useful publishers' catalogues for slides and filmstrips is that of the Slide Centre. Other publishers include JAS Educational Airphotos, Visual Publications and Women Artists Slide Library. Major slide library catalogues are those of the Design Council, Crafts Council and the Victoria & Albert Museum.

Cameras and projectors are reviewed in the general equipment sources.

Microcomputing software

Writing in 1985, Whichard could still comment on computer software thus: 'This is still too unsettled an area for coherent library collection development. Besides, it must still be determined whether computer software will become part of the public service and reference areas in academic libraries.'[17] There are now numerous examples in the UK and the US where academic libraries have taken responsibility for such services. Issues to consider include: the need to standardize on one particular make of microcomputer; whether to provide a wide range of software or to concentrate on specific programs such as word processing, spreadsheet and database; the need to provide printing facilities and training programmes. Consistent advice is difficult to find but it is perhaps most important to ensure that the parent institution has an information technology strategy which includes the library service. Once a standard microcomputer has been determined then the library should resist the temptation to have a different one. If there is no provision for a microcomputer librarian on the staff, it is wiser not to provide more than the basic programs, unless you are confident that you can train staff to answer the complex questions that will arise with a wide range of software. Not all of it is straightforward to use, whatever the claims made by the suppliers! If you can charge for printing then do so, or be prepared for the consequences of unlimited access. Finally, it is necessary to have ready access to computer technicians to keep the equipment in operation.

The librarian who has to acquire microcomputer software does not have an easy task. The bibliographic control of this format has yet to be established and it is difficult to identify sources of information which are accurate and unbiased. The wide range of equipment and computing languages exacerbates the problems of acquisition.

Increasing demand for software has resulted in the rapid growth of suppliers, and it is important to exercise caution in the evaluation of software and choice of supplier. The decision to standardize on a particular microcomputer or a limited range of microcomputers should be influenced by the software that is available or likely to be published. Software and staff training are the major costs in the use of micro-computers.

A number of institutional bodies have been established to offer advice in this area, including the National Computing Centre (NCC) which develops computing techniques and provides aids for the more effective use of computers. Members have access to a large database of information and the Centre publishes a number of guides, including a *Directory of hardware* and a *Directory of software.*

Another important source of information is CHEST which is a Computer Board national initiative established to support computing in the higher education and research community. Its primary objective is to obtain the best possible value by negotiating reduced prices with software suppliers, arranging central funding for some software purchasers and negotiating suitable licence agreements for software purchases. Its directories list software utilities, application packages and suppliers. CHEST is held on-line on the NISS Bulletin Board System and is accessible through each member institution's computer centre. It is also available in print form.

The publishers of software are numerous. They include: local education authority consortia, for example RESOURCE (Barnsley, Doncaster, Humberside, Rotherham and Sheffield) which publishes materials both nationally and locally relating to all aspects of computers in education; specialist suppliers such as Triptych Systems, which provides software for the building industry; traditional book suppliers such as Longman; Viewbook Information Education, which offers a preview disc catalogue as a sample of texts stored on computer disc; and computer manufacturers such as Apple Computers.

The major printed sources for software are in periodical form. These include general publications such as *Personal computer world,* offering guides to software and equipment, and *Which PC?* Specialist subject periodicals include *Microdecision* which provides a directory of retailers and software for business users and *Educational computing* which includes a directory of educational computing software. Finally, there are periodicals for particular makes of equipment such as *Atari user.* The latter type of periodical is essential once the library has decided on a make of microcomputer.

Specialist subject sources include the ESRC Data Archive, which publishes a software bulletin and a regular update of the computer data set held in the archive. The journal *Teaching geography* has a regular page with updating news and reviews of computer software.

There is no UK general catalogue of microcomputing software. The standard source for computing is *The computer users yearbook* and the parallel *Software users yearbook*. The US does have *the Software encyclopedia* which provides fully annotated listings for 28 500 microcomputer programs; the same company provides *Microcomputer software and hardware guide* on-line via Dialog.

Telesoftware and shareware are increasingly important sources for computer programs. The former is the transmission of programs from one computer to another by broadcast radio, television or via telephone lines. Such public domain software is designed to be widely available without licensing agreements. Shareware carries with it an obligation to pay a small fee if the software is retained. Bulletin boards for software are an important source, as are computer user groups. An excellent guide is provided by *Public domain software for librarians*.[18] *Shareware for library applications* gives detailed coverage of US material. Caution is necessary in evaluating this software for purchase. Questions include: is it free or illegal? Does it add value to the collection? And perhaps most important, is it virus free?

Several subscription services operate an exchange service. For example, the Central Program Exchange offers the subscriber a service which includes the copying of up to ten programs per year, extra programs requiring a small fee.

CD-ROM

There has been a rapid growth in the production of CD-ROM materials and most of the major information reference companies have put their databases onto the format. They also supply customized CD-ROM workstations.

The technology supplies huge amounts of data at the speed of the on-line remote database services, but apparently without the high costs for telecommunications and search charges on the host database. The software enables the data to be easily manipulated and downloaded into personalized databases. The range of items now available in CD-ROM format includes bibliographical tools, English and foreign language dictionaries, census data and general and specific subject encyclopaedias. Full-text CD-ROMs, such as *Computer library*, are also being produced. These enable students not only to carry out detailed subject searches but also to print out excerpts of the text that they require for their assignments. However, there are some costs and disadvantages to be considered by the library service. These may often include purchasing new subscriptions to and back runs of material already in stock in print format. The subscription may be on a lease basis and, if subsequently cancelled, all material will have to be returned. It is also necessary to train staff and students in order to gain the greatest advantage from the search software. Equipment costs include the microcomputer, CD-ROM player and printer, and equipment maintenance. Computer stationery costs can be high, particularly where there are full-text materials. Finally there are political and financial decisions to make in deciding when the computer journals and their back runs should be discarded to make way for the neat, compact *Computer library* disc . . . However, the technology is attractive to students because it allows them greater flexibility and speed in searching for information than do the print versions.

One of the first general guides is *CD-ROM directory*, which has sections listing CD-ROM products, company information, CD-ROM drives, books, journals, conferences and exhibitions. It is international in scope, giving information on 390 products and some 350 companies. A useful concise introduction is *CD-ROM, interactive video and satellite TV in the school library*. This gives a brief introduction to the hardware and appropriate software. It is aimed at school libraries but it will repay scrutiny by any librarian entering this field. CHEST has listed CD-ROMs that academic librarians and computer centres have shown interest in purchasing. However, there is still a lack of bibliographical tools, and diligent searching through microcomputer periodicals and publishers' catalogues is required. The publishers include Silver Platter, Multi-lingual and UMI.

CIMTECH is an important provider of information on CD-ROMs and the allied equipment. *Library and information briefings*, from Central London Polytechnic Library and Information Technology Centre, includes updates on equipment.

Physical attributes

A number of general issues concerning the physical attributes of NBM require policy decisions by the collection management librarian. These include storage, labelling, security, copyright and cleaning. A number of specific points have been illustrated earlier under the four sample categories. Reference should also be made to Fothergill and Butchart[19] which gives detailed advice concerning equipment and the specific treatment of various formats, including their cataloguing. It is, however, important to stress that the professional librarian already has a wealth of relevant experience gained from the management of collections of books and periodicals. This experience, together with an understanding of client requirements, knowledge of the physical properties of the formats, and that invaluable attribute 'good sense', are the necessary starting points.

There is nothing inherent in the physical attributes of NBM that requires them to be treated significantly differently for storage and retrieval purposes. NBM do not *have* to be shelved separately from other library materials. They are as fragile, expensive and as prone to theft as books and periodicals. The collection manager's first concern is the nature of the access required by clients. Thus, in the same library, open access to a subject collection may be necessary in order to encourage undergraduate browsing, while restricted access to an archive collection may be essential to ensure the security of materials for *bona fide* researchers. If the policy for the law library is to encourage maximum use of all formats by undergraduates, then siting the law reports, texts, on-line services, video recordings of court practice, sound cassettes illustrating particular cases, slide teaching guides and the necessary equipment in one subject area is more likely to achieve this end than separate collections housed by form in different areas of the library. NBM can be intershelved with books using specialist packing from a range of suppliers; computer discs in slip boxes, slides in photographic albums, CD discs in shatter-proof cases and so on.

Nevertheless, such an arrangement may not be appropriate where the need is to ensure access to equipment that is in heavy demand, for example a microcomputer laboratory which is provided in the library in order to maximize utilization of scarce equipment. Probably the simplest means of managing this kind of situation is to keep the necessary software at the issue counter on closed access, with students being required to book it in advance. The software is then borrowed in the normal way and returned at the end of the loan period. However, where a computer disk is available as part of the subject collection it is easy for it to be intershelved with the bookstock and borrowed from within the subject collection.

An example illustrating the requirement for maximum security arises from an off-air video recording collection that is essentially a teaching collection, accessed via a closed circuit television network. Under a licensing agreement with the broadcasters, all use has to be recorded and it also has to be available when teaching staff require an item. A closed collection therefore is provided with access via booking sheets identifying replay times.

While emphasizing the similarities with books, there are specific NBM attributes that can cause problems. It is necessary to consider the external labelling that is provided, as the information it gives is frequently insufficient for clients. External labelling should assist browsing, and, if the information is comprehensive, it saves the NBM package from being constantly opened before being dismissed as irrelevant. The labelling should list the contents, link together various parts of a production and identify the equipment standard. Standardization on particular formats will also assist the clients. Thus VHS would be the expected video-recording standard to match up with the most common domestic equipment.

As with books, security tagging may be necessary. The majority of standard library systems provide appropriate tags for NBM. However magnetic based formats such as video recordings and computer discs should not be put through the demagnetizing systems. Removing the lugs from the backs of sound and video cassettes will prevent the accidental recording over of a programme. Tapes should be stored upright so that loops do not slide over each other. Similarly they must be kept away from heat sources and in their boxes to keep out the dust. Video and sound recordings are generally well protected and do not normally require a back-up copy to be made. However, if the item is rare, for example part of an archive, the master copy should not be available, but only a duplicate provided for the client. With computer software, which is easily damaged or corrupted, it is important to make back-up copies. Care is necessary to ensure that the laws of copyright and contract are not transgressed, as there is some variation in what is permissible. It is always advisable to check with the publishers; some will allow the library to copy the original; others may be willing to supply a backup copy or will guarantee to provide a replacement copy if the original is corrupted. In a few cases there will be nothing you can do about it. Ultimately it will be the responsibility of the collection manager to weigh the demands of maximum use, optimum security, safety and availability and to formulate an appropriate policy.

Physical environment

It has to be accepted that there is a wide range of equipment and that there is unremitting technical progress. No sooner is the standard library micro-computer chosen than a better, faster and inevitably cheaper model will appear. Any decision to buy NBM equipment has to be taken accepting that it will almost immediately become obsolete. Where standards exist, it is sensible to use them and avoid buying equipment which is out of the ordinary, unless the choice can be justified on other grounds. For example, it was clear that the *BBC Domesday interactive video disc* was unlikely to develop with a wide range of software, but nevertheless it was an important development and, as a hardware item, of great interest, for example, to students of information engineering. However, in general, if a product is widely available in the domestic market then it will survive. The best advice with regard to the purchase of equipment is to plan, seek advice and, once a decision has been made, get on with it. Then the issue should not be re-examined for another three years, with a view to replacing the equipment in five years.

Incorporating equipment into the library raises issues about viewing and listening arrangements and the need for safety checks. It is crucial that equipment meets the *Electricity at work regulations 1989.*[20] A programme of regular planned inspection and testing is necessary for all equipment that will plug into a 13A socket. Cleaning of equipment should also be part of the normal maintenance programme. If clients are to work in comfort, monitors should be carefully sited away from strong reflections and chairs placed about a metre away from a 14 inch screen. Publicize criteria to ensure that staff and students are aware of the hazards of excessive use of VDUs. In the early days of NBM use in libraries, there was concern that the clients would be distracted by the equipment noise. This is now rarely a problem, although microcomputer sound systems may need attention. Laser printers should be provided in public areas in preference to dot matrix printers.

Concern about NBM and its equipment is more the result of staff trepidation than a real problem, but the need for staff training has to be recognized and provided for all staff, if this trepidation is to be overcome.

Production

In a number of academic institutions it has been common to have either a close link between the library and the institution's audiovisual production unit, or indeed for the library to be responsible for audiovisual production. Figure 8.3 shows a polytechnic library which has a publication and production service which includes off-air recording, photographic production and a video production studio. A librarian who has not found the material to satisfy a client's requirements may have one further possibility: to produce the material in-house, often via off-air recording from radio and television programmes. In the UK a licence may be purchased to record all Open University broadcasts, and the *Copyright, Designs and Patents Act 1988* [21] encourages the development and adoption of licensing schemes which will permit copying for certain fees. For example, the Educational Recording Agency is negotiating with higher education for a licence on behalf of the BBC and IBA companies.

Academic libraries also have a long history of using NBM for in-service training of staff and for user education. Examples of such programmes have included sound cassettes illustrating reference work, 'trigger' videos showing excerpts of users' behaviour in a library, and tape/slide presentations illustrating the work of a librarian for careers conventions.

However, it is important to stress that the usual criteria that would be applied in deciding to stock published material must also apply to home-produced material. Its relevance to the library and its clients should include such considerations as:

- is it relevant to the mission of the library?
- can similar material be found already in stock?
- is there already adequate subject coverage in other materials?
- can it be linked to other material in stock?
- would it have to be for reference only?
- is it designed for individual or group use?
- is the format suitable for clients?
- what physical environment is required, for example blackout facilities?
- is suitable equipment available in the library or to clients externally?
- are staff trained to handle the material and its equipment?
- what are the copyright restrictions?

The audiovisual equipment available has greatly benefited from the large domestic market that now uses video recorders, cassette recorders and microcomputers, and while care is needed to ensure regular maintenance of equipment, it is generally robust, safe and easy to use. Access to audiovisual and computer technicians is a bonus but it is no longer essential to have them on the staffing establishment.

Conclusion

In summary, the collection management of NBM involves the librarian in very similar processes to those associated with print materials, and, on the whole, NBM are no more costly than these traditional materials. It is, however, important to budget for the replacement of equipment, and an amortization procedure and maintenance schedule should be adopted. Otherwise, the daily routines of searching printed sources, contacting institutions and individuals for specialist advice and services, creating criteria for evaluation, and deciding which documents to purchase still apply. It may also be necessary to create a hire and preview system. If suitable documents cannot be traced, librarians may be in a position to produce them for their clients, although it is more likely that this activity will be linked to their own needs for training of staff and user education.

References

1. Butchart, I.C. (1980), '*AACR* 2 and the cataloguing of audiovisual materials', in G. Roe (ed.) *Seminar on AACR 2*, London: Library Association, pp.25-32, p.26.
2. University Grants Committee et al. (1965), *Audiovisual aids in higher scientific education*, London: HMSO.
3. Gilbert, L.A. and J.W. Wright (1971), *Non-book materials: their bibliographic control*, London: National Council for Educational Technology, p.43.
4. Great Britain, *British Library Act 1972*, Eliz.II, Ch. 54, London: HMSO.
5. Thompson, A.H. (1989), 'University libraries and multi media development', *Audiovisual librarian*, **15** (4), 203-205, p.203.
6. Postman, N. (1986), *Amusing ourselves to death*, London: Heinemann, p.21.
7. Lindsay, J. (1977), 'The right to know: teaching the importance of information' (Unpublished research proposal, South Hackney School).
8. Boyer, E.L. (1988) 'Connectivity' in P.S. Breivik and R. Wedgeworth, *Libraries and the search for academic excellence*, London: Scarecrow Press, pp.3-11, p.6.
9. Boyer, E.L. ref.8, p.9.
10. Lindsay, J. ref. 7.
11. Marland, M. (ed.) (1981), *Information skills in the secondary curriculum*, London: Methuen, for the Schools Council, p.9.
12. Ibid., p.32.
13. Arms, W.Y. and T.J. Michalak, (1988), 'The merger of libraries with computing at Carnegie Mellon University', *British journal of academic librarianship*, **3** (3), 153-164, p.158.

14. *Audiovisual librarian* 1-, 1973/74-, quarterly journal jointly published by Aslib and Library Association Audiovisual Group.

15. National Sound Archive (1989), *Directory of recorded sound resources in the United Kingdom*, London: British Library.

16. Tibber, M. (1989), 'The national discography', *Audiovisual librarian*, **15** (1), 25-28, p.25.

17. Whichard, M. (1975), 'Collection development in non-print materials in academic libraries', *Library trends*, **34** (1), 37-53, p.47.

18. Noble, I. (1989), *Public domain software for librarians*, London: Library Association Information Technology Group.

19. Fothergill, R.F. and I.C. Butchart, (1990), *Non-book materials in libraries: a practical guide*, 3rd ed., London: Bingley.

20. Great Britain, *Electricity at work regulations 1989*, London: HMSO.

21. Great Britain, *Copyright, Designs and Patents Act 1988*, London: HMSO.

9 Stock revision, retention and relegation in US academic libraries

Sharon Bonk and Sara Williams

American library terminology and usage differ slightly from that of their British counterparts. It is therefore necessary to define terms and set the context for their use within this chapter. Although the words relegation and retention are used in the literature, they do not stand alone as concepts within collection management. Academic librarians do indeed make decisions to retain materials in the collection (perhaps after conservation treatment or reformatting) or to relegate them to storage, or to withdraw them from the collections. Deacquisition, once a term in vogue, has dropped from use as has the short-lived newsletter, *The deacquisitions librarian.*[1] The newsletter changed both name and scope to *Collection management* after two issues, an indication of the profession's view that deacquisition, or deselection as it is now called in formal documents, cannot or should not be taken out of the broader context of collection development and management. Members of the editorial board of both the newsletter and the early years of the journal were the same persons who had done the original research which created the methodology of decision-making for collection deacquisition.

The concept of collection management includes both the theoretical aspects of collection building and the managerial aspects of collection use, space, budgeting and related matters. 'The review of collections for preservation, storage and deselection is a critical component of a library's collection management program.'[2]

Collection review, although a general term encompassing a wide range of objectives, is the term in current use closest in meaning to stock revision. Stock revision has never been used in US libraries, perhaps because to Americans it connotes January sales and the after-hours activities of stock boys in grocery stores replenishing the shelves with goods for the next day's business. The authors concede that the curiously organic terms favoured by American librarians – 'pruning', 'thinning' and 'weeding' – also fit within a grocery store metaphor. American usage may favour the organic over the mechanical because of the view that library collections are intertwined with the ever evolving academic programmes which disallow any mechanical approach to collection content decisions.

Indeed, pruning and weeding are viewed as quaint and limiting terms for processes within the broader activity of collection review. Mosher in an early key work on collection management, stated: 'The term 'weeding' will be avoided [in his essay] because it has pejorative connotations which are often not warranted, though the term entered into common parlance and will never go away.'[3]

The major American library indexing tool, *Library literature*, uses 'Discarding of books, periodicals, etc.' as its subject heading. This has not changed in fifty years, although cross references from 'Weeding' and 'Obsolescence of materials' were added in the 1940s and 1970s respectively. Secondary indexing sources, *Resources in education* and *Current index to journals in education*, do not assign subject headings to the concept which must be approached through broader concepts of 'Library materials', 'Library research', 'Space utilization', 'Library materials selection'. On-line, the primary identifier 'Weeding (Library)' can be used to access the literature directly. The Library of Congress subject heading is 'Discarding of books ...' which is used for Weeding. The related term is 'Collection development – Libraries.'

Literature review

The necessity for reviewing academic library collections to make space available for new acquisitions was recognized early. Mosher traces the identification of the problem at Harvard College back to 1725.[4] Harvard

University dealt with it formally approximately 170 years later when President Charles W. Eliot defined the principal criterion for thinning the collection as pattern of use, a principle presumably already worked out and implemented by librarian Justin Winsor. Eliot heeded dictates of campus politics, working with faculty to identify a core collection size that would encourage use. He also maintained that research libraries would need centres to store less-used but important research materials. Eliot carried his ideas beyond Harvard to the American Library Association (ALA) in 1902.[5]

Ten years before Eliot's address to the ALA, another New England patrician and thinker, Charles Francis Adams, trustee of a public library in neighbouring Quincy, Massachusetts, described the trustees' plan to deal with rapidly diminishing space: the librarian pulled from the collection less-used materials, sold them to booksellers or gave them to the more comprehensive research libraries of Harvard College, the Boston Athenaeum and the Boston Public Library.[6] This presumably solved Crane Memorial Library's immediate space problems, but probably added to the space problems of the other libraries. Adams was not without critics. S.S. Green, Librarian of the Worcester Public Library, decried the potential disservice to Quincy residents who, wanting to do research, would find the research material unavailable to them. Green went on to propose a system of mutual loans between libraries to assist students and enquirers in small towns in getting access to the materials in larger libraries.[7]

The contemporary American literature yields two distinct streams of thought: theoretical and methodological. The theoretical basis for deselection, which supports the research on methodology and practice, is gathered in several treatises and in the recent publications of the Association for Library Collections and Technical Services (ALCTS), an ALA division, formerly known as the Resources and Technical Services Division (RTSD). The basic concepts will be discussed in the following pages.

The key work on methodology of collection review for retention decisions remains that of Stanley Slote.[8] A review of the literature cited in Slote's comprehensive work and other sources reveals a paucity of articles on innovations in or refinements of methodology useful in the review of collections. Most American librarians seem to have accepted Slote's analysis of previous studies, as well as his research on collection use and collection obsolescence, as basic and will find his latest revisions to the methodology useful. Recently, Lancaster has synthesized earlier studies in a discussion of cost-effective space utilization.[9]

There has been one good practical piece on conducting a use study specifically for collection weeding.[10] Hall's methodology is based on three assumptions: that *immediate* past use is the best predictor of future use; in-house use is similar to external use; and patterns of use do not change dramatically over time. If one has appropriate circulation data, this is a useful sampling study that will assist in determining what items should be removed from the shelves.

The recently published *Guide to the evaluation of library collections* includes a relatively comprehensive bibliography of collection-assessment methodologies or the reported results of circulation studies, citation studies, in-house use studies, shelf availability studies, and interlibrary loan studies. It 'lists methods which may be used to evaluate library collections, indicating the types of libraries for which each method can be used and the advantages and disadvantages of each method.'[11]

The new codification of theory and recommended practice for all libraries, *Guide to review of library collections*, accepts that the main function of deselection is to create space for collection growth. Secondary values are 'increased convenience for the library user and economy and efficiency in the use of time by library staff. Failure to deselect materials can diminish the vitality of a collection.'[12]

Few new studies of review methodology have appeared in the literature, but one is unable to determine if this is because implementation has overtaken speculation or because little effort is really being made to review collections systematically. The time consuming nature of collection review makes it difficult to write up findings which are necessarily focused very narrowly on one institution's collections.

Much of the reported activity in collection review for withdrawal has taken place in public libraries and hence is out of the scope of this chapter. American public librarians have accepted collection use as the single most important factor in collection maintenance and have developed a variety of approaches for increasing use of materials through promotion and display, attention to the physical piece, and, whenever possible, uncrowded shelves. All of these are accomplished by routine and, from an academic librarian's viewpoint, ruthless pruning of the collections.[13,14]

Preservation is a comparatively new element in the literature on collection management. Preservation programmes have become important parts of collection management in many large academic libraries, thereby changing the nature of existing review procedures, as well as the options available to a subject specialist confronted with a book in poor condition. While Slote, writing in 1982, listed physical dilapidation and brittle paper as justification for weeding a volume, such books may form a large portion of the research collection in an academic library. The quantity of material in the largest US research libraries which is believed to be in imminent danger of dissolution is large enough to make title-by-title review in the traditional manner difficult or impossible.

The specific criteria for choosing a book for some form of preservation treatment often overlap with the criteria traditionally used as grounds for weeding or storage. Comparatively little theoretical literature exists written with preservation selection in mind. Atkinson attempted to set up a framework in which subject collections with low levels of current use but with possible future research value could be identified and micro-filmed as blocks, without review of individual titles.[15] This approach has since been adapted for cooperative projects among the largest US research libraries.

Theoretical justification for deselection

The development of theory and recommended practice for deselection and storage of library materials is partly a response to the assumption by academic librarians of the collection development responsibility formerly held by the teaching faculty. During the 1970s, librarians responsible for collection development realized that building and managing library collections should be done systematically within the context of the library's mission to support specific programmatic goals of the university. Materials selection was no longer regarded as a faculty privilege or as an art, but as the professional responsibility of librarians, a responsibility calling for disciplined endeavour with standards, objective analysis of quality, and provision for the physical care of the item after acquisition. To that end members of the Collection Development Committee of the ALA Resources and Technical Services Division produced for the first time comprehensive guidelines for collection development, including formulation of collecting policies, methods for evaluation of effectiveness of library collections, allocation of materials budgets, and review of library collections. Each guideline was issued separately between 1976 and 1978 and together as *Guidelines for collection development* in 1979.[16] Extensive revisions and expansion of the guidelines have been undertaken since the mid-eighties by the Collection Management and Development Committee. These guidelines codify the state of current practice in collection management in the US.

The production of the guidelines and their subsequent revisions is part of the expanded efforts in continuing education of librarians for collection development and management responsibilities. Other activities of the ALCTS CMDC include the creation of an ongoing series of regional institutes on collection management. These institutes have been attended by hundreds of librarians and have been well received by both experienced selectors and persons for whom collection development and management was a new responsibility. The institutes and the production of the manuals and guides are collaborative efforts of distinguished leaders in the field of collection development. Their work has provided a basis for common understandings, methods and goals, and has made possible such cooperative activities as the use of the National Shelflist Count and the RLG Conspectus.

These guides were developed through: review of the professional literature, including selected libraries' policies; review by practitioners and experts in the areas under consideration; and hearings held for interested members of the profession as the manuscript developed. The guide directly relevant to the topic of this chapter is the *Guide to review of library collections: preservation, storage and deselection.* At this writing, the guide is undergoing final revision after a public hearing at the midwinter meeting of ALA, January 1990. Publication is expected in mid-1990. The new guide updates and replaces the chapter, 'Guidelines for the review of library collections' in the 1979 *Guidelines for collection development.*

The new guide summarizes the changes in approach that have developed over the last ten years. Perhaps a pedantic distinction is the change from guideline to guide. The term 'guidelines' was thought to carry prescriptive connotations. Since each library must make decisions appropriate to its own institution, no outside group can give specific criteria for the actual decisions to be made within a library. It can only recommend procedure and issues to consider in making specific decisions.

There are two major changes which reflect changes in current thinking and practice. The new guide emphasizes the centrality of an ongoing programme of collection review. Where the earlier document implied the usefulness of such programmes, the current guide takes as given that a collection review programme should exist and recommends the contents of such a programme.

The second major change is the prominence given to review of collections for preservation. Where the earlier document included preservation as one item to consider in reviewing collections, the new publication includes preservation review as an essential element in a collection review programme.

Collection review programmes must be carefully planned and linked to needs and activities within other library departments and to needs and expectations of faculty and administration. Formal consultation with the library's constituents as the programme is planned and as a regular part of the review process is recommended so that appropriate objectives and criteria may be agreed upon that are consistent with current and future programme needs, facilities, budget and available space.

Review for storage

If a library is fortunate enough to have space into which lesser-used materials may be moved, the review process may be simplified, since there is less urgent need to withdraw materials from the collection. Because remote storage of material removes it from direct access by library users, it should not be done without careful analysis of its projected use and consideration of any potential risk to the material if it remains in an area open to the public.

Protective storage is appropriate for material likely to be stolen or mutilated. This includes material which is not considered appropriate for the rare books collection, but which may still be somewhat scarce, or which has some artifactual value, such as first editions, books with early publication dates, fine bindings or fine illustrations.

When large blocks of material are identified as lesser used material or subject to physical risk, consideration may be given to block storage. Although block storage may seem attractive, freeing relatively large amounts of space in a less labour intensive way for both subject specialists and technical services personnel who must record the location changes in the library's records, attention must be given to any parts of the block that may be used more heavily than others. Use statistics and other objective criteria for selection are rarely available for large blocks of material. Therefore, the selection of the material to be stored is usually subjective or arbitrary, rather than objective and programmatic. Remote storage of blocks of collections is generally an exception to common practice and used only in situations of extreme space limitation, or as a response to emergencies in which the physical condition of a building threatens a large block of material.

Review for deselection

The *Guide* has incorporated the perceived wisdom of all the previous use studies into its recommendations on consideration of use, or lack thereof as justification for storage and withdrawal.

> Lack of use is the most practical criterion for deselecting an item. Past use is generally considered the best single predictor of future use. Past use can be measured by circulation system records and counts, shelf time records in individual books, interlibrary loan circulation records, and in-house use statistics. It is advisable to employ subjective assessments by librarians or experts and users as well as objective use data obtained through mechanical techniques. In cases where past use cannot be practicably measured, items may be identified for deselection on the basis of estimated use, taking into account such factors as the language of the material, publication date, accession date, the subject field, and the format or nature of the material. Deselection decisions based on these factors are made title by title by subject specialists in consultation with users. Conclusions drawn on the basis of estimated use criteria may be reversed because of an item's intrinsic quality or value to a library.[17]

In reality, it is unlikely that any data are readily available about specific titles other than the date due slips in the books themselves or circulation system records. Other data needed for objective assessment, such as in-house use, interlibrary loan circulation, and title-specific circulation data, are not usually available unless a specific use study has been carried out. With the increase in the number of preservation programmes, and the consequent greater attention to cleanliness in the stacks, soon not even tell-tale layers of dust will be available to provide clues to the last time a book was removed from the shelf.

The rigour of the criteria for withdrawal of a title differs if space is available for storing part of a collection in other than prime space. The key difference in the criteria for withdrawal is that the title is considered no longer relevant to support of the academic programmes as defined in the collection development policy. Removal of duplicate copies is a part of the weeding process, but is secondary to the type of decision for outright removal of the title. Removal of an item upon replacement with one in good physical condition is also not subject to the same relevance criteria except when the artifactual value of the copy in poor physical condition is at issue.

The deselection decision needs to include: consideration of the availability of the item from another source, should unpredicted need arise; the perceived cost benefit of retaining the item over obtaining it from another source if a need arises; the finite space limitations and costs of ongoing collection maintenance.

Review for preservation

Some of the same factors considered in review of collections for deselection or storage are also relevant in review for preservation purposes. In most academic libraries with preservation programmes, a review process is set up to determine which books will be given preservation treatment and, if so, by what method. These decisions require technical judgement from the preservation librarian concerning the best methods of dealing with the book's physical state. The collection management librarian or subject bibliographer remains responsible for judgements on the book's importance to the library's collections and its probable level of use in the future.

Books in poor physical condition may be identified either as part of a systematic review of the stacks, or at the point of circulation or shelving. The latter arrangement is perhaps more common. Books needing simple repair or commercial rebinding are often treated without consultation with collection management staff, depending on the policy of the individual library.

If a book has deteriorated to the point where repair or rebinding is impossible, it may be replaced with a commercial reprint, reformatted either as microfilm or as a photocopy, withdrawn from the collection, or returned to the stacks to die a natural death.

Decisions to purchase replacements for deteriorated books, or to reformat them in some other medium, have serious implications for the library budget, and are usually preceded by the same kind of bibliographic searching which accompanies a new purchase. Both deselection and neglect of deteriorating titles are uncomfortable choices for bibliographers in academic institutions. In Atkinson's words, 'Not to preserve is . . . always to silence a voice, which, in the opinion of a number of people in the past . . . has had something to say significant enough to warrant extended consideration.'[18] Microfilm has become a widely-used alternative solution for materials which, though rarely used, are thought to have research value; in crowded libraries, it has the additional virtue of consuming less stack space than the original book.

At the University of Albany, there is a firmly established preference for hard copy as opposed to microformats. As a result, microfilm is rarely chosen as a reformatting option. The preservation review process is significant for deselection; of the books prepared for the bibliographers to consider, between thirty and forty per cent are withdrawn. Although the books under review were sent to the Preservation Office because of their poor physical condition, the usual justification for withdrawal is that the titles are no longer relevant to the collection.

Practice

Librarians responsible for collection development in academic libraries have been aware of the need regularly and systematically to review collections to remove obsolete or little-used materials from prime shelving space. Some have done this to improve the efficacy of the collection or its relevance to current academic programmes, but most reviews of the collection were done in response to the pressure of space. Some librarians have the safety net of a remote storage facility which does not require the irrevocable decision, but most do not have such a luxury. A decade ago Baatz reported that 'weeding has been minimally done' in research libraries.[19] The stated or implied mission of research libraries is to collect in anticipation of use. Consequently, routine removal of lesser used materials goes against the principles of most selectors and most faculties.

The politics of academe also inhibit an active programme of collection weeding. Tillman recently criticized the literature on deselection of material from academic libraries for lack of realism in the way in which policies are actually applied or thwarted by pressures from faculty.[20] *The Guide to review of library collections* recognizes the political implications of a review programme as one of the issues to be addressed in the development of a library's collection review programme. No guide, of course, can predict or prescribe what issues may be of specific concern to an institution, but consultation with the institution's faculty, administration, and users is part of a well-planned collection review programme. Faculty are generally not helpful during the phase of identifying candidates for storage or withdrawal, but their solicited advice or review of specific titles is important and may prevent costly or irreversible misjudgements on the part of librarians.

Naturally, some collections are reviewed on a regular basis. *Science and technology libraries* devoted an issue to the weeding of sci-tech collections. Librarians from corporate and academic libraries wrote both on the policies and practice of weeding monographs and journals. Stankus used faculty publishing records to assist in journal weeding.[21] The Massachusetts Institute of Technology Libraries' policy for weeding collections is based on consideration of changing academic programmes as well as conservation of space.[22] Burdick demonstrated a method of using *Science citation index* to supplement frequency of use data in weeding science monographs.[23] Burdick's conclusions about how citation analysis can be applied in the sciences differ from Budd's conclusions about citation analysis in the humanities.[24]

Engeldinger surveyed 550 colleges and universities on the existence of formal policies and actual practices regarding weeding of reference collections and found that very little attention is *formally* given to the role of weeding in the management of reference collections. The recorded policies and practices indicated that frequency of use, age of material, and new editions are key factors in removing items from the collection, but that availability of shelf space is the most important factor for any systematic attempt at reviewing the collection. Lack of staff time was seen to be the biggest inhibitor of systematic implementation of collection review. Most interesting were the conflicting results that indicated that 'almost half of all academic libraries do not include how much an item is actually used as part of the criteria for discarding or transferring a reference title. This is a particularly interesting observation because anticipated use determines its original selection . . . In the vast majority of cases it appears that use is determined by the subjective judgements of the reference staff and their ability to remember. Only twenty-three libraries had conducted a use survey of their collection.'[25]

Biggs and Biggs confirmed some of Engeldinger's observations through a survey of 565 academic libraries on reference collection development.

They found that 'in a substantial number of academic libraries within all types of institutions, reference selection and weeding are not guided by written policies; . . . most collections appear to be unmanageably large; low use is often a weeding criterion, and empirical use studies are rarely carried out.'[26]

The Reference and Adult Services Division of the ALA recently established a Collection Development and Evaluation Section. This development reflects increasing involvement of reference librarians in selection and evaluation of the general collections, as well as selection of reference materials. In some libraries, reference librarians have dual assignments in reference and book selection. One of the activities of the new Collection Development and Evaluation Section is to develop guidelines for maintenance of reference collections. This group will be assisted by a 1990 issue of *The reference librarian* which is focused on weeding reference collections – work that appears to respond to the problems identified in the Biggs and Engeldinger studies.[27]

The Association of College and Research Libraries has published a selection of collection development policies of small and medium-sized academic libraries.[28] Five of the eighteen sample policies included weeding as part of collection development. Most did not give specific criteria for deselection, but implied or stated that obsolescence and low use were key criteria. These policies also included procedures for soliciting faculty advice in the process. One policy is notable for the specificity of its delineation of responsibilities and activities, but states that withdrawal activities will take place as time and schedules permit. Although poor condition is stated as one criterion for withdrawal, none of the sample policies includes review of the collection for preservation. It may be that preservation awareness has not yet filtered into practice in smaller libraries; more likely, smaller libraries do not create permanent research collections.

Perhaps some of the most systematic review and withdrawal of little used material has occurred at the junior college level, institutions which do not purport to collect at any other than curricular support level. Current materials directly related to instruction, quite often at the technician level, are the only materials needed in their collections. Librarians in these institutions rarely expect to have unlimited collection growth and are not expected to build collections for unidentified future scholarly pursuits. Most two year institutions rely heavily on the collections of neighbouring colleges or interlibrary loan to supplement their collections in areas that are not of primary interest to the instructional programmes.

Research libraries

The practice among research libraries has been to withdraw books from circulating collections only in response to space demands. The authors conducted an informal electronic mail survey of the collection development officers of the Research Libraries Group to determine what systematic collection review programmes were in effect at these libraries. The respondents confirmed the observations of Baatz in his 1978 survey of Association of Research Libraries members. This result is not surprising, as historically large research libraries have preferred to store their surplus collections, while smaller academic libraries have routinely discarded volumes.

The authors asked their colleagues the following questions:

- Do you review your collections regularly to withdraw, remove to storage, or repair, rebind, or reformat materials?
- Do you review your collections in response to specific concerns such as collection evaluation, space limitation in a particular area of a building, or preservation activity?
- Do you have policies and procedures regarding review of collections for withdrawal or storage?
- Do you use information from an automated circulation system to aid in the review of a collection for weeding, preservation selection, or other collection management purpose?

The responses can be categorized into six types of activity:

- all libraries weed when space is at a premium;
- most libraries have an ongoing programme to remove lesser used materials to a remote storage facility;
- withdrawal of volumes is generally limited to duplicate copies;
- divisional or branch libraries generally review their collections on a regular schedule for withdrawal, transfer to the main library, or storage;
- reference collections are routinely culled of outdated material;

- preservation programmes have contributed to reviewing collections for allied purposes, withdrawal or storage.

The University of California campuses in the northern part of the state have had a cooperative storage facility for many years. The State of California has recently built the Southern Regional Library Facility, a high-density shelving facility designed to alleviate space constraints in the southern University of California libraries, in lieu of building more storage space for the libraries at each of those campuses. 'It is the policy of the University that the campuses must make use of the storage facilities for "seldom used volumes", and each campus was given a quota based on estimates made in 1979 of how much material in each of the libraries had not circulated in the previous ten years.'[29] If a campus library does not elect to use the facility, it will be ineligible for additional capital improvement funds from the state – a strong motivation to comply and to review collections.

One University of California campus responded to the state's mandate by establishing selection criteria for the storage facility, which they have used over the last five years to move almost 70 000 volumes of the 145 000 volume quota. The criteria include: judicious selection of duplicates in good condition; earlier editions, unless the earlier edition has better bibliographies and/or commentary by eminent writers not found in later editions; incomplete sets of a specific author if a complete set is available in the circulating collection; materials in poor physical condition. Interestingly, the campus has made a proviso that no volume be sent to storage if a faculty member does not wish it to go there. They have used these criteria to review the sciences, technology, some social sciences, art, and social science and humanities material in an uncatalogued backlog.

Other libraries have established cooperative storage arrangements with other independent academic libraries within their region. An example is the modest regional depository of the Capital District Library Council of New York State. As part of their cooperative collection development and resource sharing programme, the Council rents space for the use of all the libraries. Members must deposit material, and the centre will not maintain duplicates.

On the authors' campus a major weeding project was carried out in 1975-1977. This was in response to a serious space problem. In the initial stages there was consultation with Stanley Slote about the applicability of his work in public libraries to a university setting and the complications of not having a complete or consistent shelf-time record. Faculty were invited to review materials that had been designated for withdrawal or storage in the sub-basement of the library. Reports of that major project indicate that the selectors were hampered by not having a circulation record and therefore were conservative in their choices.

At that time, it became clear that more remote storage would be necessary as the library acquired more materials that were to be retained in perpetuity. Some discussions took place among the librarians of a number of State University of New York (SUNY) campuses, but no joint storage plan similar to those of California was forthcoming. Therefore, the University at Albany was a major proponent of the joint storage facility in the Capital District.

No major review of monographic collections specifically designed to reduce the number of volumes on the shelves has taken place since then. Collections have been reviewed as programmes were eliminated from the campus or as the direction of a department's research and teaching interests changed. For example, the nursing and business education collections were removed and transferred to other SUNY campuses which retained programmes where SUNY Albany had eliminated them. SUNY Albany also had the opportunity to choose materials from the library science collection at the Geneseo campus when that college dropped its library science programme.

Periodicals space has always been scarce, creating problems for the periodicals collection which was growing rapidly in the 1970s and early 1980s in response to campus programme expansion and the increasing number of new journals. Journals were reviewed for storage and discard in the 1976-1977 project, and again in the mid-eighties for conversion to microform, remote storage in the library's sub-basement, or at the Capital District facility. In 1988, compact storage shelving was erected in the main periodical stacks in order to increase the shelf density for the titles which selectors felt could not be stored nor converted to microform.

Two collection reviews with different operational focuses began in 1984 and continue today. Neither was designed to be the basis of collection content reviews, but they have resulted in a systematic inventory and review of the collections. The two events were the need to barcode the collection when a new circulation system was installed, and the creation of a preservation programme. The barcoding of the collection has resulted in an inventory and required selectors to review parts of the collections from the vantage point of bibliographical problem resolution.

Similarly, the retrospective conversion project carried out in conjunction with the on-line catalogue installed in 1986 resulted in collection review by selectors who were asked to review subject collections for retrospective conversion priority and at that time also to make withdrawal decisions.

It took several years to organize and mainstream the preservation programme, but that has resulted in routine review of all circulating collections for signs of physical deterioration. The procedures used by the Preservation Office at the University at Albany are fairly typical of preservation decision-making at middle-sized academic libraries with high circulation volumes. Materials in poor physical condition are reviewed by selectors who may choose from a variety of preservation treatments, replacement if available, or withdrawal.

At the University at Albany the first step in this process is a search of the on-line catalogue to determine the existence of extra copies, earlier and later editions, and the number of other titles by the same author. Such standard bibliographic tools as *Books in print*, *Guide to reprints*, and their various foreign counterparts are checked for in-print status and the existence of commercial reprints. A similar search is made for commercial microfilm using *Guide to microforms in print* and the *RLIN register of microfilm masters*.

At this point it has been found useful to consult both the RLIN and OCLC databases. RLIN is a convenient way to locate quickly titles microfilmed or scheduled for microfilming at other institutions. OCLC, which is the larger of the two databases in terms of the number of participating libraries, gives an indication of the number of libraries holding the title being searched. All this information is recorded on a form with a recommendation for treatment, and the book is set aside for review by the appropriate subject bibliographer. The bibliographer either authorizes the recommended treatment, orders that the book be withdrawn, or returned to the shelf without treatment.

The University at Albany is not unique in its use of its preservation programme as the basis of a current collection review. Based on the results of our limited survey, however, it appears that the University at Albany deselects an unusually large proportion of the materials reviewed for preservation purposes. Results of our brief survey suggest that outright deselection of a title in a research library is usually limited to duplicate copies. In a relatively rare instance bibliographers at one of the institutions surveyed are reminded that failure to make a decision actively to preserve a deteriorated title is a *de facto* decision to withdraw it.

Collection use statistics

Part of the time consuming aspect of reviewing collections for withdrawal has been having an accurate indication of the use of the title under consideration. When libraries went to mechanized and first-generation automated circulation systems in the 1960s and 1970s, many lost the traditional date due slip affixed to the book which recorded circulation due dates and provided quick reference to past use. In the literature, past use has been considered one of the few reliable predictors of future use. It is clear that this is not true for all disciplines, but the record of past circulations is indeed useful to persons making collection-retention decisions.

> The number of libraries implementing integrated or linked circulation systems has increased dramatically in the recent past. Operational relationships between bibliographic and physical access control in such libraries are much stronger. Sophisticated management reports, generated from the automated circulation system, provide more information on use, some of which is useful to collection development operations.[30]

Yet the literature does not yield much evidence of demonstrated impact or use of automated circulation on collection maintenance and development.

Hawks reported on the concept of collection management information from circulation systems. She divided the type of information into three categories: user information by patron type and library; books issued and renewed by call-number range sorted by a number of variables such as semesters – useful for comparison of trends in research interests; and identification of high demand material. Some systems may also be able to report zero activity and identify materials that have not circulated within specified date ranges.[31]

The circulation systems currently installed have varying capacities to produce the management reports necessary to link titles with circulation history. The authors' informal survey of RLG libraries revealed that all did not yet have automated circulation systems. If they did, either the systems were incapable of producing the type of information needed for collection review, or the librarians had not yet attempted to use the reports generated to review the collections.

The authors queried vendors of several circulation systems to determine if title-specific circulation counts can be supplied by the automated system. All indicated that title-specific circulation data were collected and could be reported by the system. In some instances, this information could be supplied with little effort or advance planning when the system's parameters are initially set. Circulation systems which have report-writing capabilities as contrasted to those which issue only batch reports are more likely to give title-by-title use information. On-demand reports produced in response to a variety of specific questions – for example: which books in classification QA have circulated less than x times? – are the key to generating useful collection management data.

Many systems, Geac for example, can produce a list of books circulated and renewed. Geac reports on items circulated more than n times, where n is specified at the time the batch report is to be run. The library must choose between recording reserve circulations or reshelving statistics (in-house use) as a second type of use data. The total use is cumulative from the time the book is available on the system until the counter resets after 255 uses. Although it is unlikely that many academic titles will have that high amount of use, the person using the statistical report must be aware of the system parameters. It is not possible to specify date ranges or to determine the date of last use with the batch report.

Item record extract programs can yield a number of collection management reports, such as total circulations by classification number or range by publication date, if the compile options were initially set with this purpose in mind. These extracts are very CPU intensive and do not give item-specific information. Information in the author/title file cannot be correlated with information from the user file so it is not possible to determine what type of user (faculty, undergraduate, or whatever) uses a specified subject class of materials. It is possible to write specific programs to gain this type of information if the library has an archival transactions file and has been consistent in the use of fields over time.

This description is not meant to be unduly critical of the Geac system. It is the system with which the authors are most familiar and is fairly typical of the circulation systems that offer only batch report capabilities. The brief summaries of other systems' capabilities below do not explore the limitations or pitfalls, but indicate different approaches to generating collection-use data.

Data Resources Associates (DRA) offers a report-writer as an option. Included among the standard batch programs are Item Statistic Reports that can give historical information by call number. The Uncirculated

Item Report produces a listing of items which have not circulated since a specified date. The Circulated Item Report lists items that have circulated at least a specified number of times.

The NOTIS system, used in the largest academic libraries, produces reports through IBM's SAS capabilities, thereby providing virtually limitless customized reporting. However, manipulating data via the SAS programs appears to require a resident systems programmer. NOTIS users have begun to share programs through an electronic network, thus potentially reducing individual institutions' programming time.

UNYSIS' PALS circulation module is exemplary in that it offers a variety of ways to obtain relatively current collection-use data (yesterday, month to date, previous month, year to date and previous year). However, it does not keep cumulative statistics beyond the previous year. The library must intentionally archive the tapes and write programs to gain historical data beyond that available on-line. With the data held on-line, the system is flexible and will allow a non-programmer to create snapshot reports by classification or shelflist number for the current month's activity, including the number of items in current use, and the number of in-house uses. Previous and cumulative activity is available off-line only. This type of report can quickly answer the many volume-count questions collection development officers are asked to provide as part of collection evaluations.

One of PALS' most useful capabilities is the item record in the circulation database which gives the collection reviewer direct access to item-use data: year to date circulations; total circulations; year to date browses (reshelves); total browses; total renewals; current status; number of copies; date of entry into the system. One foresees that collection reviews for storage or deselection could be greatly enhanced by the use of mobile terminals in the stacks. This is quite an improvement over reading through batch reports and matching them with a title on the shelf, or pulled from the shelf and set aside while awaiting more information before a decision is made.

DYNIX has a number of collection management batch reports as well. Its Item Statistical Class Circulation Report records monthly activity by classification range as well as by material type. There is also a 'list of titles not used since . . . ' report. The report-writer provides the ability to search the database for use by title. This provides call number, title, author, use within a specified period and grand total use. Even more specific is the use by item which provides the last recorded use, the current status, the number of copies in the system and the price paid. Item level use can be provided within specific date ranges. This combination of programs appears to be the most useful, flexible and easy to produce of all the collection management reports reviewed.

All users of these programs are quick to comment on their utility being limited by the number and quality of records in the database. Databases created by direct keying of records into a system, or data loaded into a new system from an older circulation system created by keying records, are usually full of errors, some of which may affect the value of the reports.

Summary

A review of American library professional literature reveals consensus among librarians that collections should be reviewed regularly and irrelevant materials removed. It is also generally agreed that lack of use, lack of space and poor physical condition justify removal of volumes from the collection. In practice, most academic libraries have traditionally reviewed their collections with a view to withdrawing materials only in response to serious shortages of shelving space. Lack of reliable objective means to measure actual use of materials, lack of staff time to review the collections, and the possibility of unpleasant political repercussions on campus are among the reasons why review for deselection has had less attention in practice than a study of the theoretical literature would seem to imply. The collection philosophy of academic librarianship, that research materials should be collected in advance of need and retained in perpetuity, also contributes to a reluctance on the part of librarians finally and irrevocably to eliminate a book from the collection: remote storage of little-used titles is usually preferred, if available. The development of preservation programmes has forced libraries to review systematically at least portions of their collections; the very existence of a preservation programme, however, tends to eliminate poor physical condition as justification for deselection. Preservation microfilm may be considered a form of remote storage, since it is another way of getting little-used material out of prime stack space without actually removing it from the collection. Automated circulation systems have, in theory, the capacity to produce objective data on the frequency with which individual titles are used, but this capacity has not yet been fully developed or fully exploited.

References

1. *The de-acquisitions librarian* (1976), **1** (1-2), New York: Haworth Press.
2. *Guide to review of library collections: preservation, storage and deselection* (Draft), Chicago: Association for Library Collections and Technical Services Collection Management and Development Committee, August 1989.
3. Mosher, P.H. (1980), 'Managing library collections: the process of review and pruning', in R.D. Stueart and G.B. Miller (eds), *Collection development in libraries; a treatise, Part A*, Greenwich, Conn.: JAI Press, pp.159-181.
4. Ibid., pp.161-162.
5. Eliot, C.W. (1902), 'The division of a library into books in use, and books not in use, with different storage methods for the two classes of books', *The library journal*, **27** (7), 51-56.
6. 'Sifting as a library policy', *The library journal*, **18** (4), 118-119.
7. Green, S.S. (1893), 'Adaptation of libraries into constituencies', *The library journal*, **18** (7), 219-220.
8. Slote, S.J. (1989), *Weeding library collections – III*, 3rd rev. ed., Littleton, Colo.: Libraries Unlimited.
9. Lancaster, F.W. (1988), 'Obsolescence, weeding and the utilization of space', *Wilson library bulletin*, **62** (May), 47-50.
10. Hall, B.H. (1985), *Collection assessment manual for college and university libraries*, Phoenix, Ariz.: Oryx Press, pp.70-78.
11. Lockett, B.A. (ed.) (1989), *Guide to the evaluation of library collections*, (Collection management and development guides, no. 2), RTSD CMDC Subcommittee on Guidelines for Collection Development, Chicago: American Library Association.
12. *Guide to review of library collections*, ref. 2, p.17.
13. Roy, L. (1988), 'Does weeding increase circulation? A review of the related literature', *Collection management*, **10** (1-2), 141-156.
14. Hayden, R. (1987), 'If it circulates, keep it', *Library journal*, **112** (10), 43-47.
15. Atkinson, R.W. (1986), 'Selection for preservation: a materialistic approach', *Library resources and technical services*, **30** (4), 341-353.
16. Perkins, D.L. (ed.) (1979), *Guidelines for collection development*, Chicago: American Library Association.
17. *Guide to review of library collections*, ref. 2, p.19.
18. Atkinson, R.W. ref. 15, p.342.
19. Baatz, W.H. (1978), 'Collection development in 19 libraries of the Association of Research Libraries', *Library acquisitions: practice and theory*, **2**, p.116.
20. Tillman, H.N. (1988), 'The politics of weeding', *Education libraries*, **13** (Winter), 16-19.
21. Stankus, T. (1986), 'Journal weeding in relation to declining faculty member publishing', *Science and technology libraries*, **6** (3), 43-53.
22. Lucker, J.K. et al. (1986), 'Weeding collections in an academic library system: Massachusetts Institute of Technology', *Science and technology libraries*, **6** (3), 11-23.
23. Burdick, A.J. (1989), 'Science Citation Index data as a safety net for basic science books considered for weeding', *Library resources and technical services*, **33** (4), 367-373.
24. Budd, J. (1986), 'A citation study of American literature: implications for collection management', *Collection management*, **8** (Summer), 49-62.
25. Engeldinger, E.A. (1985), 'Weeding of academic library reference collections: a survey of current practice', *RQ*, **25** (3), 366-372.
26. Biggs, M. and V. Biggs (1987) 'Reference collection development in academic libraries: report of a survey', *RQ*, **27** (1), 67-79.

27. Pierce, S.J. (1990), *Weeding and maintenance of reference collections* (The reference librarian, no. 29), New York: Haworth Press.
28. Taborsky, T and P. Lenkowski (1989), *Collection development policies for college libraries*, (Clip note no. 11), Chicago: American Library Association, Association of College and Research Libraries.
29. UCSB and the Southern Regional Library Facility. Personal correspondence from the University of California Santa Barbara, 22 November 1989.
30. Toyama, R. (1989), 'The year's work in circulation control 1988', *Library resources and technical services*, **33** (4), 331-334.
31. Hawks, C.P. (1988), 'Management information gleaned from automated library systems', *Information technology and libraries*, **7** (2), 132-133.

10 Cooperative collection development: progress from apotheosis to reality

Patricia L. Bril

Although the concept of resource sharing has been traced back as far as the library at Alexandria, the impulse toward cooperative collection development, in the sense of actual coordinated and collaborative activities, has emerged comparatively recently.[1] Instances of true cooperative endeavours in American academic libraries can, however, be found as early as 1933 when Duke University and the University of North Carolina at Chapel Hill began to share responsibility for collection coverage and, thus, to depend thereafter on one another's resources.[2]

Much of the literature chronicling the various historical attempts at genuine cooperative collection development assumes a sceptical if not cynical perspective. Indeed, there is a wealth of evidence of creative ideas and enthusiastic plans which were never brought to fruition as well as detailed accounts of problems or barriers associated with cooperation in general. To wit, 'The field is littered with networking and consortium casualties.'[3] Yet, one wonders if some of the pessimism stems from perception of a 'half-empty' cooperative cup rather than one which is 'half-full'. In the light of the many previous admonitions to cooperation and predictions of assured success, it is probably unwise to argue now that cooperative collection development has reached a certain threshold of inevitability, and hence acceptability. However, the evidence to support such an argument is compelling. The ratio between environmental incentives and barriers appears to be steadily rising.

For purposes of this discussion, 'resource sharing' is seen to be the present capitalization on past decisions about collection building and service provision, whether or not those decisions were originally directed toward cooperative goals. 'Cooperative collection development', on the other hand, is represented by intentional present actions aimed at the future realization of potentials for resource sharing. According to the 1983 RTSD *Guide to coordinated and cooperative collection development*, such activities involve two or more libraries entering into an agreement to share in the development and management of collections. And, 'Ultimately, cooperative collection development should provide a national network of dependencies and distributed responsibilities.'[4]

Let us examine some of the environmental factors which influence movement toward or resistance to cooperation.

Environmental factors

Information explosion/economic shifts

The relatively rich acquisitions budgets enjoyed by many academic libraries in the 1960s led to a corresponding de-emphasis on cooperative efforts and a revival of the quest for self-sufficiency in the building of comprehensive research collections. However, this era was short-lived and the fiscal stringencies of academe in the 1970s and 1980s have once again pushed to the fore discussions of cooperative collection development. The increase in the production of information has been well-documented and has caused even the most well-endowed research libraries to fall behind in the proportion of the world's publications (annual output approaching one million) they can hope to purchase and make available to their clientele. The escalation in serials prices and their predominance in research have exacerbated this strained situation even further.

Cooperative activities are attractive because they enhance access to a broad range of materials which are financially impossible for any one library to support. Naturally there are also costs associated with cooperation: such costs may include support of a central facility and/or staff; shared purchases; use of membership fees; and local expenditures foregone in favour of network or consortial collecting priorities. 'The reality is that libraries are pursuing cooperative collection management (just as they have pursued automation) not to reduce costs but to improve services.'[5]

Technology

Considerable progress has been made in the technology by which bibliographic data can be recorded and shared electronically. Moving well beyond the printed union catalogues and serials lists of previous decades, the major bibliographic utilities such as OCLC, RLIN, WLN, and UTLAS allow librarians to have on-line access to the holdings of libraries on a regional or national level. With the wholesale retrospective conversion of bibliographic records for incorporation in these utilities as well as in local integrated (turnkey or otherwise) automated systems, the possibilities for making use of such data increase accordingly. Highly sophisticated software applications also now allow individual libraries or consortia to analyse and manipulate data for a variety of purposes in support of cooperative efforts. In addition, the speed and quality of document delivery via telefacsimile transmission has improved immeasurably over that provided by equipment of just a few years ago. As a result, the entire character and attractiveness of interlibrary cooperation has been transformed.

Knowledge about collection characteristics and use

In the past, librarians expressed concern about the lack of concrete data which could be shared about their own and others' collections. Printed union lists and the emerging bibliographic utilities helped alleviate this situation. However, through such projects as the National Shelflist Count and the North American Collections Inventory Project (NCIP), considerably more precision may be obtained. In addition, overlap studies have contributed to the body of knowledge about relative duplication, strengths and weaknesses of collections. Furthermore, many libraries have undertaken use studies of their collections to assess patterns which might inform subsequent cooperative endeavours. The controversial study at the University of Pittsburgh suggested that nearly half of the volumes in a research collection may never be used. Other studies show that approximately 20 per cent of a collection accounts for 80 per cent of its use.[6]

Suitable models

Even when receptivity to cooperation exists within libraries, concern about the lack of suitable partners or organizational models is often cited as an obstacle.[7] Various professional groups have sought to remedy this situation. The aforementioned RTSD *Guide to coordinated and cooperative collection development* suggests a variety of preconditions for success, pitfalls to avoid, and models to consider.[8] The Association of Research Libraries Office of Management Studies (ARL OMS) produced a Systems and Procedures Exchange Center (SPEC) Kit on cooperative collection development, including examples of actual working agreements.[9] Numerous programmes and workshops on the subject have been presented, including the two-day 1985 Conference in Chicago entitled 'Coordinating cooperative collection development: a national perspective.'[10]

Higher education institutional climate

Obviously, academic library cooperation cannot be considered outside the context of the larger institutional setting. The library's collections and services, after all, exist in support of the college or university's curricular and research programmes.

The tremendous growth in the number and scope of higher education institutions during the 1960s and 1970s resulted in concomitant challenges to libraries. Early on, Downs commented on this 'overnight' transformation of agricultural, mechanical and teachers' colleges into universities: 'The financial implications for the states are staggering, if these expanded institutions are to become universities in fact as well as in name.'[11] The vastly increased number of users now requiring sophisticated (foreign, fugitive, and so on) library materials, coupled with more stringent research demands placed upon faculty, put added pressure on what in many cases are already inadequate resources.

The behavioural characteristics of these researchers must be taken into account. 'In what has been described as the "law of least effort", patrons usually place convenience of access well before quality of resource.'[12] Such behaviour may run afoul of cooperative efforts, which by definition involve a trade-off of some immediate support to local users in order to contribute materials in support of an extended network of users. Differences in the research patterns and expectations of various disciplines also should be noted. The humanist who attempts to explore the universe of knowledge on a subject may have a different tolerance for delays in obtaining materials than the scientist who values currency and relevance over comprehensiveness.[13]

Achieving an organizational structure attractive to all cooperating participants may be problematic; perceived loss of local control over collecting policies and practices may be repugnant to the library's staff and/or its institutional users. Universities which historically have competed for students, faculty, research grants, and sports honours may be less inclined to share responsibility for provision of library materials to a broader client base. Cooperative activities may be seen as a high priority within the library profession at large but a relatively low priority in terms of funding or local support within an individual institution.

Superseded cooperative programmes

Although no longer operating, several ambitious cooperative programmes are worth examining in the light of the current environment. The reasons for their demise may be instructive for future efforts.

Perhaps the most well-known cooperative collection development effort was the Farmington Plan which was initiated by ARL in 1948 in response to concern about acquiring foreign literature. The plan was a voluntary agreement of sixty American research libraries for '. . . selecting, acquiring, promptly cataloguing, and lending of foreign materials that are considered of research value.'[14] Collecting responsibilities were divided upon subject and geographic bases, dependent on the region; orders were made through assigned dealers in Europe and independent arrangements in other regions. When the Plan was discontinued in 1972 the reasons cited were: problems with dealers, duplication and gaps in coverage, disagreement about the definition of 'research value' and incongruity with existing institutional collecting priorities. In the end, many libraries moved to blanket order programmes of their own for such publications. In general, inadequate communication among participants and with vendors undermined the Plan's effectiveness. In 1959 a separate effort was initiated by the Seminar on the Acquisition of Latin American Library Materials (SALALM), in which forty libraries cooperated in the Latin American Cooperative Acquisition Project (LACAP). However, this programme was also discontinued in 1972.

Two programmes spearheaded by the Library of Congress were also important in earlier cooperative collection development. In 1961, PL-480 allowed blocked foreign currencies, obtained through agricultural trade with several developing countries, to be used to acquire multiple copies of publications. These materials were distributed to selected American research libraries. Yet, one by one these surplus currencies disappeared, with India being the last participant in the programme. PL-480 was a precursor to and was later coordinated with the National Program for Acquisitions and Cataloguing (NPAC). This programme was part of the Higher Education Act (HEA) of 1965. Title IIC of the HEA authorized funds for the Library of Congress

> ... for the purpose of 1) acquiring, as far as possible, all materials currently published throughout the world which are of value to scholarship; and 2) providing catalog information for these materials promptly after receipt, and distributing bibliographic information by printing catalog cards and by other means, and enabling the Library of Congress to use for exchange and other purposes such of these materials as are not needed for its collection.[15]

The effectiveness of NPAC was directly linked to the extent of foreign purchasing and processing which could be undertaken by the Library of Congress; unfortunately, due to budget stringencies in recent years, foreign acquisitions have received lower priority, and processing backlogs have resulted from staffing shortages.

Current national programmes

Despite the reduction or outright discontinuance of the programmes described above, some national initiatives for cooperative collection development have been sustained, and these remaining organizations continue to diversify their programmes in response to their constituents' priorities.

Center for Research Libraries

Begun in 1949 as the Midwest Inter-Library Center, this cooperative soon became national in scope. The Center for Research Libraries (CRL) now includes over 100 member libraries. Based in Chicago, CRL acquires, stores and makes available to the membership highly specialized microform sets as well as foreign serials, government documents and dissertations. In addition, indexed serials not held by four or more North American libraries are sought and maintained; a special effort has been made to hold all titles (not held elsewhere) indexed by *Biological abstracts* and *Chemical abstracts*. Much material obtained under PL-480 is retained by CRL. Suggestions for purchase are submitted and then decided upon by the member libraries. Current holdings number around four million volumes, plus more than one million microforms. Members see CRL's greatest advantages as long-term cost avoidance and increased access to materials rather than immediate cost savings. In fact, many are critical of the high membership fees. A move to a new facility solved some physical problems. CRL's future direction has undergone considerable scrutiny in recent years, and many now support efforts to scale down its coverage of serials held by a number of other libraries and to focus exclusively on more elusive items.[16]

At one time there was discussion of CRL assuming the role of a National Periodicals Center (NPC) such as the British Library Document Supply Centre in Great Britain. It has long been recognized that the Library of Congress does not serve the same sort of central role as the British Library. The NPC was proposed in 1965 legislation, H.R. 5192, but met with strong opposition from a number of constituencies. Opponents included public libraries fearing dominance of research library interests; publishers and the information industry, naturally concerned about adverse economic consequences; and, somewhat surprisingly, existing networks and consortia worried about possible government intervention and control. Many also argued that there are sufficient existing periodical collections distributed throughout the US and that they simply need to be linked more effectively together. DeGennaro offered the view that, given America's tradition of independence and decentralization, 'A single facility . . . is probably not a viable long-term solution to our resource sharing needs.'[17]

Research Libraries Group

In 1974, the libraries of Columbia, Harvard, Yale and New York Public Library joined together as the Research Libraries Group (RLG) to develop a shared computer processing system. Subsequently, other libraries joined and the Group moved from a regional to national arena of activity. The Stanford automated system BALLOTS formed the basis of the current Research Libraries Information Network (RLIN). Approximately 35 major libraries constitute the governing membership with nearly twice that number serving in affiliated member categories. With RLIN as a basis of common knowledge about member holdings, RLG has made cooperative collection development a high priority. Toward this end, the RLG Collection Development and Management Committee formulated the Conspectus, a collection assessment tool described further below. More recently, pilot studies for an RLG Long Term Serials Project have been completed for the subjects of business, chemistry and mathematics. Responsibility for support of 2 000 serials, with subscription prices of $200 or more, will be distributed among the participating libraries on a basis proportional to their relative holdings. Responsible libraries will agree to maintain subscriptions for at least five years and make them available to other RLG libraries. The project will be extended to cover additional subjects in future.[18]

RLG Conspectus

Perhaps one of the most significant breakthroughs in bringing cooperation from the position of pious platitude to actual accomplishment is the RLG Conspectus. Previously, there had been no systematic and agreed-upon method by which to compare and contrast research collections. Although the National Shelflist Count provided useful quantitative data there was no qualitative component, and the number of categories (approximately 500) was thought to be insufficient to measure, with precision, highly specialized research collections.

Developed in 1980, the Conspectus is designed to be a mapping and communication tool for libraries. Nearly 7 000 Library of Congress Classification-based categories are used. Librarians rank their collections from 0-5 in each relevant category with 0 being 'out of scope' and 5 representing a 'comprehensive' collection. Both Existing Collection Strength (ECS) and Current Collecting Intensity (CCI) are measured. In addition, language codes distinguish collecting patterns which cover all languages from those which concentrate on only one language, English or otherwise. Moreover, narrative comments can be included on the Conspectus forms. These data are then entered into the RLG Conspectus On-line for which dial-up access is available to all participants. Based on the strengths and weaknesses discerned from this instrument, Primary Collecting Responsibilities (PCRs) are assigned to encourage libraries to maintain Level 4 collections (loosely defined as 70-85 per cent of published information in a particular field) or above. The Library of Congress has agreed to serve in a backup role in any areas where Level 4 collections do not exist elsewhere; this opens the way for the Library of Congress to consider cutting back in other subject areas already well covered nationally.[19]

After initial tests and refinements, the ARL adopted the RLG Conspectus for use in its on-going North American Collections Inventory Project (NCIP), which seeks to include all the major research libraries in the US and Canada. 'The development of a national conspectus is a project of potential significance approaching that of the National Union Catalog of past generations.'[20] At this writing many participants have completed the Conspectus evaluations and others are nearing completion. In anticipation of the need for local manipulation and analysis of this vast database, microcomputer applications software is being developed concurrently by RLG and ARL OMS.

Beyond the NCIP participants, many other academic libraries and library networks have employed the Conspectus approach. The impact of the RLG Conspectus has even been felt internationally. Canadian libraries created a bilingual version, which has also allowed French libraries to experiment with the Conspectus. The British Library, a consortium of eleven Scottish libraries, and several Australian libraries have completed Conspectus projects. In addition, the Netherlands and Scandinavia have demonstrated interest in Conspectus-based collection assessments.[21]

The Conspectus approach has not been a panacea. Medium- and smaller-sized libraries find the numbers of Library of Congress categories too numerous, yet the collecting levels too restrictive. As a result, some have divided collecting levels in the lower ranges (1, 2 and 3) into subcategories, for example 3a for an undergraduate collection. In some cases, the 7 000 subject categories have been translated into Dewey Decimal Classification equivalents and/or reduced to the 500 used for the National Shelflist Count or abridged still further to some 20-25 basic subject divisions. Some believed the usefulness of the original Conspectus to be minimal for interdisciplinary and area studies. As a result, a two-track system of reporting was created to accommodate such concerns. The Conspectus also has been criticized as time consuming, impressionistic and highly subjective.[22] In response to the latter criticism, verification studies, benchmarking and comparisons with the National Shelflist Count are used to refine assessments made by subject bibliographers.

In general, there is agreement on the need to move beyond the process of the Conspectus to the content in achieving cooperative aims.[23] Many observe that PCRs have only been assigned in obvious cases which merely reinforce the *status quo* and that no substantive cooperative dependencies have emerged.[24]

On the positive side, others cite that the process of Conspectus assessment has facilitated discussion with other libraries because a common frame of reference now exists. Stam believes the 'Conspectus constitutes an insurance policy against reduced budgets, the framework for redistribution of our own financial resources and the groundwork for wide access.'[25] The Conspectus results have also provided a useful basis for formulation or refinement of collection development policies; examination of bibliographers' workloads; representation of the library's position to institutional administrators/faculty/accreditation agencies; and attraction of external funding or donations. The Conspectus has even been heralded as an excellent training tool for new bibliographers.[26]

Local, state and regional programmes

In addition to the high-profile national efforts in cooperative collection development, a number of regional, state and local projects are also thriving. In fact, despite advances in technology which are designed to mitigate geographic barriers, the physical proximity of libraries continues to be a strong determinant in the success of attempts at cooperation. The existence of reciprocal borrowing privileges and rapid document delivery contribute to users' comfort with resource sharing. As noted by Hewitt and Shipman in their 1983 survey of ARL members to determine the level and nature of cooperative collection development, any attempt to encapsulate the highly dynamic current situation is akin to trying to hit a moving target.[27] However, a number of well-established as well as fledgling programmes deserve mention. For convenience sake, they are divided into two categories, those programmes which include academic libraries exclusively, and those which cut across types of libraries.

Academic library programmes

Already mentioned is the long-standing success of the Triangle Research Libraries Network in North Carolina, which now also includes North

Carolina State University in addition to the founding members, Duke University and the University of North Carolina at Chapel Hill. Each library alerts the others to expensive purchases, and internal justification for new serials titles must take into account availability elsewhere within the Network. Although occasionally special funds are attracted by the Network, most support comes from the ongoing budgets of the individual libraries.[28]

Another well-established cooperative is the Hampshire Inter-Library Center (HILC) which, since its founding in 1951, has evolved from a central depository for little-used items to a distributed arrangement in which each of the five academic library members assumes responsibility for holding and sharing certain titles. Much of the cooperation is focused on serials and last copy agreements. Dues support the Center's operation.[29]

In California, the nine-campus University of California (UC) system has operated a Shared Purchase Program since 1976. Annually a percentage (now 3 per cent, approximately $300 000) of the combined UC acquisitions funds are allocated for central purchasing. Stanford University, which already had a long-standing tradition of resource sharing with the nearby UC Berkeley campus, joined the Shared Purchase Program in 1978; accommodations for this mix of private and publicly supported institutions have been accomplished. However, the lack of a common on-line system inhibits direct access to members' holdings. Titles are suggested by each of the campuses and the collection development officers vote to determine which titles are bought and where these items will be housed. Users are alerted to such items through entries in the UC On-line Catalog, MELVYL, and through appropriate indexes or finding lists retained by all libraries.[30] Until recently, the shared purchases were normally expensive microform sets or other esoteric items. However, one of the latest decisions was to purchase rights to the magnetic tapes for MEDLINE and Institute for Scientific Information (ISI) *Current contents*. These databases have been mounted centrally on MELVYL for mutual access.[31] The UC is also embarking on a cooperative approach to holdings of scientific journals in translation, Pacific Rim trade journals, and East Asian newspaper backfiles. The personnel costs associated with the mechanics of these programmes and their attendant meetings are seen to be far outweighed by extended access to materials and valuable face-to-face communication among the collection development officers.[32]

Since 1981 the New York coordinated collection development programme has formed an integral part of the New York Reference and Research Library Resources System (3Rs). Under this programme, all public and private academic libraries in the state (over 175 in total) are eligible for grants, based on enrolment, which range from $4300 to $75 000.[33] Grants are awarded by the state on a competitive basis, taking into account evidence of regional analysis of collections, identification of needs, and formulation of a rational plan to meet those needs through cooperative collection development.

In order to facilitate the very labour-intensive process of collection analysis, several cooperative efforts have focused on extracting comparative data from bibliographic utilities. The Committee on Institutional Cooperation (the Big Ten universities plus the University of Chicago) have used both the RLIN and OCLC databases to compare holding patterns in selected subject areas.[34]

In a collective evaluation project, a consortium of seventeen North Texas academic libraries has experimented with OCLC archival tapes to generate data for Conspectus subject categories.[35] In response to needs such as that of the North Texas experiment, the OCLC and AMIGOS bibliographic networks have jointly developed a CD-ROM Collection Analysis system which allows libraries to examine their own holdings in relation to those of a standardized peer group or a user-specified peer group of libraries. Gaps, overlap and unique titles can thus be ascertained. The effectiveness of this system is, of course, dependent upon the accuracy and completeness of the bibliographic database. And, at present, only ten years of coverage are provided.[36]

In Alabama, as part of a statewide effort to upgrade the higher educational system, funds are being allocated each year to institutions to develop their library collections in support of academic programmes. Efforts are coordinated by the Network of Alabama Academic Libraries (NAAL), sponsored by the Alabama Commission on Higher Education. Conspectus results are used to demonstrate the level of need in specific programme areas. 'Alabama . . . is considering its total academic library resources as one research collection.'[37] The emphasis is on *local* collection building rather than shared purchase; libraries are encouraged to build on historical strengths and core collections. Both one-time and ongoing funding is provided and five-year reviews require institutional proof of commitment of such funds to library resources. The state also compensates net lenders and supports free facsimile transmission throughout the network.[38]

Multitype library cooperatives

Alaska was one of the first states to adapt the RLG Conspectus to the needs of a small and multitype library environment. The situation in Alaska is particularly conducive to cooperative ventures: the population is sparse and libraries are relatively isolated throughout this large state. In addition, the economy is highly dependent on the natural resource market. Assurance of adequate information resources, even during lean financial times, was a high priority.[39]

The Alaskan Conspectus experience formed the basis for the more extensive Pacific Northwest Conspectus funded by the Fred Meyer Charitable Trust for the five-state cooperative, Library and Information Resource Network (LIRN). The Network involves 240 libraries. A flexible Conspectus approach allowed libraries to select Dewey or Library of Congress classification versions, with varying levels of subject categories and intensity indicators.[40]

As a subset of LIRN, the Valley Library Consortium formed the Valley Automated Library Network (VALNET). VALNET serves a relatively small and isolated region of Idaho and Washington. One cooperative outcome is an agreement to rotate purchases of expensive continuations to assure at least one current edition is held within the region.[41]

The New York Metropolitan Reference and Research Library Agency (METRO) is also using the LIRN-modified Conspectus. In addition to learning more about one another's resources through this effort, central funds are being pooled to strengthen resources in one subject area per year within the region.[42]

In Colorado, the Colorado Alliance for Research Libraries (CARL) began as an exclusively academic library consortium but has expanded to include a mix of library types. Again, a modified Conspectus project was undertaken and the Colorado Comparative Matrix (CCM) was developed to identify collection strengths and weaknesses. In addition, the collection development policies of all libraries are available on-line. Cooperative collection development activities are pursued by CARL's Committee on Library Acquisitions (COLA). Pooled resources of not more than 1 per cent of the CARL libraries' combined budgets are used for shared purchase of such items as expensive sets. The goal is 'to manage or access the collections of its members as if they were one collection.'[43]

A relatively new entrant to the field is the North Bay Cooperative

Library System, which involves seventeen libraries in Northern California. Agreement is being sought on primary and secondary collection responsibilities with mechanisms by which each library would route suggested titles to the most appropriate institution to consider for purchase.[44]

Illinois is perhaps the leading light in statewide resource sharing. Reciprocal borrowing agreements, a common circulation system (LCS), and a developing common on-line catalogue (ILLINET On-line) have done much to inspire further cooperation in the arena of collections. One of the more interesting results is that the University of Illinois, the largest library in the state, is actually a substantial net borrower. In fact, 50 per cent of the materials it borrows are held in its own collections but are either missing or otherwise unavailable. The Illinois experience supports the notion that *all* libraries, not just smaller ones, have much to gain from cooperation. Illinois is perhaps unique in not adapting the RLG Conspectus model but rather in developing its own Illinois Collection Analysis Matrix (ICAM) based upon quantitative (National Shelflist Count) as well as qualitative assessments by bibliographers. The Illinois Board of Higher Education has subsequently provided grants to purchase expensive or little-used items not readily available within the state. With LSCA funds, a strategic plan for a comprehensive multitype network system has been formulated and a statewide coordinator has been appointed. Cooperative collection development is a major component of the plan.[45]

Special applications/refinements

Most of the cooperative activity described thus far has related to general library collections. However, there have also been a number of cooperative initiatives, or refinements of broader applications, in specialized subject areas.

The RLG Conspectus has been instrumental in cooperative collection planning for law libraries, music libraries, East Asian Studies libraries, and the Seminar on the Acquisition of Latin American Library Materials (SALALM).[46] A consortium of five private colleges in Idaho and Montana are cooperating specifically in holdings of education materials.[47] One particularly interesting study, funded by CONOCO, examined research collections in geology and German literature. When subject bibliographers had information available to them about other libraries' holdings, they expressed a willingness to forgo 40 to 50 per cent of their suggested purchases. Their primary concern was that the material be held somewhere within the region.[48]

A number of cooperative efforts have focused almost exclusively on serial literature. This is especially true in medical libraries, where reliance on serials is strong. Roberts provides a good overview of current efforts, including that of the Pittsburgh Regional Library Center, which has a two-stage cancellation notification process to allow input from nearby libraries before subscriptions are actually dropped. Also mentioned is an agreement between Washington State University and the University of Idaho libraries to stagger binding of journals to assure availability to users in the region at all times.[49]

In the Greater Midwest Regional Medical Library Network, Millson-Martula highlights a Conspectus analysis of holdings, augmented by additional medical descriptors and objective indicators of size and physical condition of materials. The Network is pursuing a goal of coverage in any given subject with three Level 4 collections in the region. Pooled funds are directed toward filling in identifiable gaps.[50]

With the current emphasis on rationalizing expensive serials holdings, the need to browse contents of journals not owned by one's library has increased. Commercial products, ISI's *Current contents* and CARL's *Uncover* are now being incorporated in many libraries' on-line catalogue environments.[51] In other cases more basic means are used, such as exchanging photocopies of journal contents pages with libraries within a cooperating group.

Materials held in special collections are, by definition, problematic in terms of cooperation, because many represent unique and/or fragile items. However, Smith examines the types of agreements which have been explored by some libraries in coordinating development of highly specialized collections, including a case study of the North Carolina experience.[52]

Because collection management involves retention as well as initial selection decisions, cooperative endeavours must extend their attentions to weeding, storage and preservation issues. Obviously, the complexity of weeding is affected by prior agreements of libraries to assure Primary Collecting Responsibilities. Successful storage centres have been developed by some cooperatives such as the University of California's Northern and Southern Regional Library facilities. The establishment of acceptable ownership and access policies is important to the smooth functioning of centralized storage units.

The Research Libraries Group has also established the category of Primary Preservation Responsibility (PPR) and encourages participation of libraries outside RLG to extend potential coverage. Nevertheless, questions persist: how many copies should be preserved and in which format? Atkinson has developed a useful typology to apply in preservation decision-making. In stressing that 'quantity is quality in a research library' and the concomitant need to preserve 'trash' in order to put 'quality' materials in perspective for posterity, libraries are challenged quickly to coordinate responsibility for such coverage and to record decisions in shared bibliographic databases so as to avoid duplication of effort.[53]

Looking to the future

As libraries strive to move farther along the continuum from simple resource sharing to more sophisticated applications of cooperative collection development, several issues must be resolved.

Coordination and leadership

It is unlikely, and many believe undesirable, that a centralized agency such as the British Library Document Supply Centre will emerge preeminent from the diverse American networking and consortial arena described above. Yet there is a genuine need for a greater degree of coordination of cooperative collection development activities across network boundaries. The Library of Congress is not assuming this role. Fortunately, some leadership is emerging from such national organizations as RLG and ARL as well as a few state agencies for higher education. In addition, the professional associations are providing a variety of fora for discussion of this issue and are producing practical guidelines. On an international level, some intersection must also be made with UNESCO's Universal Availability of Publications (UAP), a core programme of the International Federation of Library Associations (IFLA). And the implications for coordinated resource development of the political changes in Eastern Europe, coupled with the European Community changes in 1992, must be considered.

Some fear that as individual libraries enter into more and more cooperative agreements, at different levels and with varying conditions, it will become increasingly difficult to decipher and disentangle the web of commitments. Certain agreements may restrict participation in others. How unfortunate it would be if these very positive impulses toward cooperation were thwarted by the resultant confusion of an overlapping series of arrangements.

Because the nature of most cooperative plans is entirely voluntary, enlightened self-interest and moral suasion are probably the chief motivations to participation. Without strong assurances that cooperating partners will not renege on collecting obligations, libraries may be hesitant to enter into alliances; there is an understandable fear of having to acquire materials retrospectively, at great expense or effort, should such alliances eventually collapse. Weber observes that cooperation seems to work best among universities of equal status or widely different status; the middle range of institutions are less inclined to pursue or be satisfied with the results of resource sharing.[54] Hewitt and Shipman also found that cooperation was more prevalent among the largest and smallest ARL members, again suggesting the middle ground to be far less fertile in cultivating cooperation. They also discovered concentrations of cooperative collection development in the easternmost and westernmost parts of the United States.[55] While there may be plausible explanations for lower rates of cooperation among middle-sized and/or Midwestern institutions, these are just a few examples illustrative of the highly complex profile of cooperation. More systematic coordination and development of extant programmes might also result in serving better those sorts of libraries which thus far, for whatever reason, have not found the available opportunities for participation to be attractive.

Determination of collecting responsibilities

In a cooperative environment, libraries cease to be judged solely on the size of their collections; such factors as speed of access, cost of provision and user satisfaction rate must also enter into any evaluative equation.[56] However, in all of the rhetoric about access instead of ownership, one must not lose sight of the fact that the materials must be identified, selected and retained somewhere in the first place, or the need for access thereto becomes a moot point. Libraries must be careful not to slip into the more circumscribed role of serving merely as information brokers.[57]

Most agree that more than one copy of all but the most exotic material should be acquired by the nation's libraries in the aggregate. This provides an insurance policy to protect against possible destruction of an item by decay, natural disaster, or criminal/military acts.[58] The degree of overlap in existing collections is not nearly as great as one might expect. For small and medium-sized libraries, overlap rarely exceeds 50 per cent.[59] Studies of large research collections reveal that unique items often account for over 70 per cent of a given library's holdings.[60] On the other hand, even the combined resources of the RLG libraries and the Library of Congress do not represent the entire universe of published information. This fact presents a strong argument against the purely *laissez-faire* approach to cooperation, in the hope that libraries somehow will serendipitously select materials which complement rather than duplicate one another's collections. Overall coordination of individual collecting patterns is essential to ensure as complete coverage of the world's literature as possible.

To achieve such coordination, Primary Collecting Responsibilities must extend beyond confirming the *status quo* for categories on which all acquiesce because of historical precedent. PCRs must also be assigned in categories where more difficult commitments and concessions will need to be made. Ironically, some have observed that the post-Conspectus era is one in which even more Level 4 Current Collecting Intensities are pursued as *de facto* arguments for larger budgets.

Related to the assignment of PCRs is the issue of defining core collections, with the assumption that the areas ripest for resource sharing lie outside the core. Herein lies what could become a rather circular exercise in which librarians attempt *ex biblioteca* to determine what in future will be little-used items. One method recommended for distinguishing core from peripheral materials is to approach the question from a functional rather than subject-based perspective, that is, to consider within the core reference sources, current journal literature and basic instructional materials.[61]

Much has been said about moving from collection-centred to client-centred cooperation. Naturally each library seeks to build, within its financial means, the collection most responsive to the present and future needs of its clientele. However, some librarians caution that over reliance on use or user studies may diminish the role of the librarian selector and result in demand-driven collections, which would be characterized by their homogeneity as well as high use.[62] It is a challenge for librarians to develop the means to satisfy immediate local resource needs, without abdicating the responsibility to contribute to the provision of information on a global basis for future generations.

Technological development

Emerging technologies will continue to influence the character of our cooperative activities. Advances in resource-sharing technology make cooperative collection development more palatable to users by increasing the speed and quality of access to information. Ferguson describes five highly innovative but small-scale electronic information delivery projects in the Northwest by the Fred Meyer Charitable Trust, including the application of simultaneous remote-searching techniques.[63] The current technological transformation of facsimile transmitters, from slow cumbersome machines to fast versatile systems, provides a classic example of how quickly the widespread acceptance of a previously ineffectual technology can occur. Better on-line links to acquisitions as well as cataloguing data of other libraries would open the way for more proactive rather than reactive decisions when libraries are considering purchase of non-core items. Microforms are often the object of resource-sharing efforts but are seen by many to be an interim medium. The development of an alternative to current microformats or at least better means of sharing such material, for instance by discovering less costly methods of digitizing images to be stored electronically, could have a dramatic impact on document delivery.

In the foreseeable future, libraries will be pursuing cooperative means to collect, share and preserve traditional formats for posterity. However, these means may become increasingly technologically sophisticated. Concurrently, issues involving the cooperative provision of non-traditional formats must be faced, along with their attendant concerns of licensing, copyright, and so on. Thus far the widely discussed phenomenon of the paperless society has not advanced as rapidly as originally predicted by those such as Lancaster. However, if and when electronic publishing is pursued on a larger scale than currently, the maintenance of backfiles, among many other issues, must be addressed. Visionaries such as Ted Nelson of Autodesk continue to predict a sort of seamless web of knowledge nodes:

> ... Project Xanadu, a plan to use the world's computers as so many windows on all the writing ever produced ... All this literature would be stored in one huge electronic file accessible from any PC or other computer. Anyone could browse randomly in this digital repository, choose any number of passages, and assemble them into a new document that would become another part of the Xanadu collection.[64]

What role libraries would play in such a scenario is highly indeterminate but nonetheless challenging.

Institutional and user relations

Obviously, librarians cannot pursue cooperative collection development in a vacuum. Our collections should not only reflect current academic programmes and research priorities but also, as far as possible, should preserve those of the past and anticipate those of the future. This is clearly an area where libraries must assume a leadership role within their respective institutions. For better or worse, the most effective cooperation will also have the most visible impact on the parent organization. Library administrators need to be prepared to articulate the advantages promptly and persuasively. Individual universities have no more hope of achieving self-sufficiency by providing curricular and research programmes in all fields of knowledge than libraries do of independently satisfying all of the institution's information needs. Greater rationalization of graduate and research activities would undoubtedly simplify the pursuit of cooperative collection development. 'Librarians are in an excellent position to provide much information and guidance in helping their institutions make difficult choices . . . Library cooperation is a necessary – although insufficient – condition for the strengthening of higher education [in this country].'[65]

Librarians and university funding agents must be cautioned against viewing cooperative collection development as primarily a budget-cutting measure. Indeed, there will be benefits realized in terms of foregone purchases as well as some staff and space savings. But the countervailing cost to borrow (provide access to) an item not owned continues to be substantial. At present, outside of Illinois few libraries experience interlibrary loan rates above 1 per cent of their total circulation figures.[66] If resource sharing is pursued on a much grander scale in future, this percentage could increase dramatically. Libraries must then face the problem of determining when it is actually less expensive to purchase an item than provide access to it. Related to this matter is the very real dilemma posed by publishers who may simply increase the per-unit price of an item when the number of purchasers declines. And, of course, the question of user fees arises when materials are secured via on-line and/or document delivery services rather than through the traditional acquisition function. Should the user be asked to pay for access to an item because the library has chosen to allocate its funds for other materials and/or services? There is great variety in how libraries approach this matter today, and periodic reassessment will be necessary as the complexion of resource sharing continues to change.

Conclusion

If at present the notion of resource dependency connotes a weakening of individual institutions, libraries have an important task before them: to instil the concept that sharing strengthens the overall resource fabric. If the lofty goals of cooperative collection development are to be realized, Battin's exhortation is one which needs to be repeated until it is inculcated within the entire academic community:

> ... the process of scholarship cannot be confined to one building, to one institution, to one region, or even to one political jurisdiction. ... We must provide the intellectual and conceptual framework for a coordinated information process and create the interinstitutional capabilities to assure the continuing, unobstructed flow of information across local, regional, and national boundaries.[67]

References

1. Sohn, J. (1986), 'Cooperative collection development: a brief overview', *Collection management*, **8** (Summer), p.1.
2. Hewitt, J.A. (1986), 'Cooperative collection development programs of the Triangle Research Libraries Network', in W. Luquire (ed.), *Coordinating cooperative collection development: a national perspective*, New York: Haworth Press, p.139.
3. Battin, P. (1980), 'Research libraries in the network environment', *Journal of academic librarianship*, **6** (May), p.70.
4. Mosher, P.H. and M. Pankake (1983), 'A guide to coordinated and cooperative collection development', *Library resources and technical services*, **27** (Oct/Dec), p.420. (This guide is currently under revision.)
5. Bennett, S. (1984), 'Current initiatives and issues in collection management', *Journal of academic librarianship*, **10** (Nov), p.260.
6. Roberts, E.P. (1987), 'Cooperation, collection management, and scientific journals', *College and research libraries*, **48** (May), p.248.
7. Hewitt, J.A. and J.S. Shipman (1987), 'Cooperative collection development among research libraries in the age of networking: report of a survey of ARL libraries', in J.A. Hewitt (ed.), *Advances in library automation and networking*, Greenwich, Conn.: JAI Press, p.198.
8. Mosher, P.H. and M. Pankake, ref. 4, pp.417-531.
9. *Cooperative collection development*, (SPEC Kit III), Washington, DC: Association of

Research Libraries, Office of Management Studies, 1985. (Also available as ERIC Document #ED 255 216.)

10. The proceedings of this conference are collected in W. Luquire, ref. 2. The conference was designed to explore the state of the art as well as suggest model criteria for the State of Illinois.

11. Downs, R.B. (1970), 'Future prospects of library acquisitions', *Library trends*, **18** (January), p.417.

12. Rutstein, J.S. (1985), 'National and local resource sharing: issues in cooperative collection development', *Collection management*, **7** (Summer), p.6

13. Branin, J.J. (1986), 'Issues in cooperative collection development: the promise and frustration of resource sharing', in J.L. Engle and S.O. Medina (eds), *Issues in resource sharing*, Atlanta: Southeastern Library Network, pp.13-14.

14. Edelman, H. (1972), 'The death of the Farmington Plan', *Library journal*, April, p.1251.

15. United States. Higher Education Act, 1965. Statutes at Large, 79, sec.231, 1228.

16. Thomas, S.E. (1985), 'Collection development at the Center for Research Libraries; policy and practice', *College and research libraries*, **46** (May), 230-235.

17. DeGennaro, R. (1975), 'Austerity, technology and resource sharing: research libraries face the future', *Library journal*, **99** (May), p.921. For a discussion of the National Periodicals Center see M. Biggs (1984), 'The proposed National Periodicals Center, 1973-1980: study, dissension and retreat', *Resource sharing and information networks*, **1** (Spring/Summer), 1-22.

18. Sartori, E.M. (1989), 'Regional collection development of serials', *Collection management*, **11** (Spring), p. 73; and memo from J. Boisse to RLG Board of Governors Programs Committee, 25 January 1989.

19. Gwinn, N.E. and P.H. Mosher (1983), 'Coordinating collection development: the RLG Conspectus', *College and research libraries*, **44** (March), 128-140.

20. Gwinn, N.E. and P.H. Mosher, ref. 19, p.139.

21. Farrell, D. and J. Reed-Scott (1989), 'The North American Collections Inventory Project: implications for the future of coordinated management of research collections', *Library resources and technical services*, **33** (January), 15-18.

22. Stam, D.H. (1986), 'Collaborative collection development: progress, problems and potential', *IFLA journal*, **12**, p.13. For discussion of additional reservations about the Conspectus approach, see D. Henige (1987), 'Epistemological dead end and ergonomic disaster? The North American Collections Inventory Project', *Journal of academic librarianship*, **13** (September), 209-213.

23. Branin, J.J. ref. 13, p.33.

24. Bennett, S. ref. 5, p.258.

25. Stam, D.H. ref. 22, p.15.

26. Ferguson, A.W. et al. (1988), 'The RLG Conspectus: its uses and benefits', *College and research libraries*, **49** (May), 197-206.

27. Hewitt, J.A. and J.S. Shipman, ref. 7, p.195.

28. Hewitt, J.A. ref. 2, pp.146-147.

29. Bozone, B.R. (1986), 'HILC at thirty-four: a view from within', in W. Luquire, ref. 2, pp.151-160.

30. Buzzard, M.L. (1986), 'Cooperative acquisition within a system: the University of California Shared Purchase Program', in W. Luquire, ref. 2, pp.99-113.

31. Lynch, C.A. and M.G. Berger (1989), 'The UC MELVYL MEDLINE System: a pilot project for access to journal literature through an online catalog', *Information technology and libraries*, **8** (December), p.375.

32. Buzzard, M.I., ref. 30, p.110.
33. Neumann, J. (1986), 'The New York State experience with coordinated collection development: funding the stimulus', in W. Luquire, ref. 2, pp.115-128.
34. Sanders, N.P. et al. (1988), 'Automated collection analysis using the OCLC and RLG bibliographic databases', *College and research libraries*, **49** (July), 305-313.
35. Nisonger, T.E. (1985), 'Editing the RLG Conspectus to analyse the OCLC archival tapes of seventeen Texas libraries', *Library resources and technical services*, **29** (Oct/Dec), 309-327.
36. Pitkin, G.M. (1988), 'Access to articles through the online catalog', *American libraries*, **19** (October), 769-770.
37. Cohen, L.M. (1988), 'Resource sharing and coordinated collection development in the network of Alabama academic libraries', *Collection management*, **10** (3/4), p.153.
38. Cohen, L.M. ref. 37, pp.155-158.
39. Stephens, D. (1986), 'A stitch in time: the Alaska Cooperative Collection Development Project', in W. Luquire, ref. 2, pp.173-184.
40. Oberg, L.R. (1988), 'Evaluating the Conspectus approach for smaller library collections', *College and research libraries*, **49** (May), 187-196.
41. Oberg, L.R. (1986), 'A model of cooperation: the VALNET Project', *Library journal*, **111** (November), 50-53.
42. Ferguson, A.W. et al., ref. 26, p.200.
43. Rutstein, J.S. ref. 12, p.12.
44. Pettas, W.A. (1989), 'Cooperative collection development: an inexpensive project in Northern California', *Collection management*, **11** (1/2), 59-67.
45. Meachen, E. and G.R. Scharfenorth (1989), 'Cooperative collection management in higher education: the IACRL/IBHE initiative', *Illinois libraries*, **71** (January), 46-53.
46. Ferguson, A.W. et al., ref. 26. p.201.
47. Idaho and Montana Consortium for Collection Development. *Library journal*, 1989, (May), p.27.
48. Mosher, P.H. (1987), 'Cooperative collection development equals collaborative interdependence', *Collection building*, **9** (3/4), p.31.
49. Roberts, E.P. ref. 6, pp.247-251.
50. Millson-Martula, C.A. (1989), 'The Greater Midwest Regional Medical Library Network and coordinated cooperative collection development: the RLG Conspectus and beyond', *Illinois libraries*, **71** (January), 31-39.
51. Dillon, M. and C. Mak (1989), 'Collection analysis CD – a new approach to collection assessment', *Library hi-tech news*, November, 3-5.
52. Smith, M.M. (1985), 'Cooperative collection development for rare books among neighbouring academic libraries', *College and research libraries*, **46** (March), 160-167.
53. Atkinson, R.W. (1986), 'Selection for preservation: a materialistic approach', *Library resources and technical services*, **30** (Oct/Dec), 341-353.
54. Weber, D.C. (1976), 'A century of cooperative programs among academic libraries', *College and research libraries*, **37** (May), p.214.
55. Hewitt, J.A. and J.S. Shipman, ref. 7, p.206.
56. Dougherty, R.M. (1988), 'A conceptual framework for organizing resource sharing and shared collection development programs', *Journal of academic librarianship*, **14** (November), 287-291.
57. Battin, P. ref. 3, p.71.
58. Mosher, P.H. and M. Pankake, ref. 4, p. 426.
59. Downs, R.B. ref. 11, p.118.

60. Mosher, P.H. (1986), 'A national scheme for collaboration in collection development: the RLG-NCIP effort', in W. Luquire, ref. 2, p.23.
61. Atkinson, R.W. (1989), 'Old forms, new forms: the challenge of collection development', *College and research libraries*, **50** (September), 507-520.
62. Bennett, S. ref. 5, p.259.
63. Ferguson, D.K. (1987), 'Electronic information delivery systems: reports on five projects sponsored by the Fred Meyer Charitable Trust', *Library hi-tech news*, **5** (Summer), p.65.
64. Barney, C. (1983), 'The prophet from Xanadu', *PC world*, March, p.293.
65. Munn, R.F. (1986), 'Cooperation will not save us', *Journal of academic librarianship*, **12** (July), p.167.
66. Rutstein, J.S. ref. 12, p.6.
67. Battin, P. ref. 3, p.68,70.

11 The view from the British Library

Barry Bloomfield and Michael Smethurst*

Once upon a time – not so very long ago – the national library was a temple of learning whose collection management policy emerged or was handed down as from on high and whose function was that of a repository for the national printed archive and a treasury for its manuscript heritage. As a last resort of exalted scholarship – and scholars – such institutions were popularly thought to contain every book ever printed, and even to enter their doors marked readers with a little of the odour of sanctity. This myth came to an abrupt end in the UK with the founding of the British Library in 1973.

Statutory obligations of the British Library

The stage had been set with the report of the Dainton Committee[1] in 1969 and this had been followed by a Government White Paper[2] in 1971 which explicitly stated that 'The objective of the British Library will be to provide the best possible central library services for the United Kingdom'

*The authors wish to state that the opinions expressed in this chapter are entirely personal and are not necessarily the views of the British Library, nor should they be construed or interpreted as other than expressions of personal professional opinion.

259

and this aim was further defined as involving 'preserving and making available for reference at least one copy of every book and periodical of domestic origin and of as many overseas publications as possible . . . providing an efficient central lending and photocopying service in support of the other libraries and information systems of the country; and providing central cataloguing and other bibliographic services . . .'. The subsequent British Library Act[3] simply said 'This Act shall have effect with a view to the establishment for the United Kingdom of a national library . . . consisting of a comprehensive collection of books, manuscripts, periodicals, films and other recorded matter whether printed or otherwise' and laid upon the new British Library Board the 'duty . . . to manage the Library as a national centre for reference, study and bibliographical and other information services, in relation to both scientific and technological matters and to the humanities'.

From these statutory bases the new British Library has had to fashion its own collection management policies and at the same time to merge a number of different institutions into one new body and reconcile traditions, staffing establishments and grades, and collecting policies, almost all of which were significantly different. Colleagues who had formerly been rivals became after 1973 members of the same British Library – but it is fair to say that this process took much time and effort and even now it is not fully accomplished. (Those interested in a more detailed review of the early years may consult the extensive literature.)[4]

There are other national libraries and other libraries entitled to the privilege of copyright deposit but it is important to understand at the outset that the British Library is the national library for the UK and that it serves equally science and technology, the humanities and the social sciences. Further, it is responsible for providing both reference and lending services and a central photocopying service together with a centralized cataloguing service. It has been understood that on it rests the responsibility to provide the best central library services for the UK and, although nominally at arms length from direct government control, it is the only library funded by its parent government department, the Office of Arts and Libraries. The Research and Development Department of the British Library acts as a channel for funds granted to other libraries under provision 1.3(b) of the British Library Act and that same department has also overseen the disbursement of funds for preservation and conservation generously granted by the Wolfson Foundation. All these affect the British Library's view of collection management for it is absolutely clear that it cannot, with its own resources and collections, achieve the objectives its statutory role demands. It must act in cooperation or coordination with other major research and academic libraries, even though it will often seem that disproportionate effort is needed to achieve small results. The truism that no library is nowadays independent applies as much to national as to other libraries; the effort to achieve satisfactory coordination and results on both national and international fronts will in the future have more significant implications for the British Library's collection management policies.

Current role of the British Library

Allied to this problem is one peculiar to the British Library: how to establish clearly what is its precise role and what public does it serve? Is the British Library to be, what it increasingly is, a library of first resort for scholars; or should it retain its role as a library restricted to advanced scholarship and serving those scholars and other libraries? This discussion becomes increasingly important as the date for the occupation of the new building at St Pancras comes nearer, since the Library aims to attract to this building many with non-scholarly interests to enjoy its expanded exhibition programme, even including those of school age. Once there it is not likely that all of them will depart without wanting to use the huge library resources concentrated in that large new building. The library of the Centre Pompidou, it is reported, has on occasion received as many as 16 000 readers on one day; if that were to happen in the new British Library at St Pancras the whole character of the Library would necessarily change and the impact on collection management would be tremendous. So, in addition to the problem of defining the role and public of the new British Library, there is the possible impact of the new building at St Pancras to take into account. In effect, after 1996 the British Library will be a library on two sites: St Pancras and Boston Spa. This should simplify the problems of defining a clear collection development policy, but with two strong collections and concentrations of staff it may prove even more difficult than past experience has already demonstrated to weld the two into one institution.

On top of these problems there is the recurring difficulty of building collections that will satisfy the needs of research workers in the future. The problem is complicated by the fact that funds for acquisition and preservation are now restricted and, in real terms, sharply reduced not only in the British Library but in almost all other major research and academic libraries. Shared poverty is never enjoyable and does not build strong library collections. To divert acquisition funds from pressing contemporary needs to provide for an unspecified future is generally unpopular and as likely to be unprofitable as not. Since most libraries cannot cope with the present influx of published material the outlook for speculative provision against future needs is bleak – and here funds for preservation are often as important as funds for acquisition.

As the national library for the UK the British Library also has the duty of acting in conjunction with other similar central national libraries both in non-governmental and inter-governmental bodies. It needs to be represented on committees and at conferences, and such activities will often affect collection management policies not just for central national libraries but for others too. The attempt by the European Communities to evolve a library development plan on a European scale is one area where the British Library has represented, in coordination with others, national interests in library matters. And the fact that the Government deals with European matters through its appropriate department means that the Office of Arts and Libraries is also necessarily concerned.

So, to summarize the preamble to this chapter, there are a number of given or assumed factors which influence the British Library in its view of collection management not only for its own collections but nationally. These can briefly be set out as:

- the BL's position as the national library for the UK;
- the statutory obligations laid upon the BL in the BL Act;
- the problems of fashioning a unified collection management policy and uniting previously different and independent institutions in one framework;
- the BL's duty to liaise with and support other libraries to achieve the best national library service;
- the impossibility of the BL's being able to satisfy all demands made upon it, especially in a time of financial retrenchment;
- the problem of clarifying the role of the BL and identifying the public it serves;
- the impact of the new building at St Pancras on the use of the collections, allied to the concentration of the BL on two main sites;
- the difficulty of building research collections for the speculative

needs of future scholars and preserving those existing against destruction through use or neglect;

- the BL's need to represent the UK's library interests internationally, which may affect collection management policies for example within any European library development plan or coordinated initiative.

Collection policies

The British Library in determining its collection development and collection management policies seeks to recognize its unique position. On the one hand it has responsibility for collecting and maintaining the annual output of British publications, to form the national printed archive; on the other hand it has one of the largest and most comprehensive collections in the world, and its responsibilities relate to its pre-eminent role as an international research library. Yet it has also to combine the reference functions as a research library with its international and national document-supply function from what is probably the world's largest centralized collection of scientific literature.

As a library of first resort for scholars in the humanities, the maintenance and extension of the Library's reference collections are of prime international importance. Its importance as a research library lies, for them, in the fact that in its reading rooms they can consult an unparalleled range of related material. As a library of last resort, serving, through the Document Supply Centre, libraries all over the world, the Library seeks to maintain a very high satisfaction rate to those seeking material through interlibrary loans.

The problems faced by the Library in seeking to define the priorities which it should follow in collection development and collection management as a library of both first and last resort have increased in difficulty as the real resource of government grant-in-aid has fallen, and as the Library's dependence upon revenue-earning services has increased. There are no easy solutions to these problems, but, in a period of continued under-resourcing of libraries in the UK and elsewhere, the resolution of the conflicting pressures on the Library becomes of critical importance.

In developing a long-term strategy for collection development and management the Library's intention, as given in *Gateway to knowledge* [5] is to work with others to achieve comprehensive access to recorded knowledge. 'In the next five years we shall be obliged to spend less on adding to and caring for the collection but we shall seek to make progress both in the better organisation and exploitation of our own resources, and in our cooperative arrangements with other libraries. This means we shall build on the strengths we already have; and we shall make clear the areas where we shall expect others better placed than ourselves, to carry the central collection responsibility.'[6]

The successful development of a constructive programme for collection management, to build on the strengths of the Library and to make clear to others where we shall no longer be seeking to carry a central collecting responsibility, is highly dependent upon the Library's ability to create a robust coordinated approach to collaboration with other libraries, which recognizes the political and economic realities and overcomes the many obstacles which have hindered all previous attempts at cooperative collection development in the UK.

National plan for libraries

This makes the long-standing debate on the need for a national plan for libraries more than a mere academic exercise. Indeed, it can be argued that only by the development of a national plan can the overall resources available for library collections in the UK be most effectively used to support research and scholarship. The need for a national plan has long been recognized by many concerned with the effects of the devolved systems of funding support for research libraries in this country. The University Grants Committee (UGC)'s *Report of the Committee on Libraries*, (the Parry Report) published in 1967 saw the establishment of the British Museum Library departments as the British National Library to be 'a prerequisite of a national plan for foreign acquisitions in which the national library should play a major part'.[7] But it also identified one of the problems inherent in the British system of funding research libraries and in developing a cooperative policy for acquisitions: 'Objections raised in evidence were that individual institutions would have to surrender their autonomy in the choice of books.'[8]

Cooperation

Writing in 1978 on the work of the National Central Library, Urquhart expressed the problem of resourcing cooperative development in similar terms: 'the actual method of financing libraries militates against library cooperation, for the direct paymaster of a library – an academic institution, a local authority or a research institute – is concerned with using the resources allocated to their institution primarily for the purpose of that institution.'[9] The continued pressure by the Library Association, SCONUL and other professional groupings during the last 15 years to have the need for a national coordinating agency recognized by government has met with little success, although it directly led to the formation of the Library and Information Services Committees and Councils (LISC) for England, Wales, Scotland and Northern Ireland. That these should have been established as separate committees illustrates the political problems of better coordination between libraries at a UK level. The separation of committees emphasizes rather than diminishes the boundaries between the differing ministerial responsibilities in respect of libraries in each of the countries. The National Libraries of Scotland and Wales and the British Library have quite separate political masters and paymasters; the university libraries rely on block grants made to their parent institutions by the Universities Funding Council which, although it has a Scottish committee, functions at a UK level; the polytechnics are separately funded through their own body, and the public libraries through their local authorities.

LISC and LIPs

LISC sought, in its series of reports *The future development of libraries*[10] to strengthen its own role as a coordinating body, and placed particular emphasis upon the creation of coordinated strategies for improving access to collections at local and national levels. In its third report[11] its proposals for Local Information Plans (LIPs) recognized the political difficulties of achieving a national plan, and the lack of success of the 'top-down' approach to national coordination. It advocated a 'bottom-upwards' approach to integrated provision through local area planning based on the model of the local authority planning structures. The development of LIPs has been assisted in England and Wales by funding support from the Office of Arts and Libraries which is administered in consultation with the BL Research and Development Department. It is too early to say whether the scheme will have more than a limited success in coordinating library provision at a local level, and since the emphasis lies primarily in improved local access to information, the influence upon national collection development policies may be limited. It is, however, a recognition by government that it has a role in enabling better local coordination through funding support. In respect of the better utilization of local library resources, the success of Local Information Plans could be of major importance to the British Library in its development policies for the Document Supply Centre and the relationship between the Library's document supply function and its reference function. The further development of centralized lending collections to improve local access to information could well be modified, especially if LIPs can provide a wider range of information and documents economically and efficiently. The work of the new interlending coordinating body the Library and Information Cooperation Council (LINC) could also be extremely important in establishing better coordination between LIPs, the Regional Library Systems and the Document Supply Centre.

The benefits of any improved coordination through the development of LIPs will almost certainly be almost entirely in respect of access to scientific, medical and factual information; provision for the scholar in the humanities and the historically-based social sciences is not likely to be significantly changed by better access to local resources, given the comparative weakness of those local resources in the range and depth of humanities research material. There are few truly significant research collections of depth and breadth in the humanities outside the larger university libraries, the libraries of specialized institutes, and the three national libraries. The British Library's reputation in the humanities and social sciences as a comprehensive research library leads to the frequently held assumption that it should be able in the future to collect comprehensively. The view that the Library has resources to support comprehensive collection development is one of the difficulties which the Library has to overcome in pursuing new policies. The resources are not adequate to follow the concepts of universality ascribed to Panizzi. Given the growth in world literature in the twentieth century, Panizzi's collection development policies are unattainable; given the cut in real resources in recent years, the extension of acquisition policies which the Library followed in the first five years of its existence cannot now be maintained. The old traditions of the British Museum Library, based upon maintaining the development of its own collections without regard to the growth of research collections elsewhere, although they may be regarded as the source of its present richness, cannot be defended rationally against the reality of an overall decline in resources for collection development in the country as a whole; and, indeed, those with good knowledge of the collections can readily point to major areas of weakness, and to areas of collection development which were not covered during the earlier part of this century.

Collaboration

In seeking partnership for collection development, the British Library is only too aware of the problems imposed by the lack of a formal national plan. However, it cannot itself afford to divert substantial funds to other libraries to support their collaboration in a national strategy although grants given under provision 1.3(b) of the British Library Act can support local development in the national interest. It would not welcome the diversion of existing funds by the Office of Arts and Libraries from the severely limited funding given in grant-in-aid to the Library, in order to provide for centrally funded collection development.

Politically, the Library is addressing this problem by drawing attention to the collective weakness inherent in the system of separated responsibility for funding research libraries. In what is inevitably a slow and initially unrewarding process, the Library is seeking to establish, through meetings with the UFC and the Committee of Vice-Chancellors and Principals (CVCP), the need for joint initiatives, and for the proper recognition at government level of the interdependence between the British Library and the major university libraries in the development and maintenance of research collections. During the last three years some progress has been made, but much remains to be done. Universities will not readily acquiesce in any further diminution of their autonomy; they will not readily support ear-marked funding for libraries in general, since it is seen as a loss of autonomy, although they may more easily accept the ear-marking of additional funds for particular national responsibilities. At a professional level, there is a willingness to cooperate and a clear recognition of the fragility of the present system of informal collaboration at a time when resources are severely limited. But without additional resources, few are able to guarantee that they can modify their own policies to remedy the national problem.

At the same time, the Library is seeking to promote a wider understanding of the problems of collection development. In recent years, through a series of colloquia it has brought together scholars and librarians in particular subject areas to discuss the problems peculiar to the discipline under consideration, from matters relating to bibliographical control to acquisitions policies. The Library's policy has been to publish the proceedings of each colloquium and whenever possible draw upon the views of experts in the further refinement of its own policies of collection development. Subjects covered in this way include Canadian, Australian, African, South Asian, Chinese, Japanese, and German Studies as well as Incunabula.

The wide consultation and seeking of expert opinion is both necessary and valuable in guiding the Library towards wise and practical solutions to the complex problems which it faces in redrawing its own priorities for acquisition. An important feature of the colloquia is that they are not limited to British participants, and the international context in which the Library works is always well identified. Indeed, the Library would be failing to fulfil its obligations to international scholarship if it merely developed policies in a national context. Much effort in recent years has been directed towards international collaboration. In Oriental Studies, joint projects have been established with centres of excellence in Europe, covering both bibliographical listing and acquisition of materials. In respect of the literature of Africa, for example, the Library is establishing a collaborative arrangement with the Bibliothèque Nationale in Paris under which the BN will give priority to the acquisition of material of former French colonial territories whilst the British Library gives priority to the material of former British colonies. This is a particularly valuable area of collaboration, especially in respect of official publications which are both notoriously difficult to acquire on a regular basis and difficult and expensive to control as bibliographical items.

The Library fully recognizes the importance of its policy decisions in respect of the collaborative and coordinated strategies which must be formulated in the context of a European framework. It has not shrunk from offering initiatives under the European Action Plan which is being developed by DG XIII. The Library is proposing a number of collaborative projects ranging from an integrated development of CD-ROM publications of national bibliographies to a programme for the development of national union catalogues of microform masters. Whilst strictly outside the topic of collection management in this discussion, the development of compatible files of bibliographical data is entirely relevant to the larger issues of collaboration in collection development since these files can offer for the first time immediate access to the existing holdings of the major research libraries in Europe, and, given the proper exploitation of the technology now available to libraries, facilitate the creation of informed and sensitive policies which relate to the holdings of other libraries.

This same ease of communication offers greater scope than ever before to purposeful collaboration within the UK. The CURL group of libraries (the Consortium of University Research Libraries, which has within its membership the Bodleian, Cambridge, Leeds, Manchester, Edinburgh, Glasgow and London Universities) is currently creating its own database of the current catalogues of its members and, under the terms of a grant from the UGC, will make these available on JANET (the Joint Academic Network). The British Library has observer status at the CURL meetings, and there is growing cooperation between CURL and the BL, which can be developed in practical ways when an increasing body of catalogue data is available on-line from CURL and from the BL. The importance of Oxford and Cambridge as libraries of legal deposit within the CURL network, as well as their importance as the two major university research libraries in the UK, cannot be underestimated in any consideration of the better coordination of national policies.

Shared cataloguing

The British Library is seeking to develop a special relationship with CURL and with the National Libraries of Scotland and Wales. This is at present being strengthened at several levels. Over the last two years a series of meetings with the five other libraries entitled to legal deposit has sought to develop a workable scheme for the shared cataloguing of the current intake to the British printed archive. The growth in recent years of newly published British imprints has been extraordinarily high: in 1980 the *British national bibliography* recorded some 48 000 items; in 1989 some 68 000 items; and it forecasts that 90 000 items will be published in 1995. Merely to keep pace with the additional material to be catalogued outstrips any gains in efficiency which the British Library could possibly achieve in its cataloguing performance. The inevitable result of this growth will be a growing backlog of material awaiting cataloguing, and hence a failure on the British Library's part to achieve a good measure of currency in publishing and providing bibliographical records to other libraries (which in turn limits their performance in terms of any cooperative acquisition policy for British material). The appointment of a large number of additional cataloguing staff to deal with the extra work will require substantial additional funding if the cost is not to be met by the damaging solution of paying for it by cuts in the Library's funding for foreign acquisitions. The Library is therefore seeking to share the burden with the other deposit libraries by an agreement under which they would between them catalogue up to one-third of the intake, supplying records in machine-readable form to a common standard in return for free access to the British Library's database of current British imprints. A pilot scheme is now in operation but there remain a number of difficulties, not the least of which is achieving a compatibility of records within a minimal UK MARC structure.

Discussions are also continuing to extend the principles of this sharing of effort into foreign language material. The development of the CURL database and the conversion of the British Library catalogue (BLC) into machine-readable form suggest that record sharing for foreign acquisitions could be accomplished with mutual benefit to all the libraries concerned. The British Library has mounted the partially completed conversion of the BLC on its BLAISE-LINE files which are available through JANET, and within three years the full general catalogue of the Library should be available as an on-line public access catalogue (OPAC) on JANET. We believe that this facility for accessing our current and older records could be of enormous value to other libraries in planning at a practical level rational and cost effective acquisition programmes. If, within the Library, we can further develop a common database between the reference services and the lending services and network this, at the same time linking the database with document retrieval services, then we have in JANET an enormously important and effective tool for the better coordination of collection development and management.

Conspectus

Conspectus, or 'The Conspectus' as American colleagues usually refer to it, can be used as a key to unlock these common or distributed databases by indicating where library collections are strong or weak. It is a technique for recording those strengths and weaknesses, both current and retrospective. Its great advantage compared to previous techniques is brevity, combined with the ability to handle, process and revise assessments by means of the computer.

The Research Libraries Group (RLG) in North America is an association of major research and university libraries formed in 1974. Its purpose is to coordinate the continent's library resources and activities so as to get the best value from them and to support research and academic activity in the most efficient fashion. In 1980 the Management and Development Committee endorsed a recommendation for the formulation of a collection development policy statement that was to include information on the levels and effectiveness of the major libraries' existing collections and their current collecting intentions. (The intention was to include the collections of the Library of Congress (LC), although LC was not and is not a member of RLG.) In effect, the final intention was to devise a national statement of collection policy for the principal research libraries in the US and Canada.

Basically the Conspectus system is simple and flexible and rests primarily on the professional judgement of librarians – which is its major strength. The whole field of knowledge is divided into a series of sets or subject divisions. In the beginning these were based on the segments of the Library of Congress classification, but there are now in existence concordances to convert these sets to other library classifications. Libraries record their collection data on a series of worksheets arranged by these subject descriptors each of which is identified in the Conspectus by a unique three-letter code, followed by a running number. Each of these subject groups can be considered by libraries and there follow three columns to be completed: Existing Collection Strength (ECS), Current Collecting Intensity (CCI), and Comments. ECS and CCI are recorded on a scale running from 0 (the lowest) to 5 ('Comprehensive' coverage) while a subsequent alphabetic code indicates the linguistic scope of the collection: E equals English language only; F indicates selected foreign language material, mostly European; W means material is collected in all languages; and Y that the collection is primarily in one major language. Obviously many library collections are so extensive and so complex that such a simplistic notation cannot be sufficiently specific and the library undertaking the description, or Conspector, can use the added Comment column and also include what are known as 'scope notes'. (The BL Conspectus has adopted this device a good deal.) The description of any library collection in this systematic fashion on a series of worksheets is then transferred to a computer-based system which can be interrogated by librarians, users and others to discover what are the strongest collections in a variety of subjects, where they are located, what gaps appear in collections, nationally or locally, and many other questions. It is obvious that a systematic listing of collecting strengths cumulated in this fashion will be of great utility in federal institutions.

The British Library initiated a Conspectus review as a necessary preliminary to the more precise formulation of a collection development policy in 1983: clearly Conspectus was an appropriate tool for the BL to use. The impetus towards this was given by Alex Wilson, then Director General of the Reference Division, and there was a good deal of discussion among colleagues. The full story of the implementation of the Conspectus can be gleaned from Stephen Hanger's article in the *Journal of librarianship*.[12] There was full cooperation from all the selectors in the BL in Humanities & Social Sciences (H&SS) and Science Reference and Industry (SRIS), and gradually after a good deal of hard work by Brian Holt and Stephen Hanger a pattern of assessment and information began to emerge. It will be no surprise to learn that everyone gained a good deal from the exercise, and this is one of the main benefits of undertaking a Conspectus-type survey. The results were published in *Conspectus in the British Library*[13] and presented to the Advisory Council and appropriate Advisory Committees in the British Library. Most were shocked to learn that we judged our collecting strengths in certain areas as below research level and that in many areas the BL does not aim to collect at all. (Appendix 5 of *Conspectus in the British Library*, on the Exclusions Policy, was a considerable talking point, but this method was adopted because the BL could not easily define its basic acquisitions policy, so the contrary stance was adopted to define what the BL did not do.) In today's hard economic circumstances the BL cannot afford to expand coverage, indeed it is looking more often than not to lean on other libraries' resources to avoid costly duplication and make the most effective use of scarce resources. The BL has been drawn into discussions of research library provision for art history and law, both subjects for which the BL does not see itself as the first or principal resource for scholars, but so far it has not been possible for the National Art Library in the Victoria & Albert Museum (V&A) or the major legal libraries to assume prime responsibility for literature provision in those areas.

The National Library of Wales also decided to undertake a partial Conspectus survey, changed its mind in mid-stream, and undertook a complete survey of the collections which at the time of writing is in progress and due to be completed in late 1990.

In Scotland, the National Library, the two major public libraries in

Glasgow and Edinburgh and each of the eight university libraries also applied Conspectus to their collections. The work was coordinated by the National Library of Scotland and by the Scottish Committee for cooperation between the eleven libraries, which was chaired initially by J.M. Smethurst and later by H. Heaney, Librarian of Glasgow University. The decision to undertake Conspectus in Scotland arose from wider discussions between this group of Scottish librarians on the need for greater collaboration and coordination in acquisition and preservation policies. As a group, the university librarians had been under considerable pressure from the Scottish Committee of Principals to examine the concept of a single federal university library which would serve each of the eight universities. Aware of the many difficulties and problems which would need to be resolved, and for which there might not in any case be a political solution acceptable to the universities themselves, the group responded to this pressure by proposing the development of commonly accessible machine-readable catalogues (the SALBIN scheme), and the analysis of collections by Conspectus as a broad mapping tool which could be used in conjunction with the networked catalogues, and also be valuable for coordinating acquisition and preservation policies. Implementation of Conspectus in Scotland has been built upon a successful and productive period of collaboration over some twenty years, in which the National Library of Scotland played an important role. The close working relationships between the libraries, and the strongly binding national context in which they worked, helped overcome a number of the practical difficulties, particularly in the interpretation of the levels of coding and in the definitions of the subject areas. The Conspectus in Scotland, by its comprehensive coverage of the major research libraries, makes a particularly strong contribution to the development of a national database for the UK. The Scottish group has been very supportive of this, and also of extending the concept of a network of linked national databases in Europe.

The data from the Scottish surveys and the BL surveys have now been entered into a joint database in the BL. Conspectus has been discussed by SCONUL on a number of occasions and by the Library Resources Coordinating Committee (LRCC) in the University of London, but while some colleagues have been in favour others have been against undertaking such work in a time of little money, while many have been unconvinced and have waited upon events.

The advantages of cooperation in mapping the strengths and weaknesses of library collections are obvious. What are the dangers? Forced coordination by the UFC must be a possibility; but this is happening in any case and collections are on the move as academic departments are rationalized as never before. Might it not make the deliberations of the UFC more informed if they could have a reliable map of library collections?

These are perceived to be the other uses of Conspectus if it covers sufficient major libraries:

- the facility for librarians and scholars to search for data;
- the allocation of Primary Collection Responsibility (PCR) to major libraries to prevent duplication, although this does assume a plan of collecting on a regional, national or international scale;
- using its data as the basis for a National Inventory Plan (NIP) as the Americans and Canadians are doing;
- the coordination of preservation responsibility for various allocated areas.

Other uses may well arise, and these possibilities are by no means exhaustive.

The BL would like to see a spread of Conspectus surveys in the major libraries of Europe so that their data may be added to what already exists. University and research libraries should undertake complete or partial Conspectus surveys to reveal their strengths and weaknesses. This will demand the development of national, literary, and historical schedules for the countries which participate – some of this work is already being undertaken by LIBER.

What are the problems to be faced? First, to encourage other libraries to take part. Second, to assure colleagues that the methods of judgement are valid for libraries across the board. Briefly, in measuring the strengths of collections we are measuring not only quantity but also quality, and there are basically three ways of doing this:

- by measurement in metres (if you have a collection on economic history measuring 300 metres it is likely to be stronger than a similar collection in another library measuring only 10 metres);
- by checking the library's holdings against a standard bibliography and noting the gaps, etc.;
- by a personal individual assessment by librarians or scholars. (Or by any combination of these three.)

The last method obviously contains difficulties, but the professional experience and judgement of librarians will soon introduce a note of reality into the assessment. If a 5 mark indicates the highest comprehensive collection and the BL awards itself such a mark only in about half a dozen instances, then a college librarian judging his/her holdings will soon realize and begin to assess the true worth of his/her collections. But there do exist validation exercises in a few subjects and areas and the BL has undertaken one in the art history field – which happily confirmed our own rating. The V&A undertook the same validation and came out with a slightly higher score than the BL. So validation is possible and desirable. The major problem in the future will be: who is to conduct and devise these validation exercises? At present the appropriate RLG Committee is doing this, but can it be expected to do so on a world-wide scale in the future?

So Conspectus is a useful tool for libraries in cooperation to achieve a machine-readable record, easily amended and consulted, of the strengths and weaknesses of library collections in a given area, region or country. Cooperation in the creation of records, particularly those relating to the national printed archive, to which we have already referred, is a further important step to achieving greater coordination in the management of that archive. But two other major developments are needed if we are to see fully effective management of the archive and additions to that archive. Neither will be easily accomplished, but successful cooperation in record creation helps greatly in identifying the most difficult problems and making them more readily amenable to practical solutions. The first is coordinated management of conservation of the national archive.

Conservation

In 1988 the Andrew W. Mellon Foundation of New York made a grant to the British Library of $1.5 million for preservation purposes. An appreciable part of this grant was applied by the Library to accelerate work on the Register of Preservation Microforms and to convert it to a national register with entries from other libraries recorded so as to avoid needless duplicated effort. At the same time that the Mellon Foundation made its grant to the British Library grants of half a million dollars were also made to the Bodleian Library, Oxford and the University Library Cambridge with the promise of further matching funds at a later date, and these grants were also to encourage a programme of coordinated preservation microfilming in these great libraries, on the understanding that reports on the material microfilmed would be included in the British Library's Register of Preservation Microforms.

At the time of the grant from the Mellon Foundation the Register included some 25 000 entries almost exclusively derived from material microfilmed in the British Library since 1983 often at the request of outside customers. There has been no attempt so far to include other material microfilmed by other departments or divisions in the Library although it is known that holdings of archival negatives are extensive. (For example, the holdings of the Newspaper Library at Colindale, the India Office Library and Records and other sections of the Bloomsbury departments are very large indeed.)

The Register of Preservation Microforms now contains about 45 000 entries and became available on-line through BLAISE in September 1989.[14] During 1990 it will begin to include reports from the Bodleian Library, the University Library Cambridge and other national libraries enjoying copyright deposit, and discussions are beginning to plan for the gradual introduction of material in other departments of the British Library and in other university libraries. A priority is to include newspapers microfilmed cooperatively under the NEWSPLAN programme in the various regions of the UK. Some other reports have been included under the programme of work undertaken on behalf of the Nineteenth Century Short Title Catalogue where, for example, material from the National Art Library in the Victoria & Albert Museum is included. The British Library strongly supports this initiative to coordinate microfilming resources and make the best use of scarce finance. The last thing wanted nationally is for each library to microfilm the same titles, having selected them as priority items for preservation; easy access to the Register of Preservation Microforms should obviate this and promote preservation policies and collection management nationally and internationally, for the Research Libraries Group supports a similar register and cooperative effort in North America. Both registers will be mutually available in the future.

The Mellon programme illustrates well how the injection of earmarked funding into the system can stimulate coordination of policies and achieve immediate practical results. The first stage of an ambitious but pragmatic programme of filming nineteenth-century material at risk in the British Library, the National Libraries of Scotland and Wales, the

Bodleian and Cambridge has begun. Under the scheme each library has undertaken to give priority to an agreed and discrete selection of material, and to supply to the British Library a master film in order that copies can be made available to others from a central source. It is expected that the programme will be further developed with other major libraries. The Library intends to provide funding, probably at the level of 50 per cent of costs, to other libraries which agree to take responsibility for filming titles known to be at risk, and submit master films and a machine-readable record to the National Register.

Coordinated acquisition

The second development, and the more difficult by far, is to look for greater coordination in the acquisition of material to the archive, and to achieve through this a national policy which will lead both to better coverage of all British publications and a better use of the overall resource in maintaining and giving access to this archive. The UK is fortunate in having five legal deposit libraries entitled either by right or by claim to receive a copy of each newly published printed work. It is also fortunate that a sixth deposit library, Trinity College Dublin, has (since the independence of Eire) maintained its privilege to acquire British publications under the 1911 Copyright Act in return for the British Library's privilege of receiving a copy of each Irish publication. The benefits to scholars of the archive being available in five centres are substantial; the cost to each of the libraries is, however, also substantial, and, in terms of the additional building costs for storage, has to be well justified. In 1988 the British Library commissioned a study of its acquisition and retention policies under the chairmanship of Dr Brian Enright, Librarian of Newcastle University, which included in its terms of reference the examination of policies relating to the acquisition and retention of material under the Copyright Act of 1911.

Selection for survival

The review was completed in 1989, and the report of the review team was published in October 1989 by the British Library under the title: *Selection for survival*.[15] The review was very wide ranging in its examination of the

Library's acquisition policies and collection management, and identified some thirty major policy issues which the team believed should be subject to further investigation and review. Many of these are related to the broad responsibilities of the Library under the British Library Act, and how these can be met or modified in a period of severely limited resources. Among specific issues that of legal deposit has received the widest public attention. The Library has responded by giving to the Director General of Humanities & Social Sciences corporate responsibility for collection management across the Library, and the task of further investigating the issues and proposing measures for implementation. To date (Spring 1990) the working programme has concentrated on areas in which immediate action is considered to be essential, taking account of the Library's priorities in the next five years. These include improved selection methods at the intake stage to deal with the problem of reprints which are deposited under the publishers' understanding of the requirements of the Act. Over 5 000 apparent reprints are received annually from UK publishers, none of which is required under the Act and the regulations relating to its interpretation; the cost of processing these items and storing them is estimated to be at least £17 000 per annum, and as the review group pointed out the costs of maintaining material not selected by the Library and of little or no value to its work as a national archive or research library are an increasing burden over the lifetime of the materials. A second area which is being examined is that of material which is either completely outside the scope of the 1911 Act or which is not considered to be within the area of the Library's competence or requirements of the Act. This material covers a wide range of artefacts which are unlikely ever to be sought in the Library such as blank annual diaries, large print reprints, blank crossword puzzle books and a variety of children's toys and games with printed instructions.

Here scholarly needs might be fulfilled by keeping a representative sample. The Library does not, however, wish to modify its policies without reference to the other legal deposit libraries. It wants to ensure that, where necessary, a reassignment of responsibility takes place so that material in categories which others feel to be important in terms of future usefulness might be preserved centrally if the Library ceases to retain it. It is therefore discussing the formulation of a policy of shared responsibility for deposited material with other libraries. In these discussions, which concentrate on the fringe areas already mentioned, the Library believes that shared coverage might lead to substantial savings in each of the deposit libraries and at the same time might result in a freeing of resources which would enable each to concentrate more effort into obtaining material which should be deposited but which at present is not. These are difficult matters on which to get a rational consensus and on which to build robust policies likely to win universal approval.

There is clearly a strong body of opinion which believes that the British Library should hold every printed item no matter what its current value to scholarship or research, on the assumption that it is not possible to predict its future importance. It is equally apparent that without a substantial increase in funding the Library could only undertake this by putting its conservation policies at even greater risk – we do not now have the level of resource which guarantees the maintenance of the printed archive, and the processing, storage and maintenance of a far greater annual intake of material adds significantly to recurrent costs. The Library is also seeking to recognize, in its modification of the deposit intake, that publishing at the end of the twentieth century is greatly different to the practice in 1911 when the legislation was last reformed, both in its scale and in its content. Furthermore, in seeking to exercise better control of legal deposit material, the Library is also mindful of the need to establish bibliographical control and collection development policies for that material which is now so extensive but which has never been subject to legal deposit – sound recordings, audiovisual material, microforms, and, of course, electronic material. The Library is already lobbying for an extension of legal deposit to include the right to claim material in new media. As this material proliferates, it is probably far more important for the needs of future historians, sociologists and other scholars to ensure that major publications in non-print form are acquired, preserved and maintained than to expend increased resources on the collection and maintenance of material at the extreme edges of conventional printing and publication.

Conclusion

Much has been written in recent years about the failure in the past to create workable policies for cooperation between libraries in the acquisition and retention of material of lasting value, and there are those within the information profession who are convinced that there is little to be gained from further pursuit of national policies for coordination. These views represent in many ways sound realism given the political and economic obstacles to practical coordination. They are reinforced by the lack of resources in libraries throughout the UK, and the pressure this places upon librarians to concentrate upon minimizing the political results of poverty by ensuring a seemingly equal distribution of misery to each subject within their interests. But it is also important to recognize that libraries have invested huge sums in the initial development of automated systems that give not only better control of the collections and of acquisition, but also allow cheap and effective communication between library systems and the prospect of cheaper transmission of information held in documents and in electronic media. That investment demands a more integrated and coordinated approach to collection building and preservation of collections, and indeed the investment can only be fully justified in terms of improved access to the widest range of materials held in distributed centres. The British Library, in reconsidering its own policies, recognizes that separately each library can only effectively hold a smaller and smaller proportion of the world's needed literature, and that its own collections cannot be maintained and extended to make good that loss elsewhere unless technology is used to promote a workable and reliable network of interdependent collections, through policies coordinated in the national interest. We believe our new initiatives will be of the greatest value in developing practical national plans.

References

1. National Libraries Committee (1969), *Report* [Chairman: Sir Fred Dainton], London: HMSO, (Cmnd. 4028).
2. Great Britain, British Library (1971), White Paper, London: HMSO, (Cmnd. 4572).
3. Great Britain, British Library Act 1972, Eliz.II, Ch. 54, London: HMSO.
4. Bloomfield, B.C. (1981), 'Progress in documentation: the British Library, 1973-80', *Journal of documentation*, **37** (3), 107-24.
5. British Library (1989), *Gateway to knowledge: the British Library strategic plan 1989-1994*, London: The British Library Board.
6. Ibid., p.24.
7. University Grants Committee (1967), *Report of the Committee on Libraries* [Chairman: T. Parry], London: HMSO.
8. Ibid., p.77.
9. Urquhart, D.J. (1978), 'The National Central Library – a historical review', *Journal of documentation*, **34**, p.280.
10. Great Britain, Department of Education and Science, Office of Arts and Libraries, (1982), *The future development of libraries and information services: the organisational and policy framework*, and *Working together within a national framework*, London: HMSO.
11. Great Britain, Department of Education and Science, Office of Arts and Libraries, (1986), *The future development of libraries and information services: progress through*

planning and partnership. Report by the Library and Information Services Council, (Library information series no. 14), London: HMSO.

12. Hanger, S. (1987), 'Collection development in the British Library: the role of the RLG Conspectus', *Journal of librarianship*, **19** (2), 89-107.
13. British Library (1986), *Conspectus in the British Library*, London: The British Library.
14. Ferris, V. (1989), 'Don't film it if you're not recording it', *Library conservation news*, **22** (January), 3-8.
15. Enright, B.J. (1989), *Selection for survival: a review of acquisition and retention policies*, London: The British Library Board.

Glossary

ADONIS project	Article Delivery over Network Information Services
ALA	American Library Association
ALCTS	Association for Library Collections and Technical Services
AMIGOS	Access Method for Indexed Data Generalized for Operating System
ARLiN	Association of Research Libraries Network
ARL OMS	Association of Research Libraries Office of Management Studies
ASCII	American Standard Code for Information Interchange: a standard for converting alphanumeric data into digital code for machine storage
ASIG	Australian Serials Interest Group
BALLOTS	Bibliographic Automation of Large Library Operations using a Time Sharing System
BBC	British Broadcasting Corporation
BFI	British Film Institute
BL	British Library
BLAISE-LINE	British Library Automated Information Service
BLAISE-LOCAS	British Library Automated Information Service Local Cataloguing
BLCMP	Originally Birmingham Libraries Cooperative Mechanisation Project, now known as BLCMP Library Services Ltd.
BLDSC	British Library Document Supply Centre
BLPES	British Library for Political and Economic Science
BNB	British National Bibliography
BNBMARC	British National Bibliography MARC
BNFVC	British National Film and Video Catalogue

BOOKBANK	Whitaker's *Books in Print* on CD-ROM
BTEC	Business and Technician Education Council
BUFVC	British Universities Film and Video Council
CARL	Colorado Alliance for Research Libraries
CCI	current collecting intensity
CCM	Colorado Comparative Matrix
CD-ROM	Compact disc read only memory
CHEST	Combined Higher Education Software Team
CIMTECH	National Centre for Information Media and Technology
CIP data	Cataloguing in Publication data
CMDC	Collection Management and Development Committee
COLA	Committee on Library Acquisitions
COPOL	Council of Polytechnic Librarians
CPU	Central Processing Unit
CRL	Center for Research Libraries
CURL	Consortium of University Research Libraries
CVCP	Committee of Vice Chancellors and Principals
DRA	Data Resources Associates
DSC	Document Supply Centre
ECS	existing collection strengths
ESRC	Economic and Social Research Council
FTE	full time equivalent
GCSE	General Certificate of Secondary Education
GPO	US Government Printing Office
HEA	Higher Education Act, 1965
IBA	Independent Broadcasting Authority
ICRISAT	International Crops Research Institute for the Semi-Arid Tropics
IFLA	International Federation of Library Associations
ILL	interlibrary loan
ILLNET	Illinois Library and Information Network
INFROSS	Information Requirements of the Social Sciences
ISBN	international standard book number
ISO	International Standardizing Organization
ISSN	international standard serial number
JANET	Joint Academic Network
LACAP	Latin American Co-operative Acquisitions Program
LASER	London and South Eastern Library Region
LCS	Illinois State common circulation system
LIP	Local Information Plan
LIRN	Library and Information Resource Network
LISC	Library and Information Services Council
LISA	Library and Information Science Abstracts

LISU	Library and Information Statistics Unit
LSE	London School of Economics
MARC	machine readable cataloguing
MEDLINE	Medlars [Medical Literature Analysis and Retrieval System] on-line
MELVYL	On-line catalog, University of California
METRO	New York Metropolitan Reference and Research Library Agency
NAAL	Network of Alabama Academic Libraries
NASIG	North American Serials Interest Group
NBM	non-book materials
NCC	National Computing Centre
NCET	National Council for Educational Technology
NCIP	North American Collections Inventory Project
NEMROC	North East Media Resources Organising Committee
NISS	National Information on Software and Services
NIVC	National Interactive Video Centre
NOTIS	Northwestern On-line Totally Integrated System
NPAC	National Program for Acquisitions and Cataloguing
NSP	non-subject parameter
OCLC	Online Computer Library Center
OPAC	online public access catalogue
OSI	open systems interconnection
PCR	primary collecting responsibility
RESOURCE	a local education authority software publishing consortium, whose members are Barnsley, Doncaster, Humberside, Rotherham and Sheffield.
RLG	Research Libraries Group
RLIN	Research Libraries Information Network
RTSD	Resources & Technical Services Division (of the American Library Association)
SALALM	Seminar on the Acquisition of Latin American Library Materials
SALBIN	Scottish Academic Libraries' Bibliographic Information Network
SAS	Statistical Analysis System
SCONUL	Standing Conference of National and University Libraries
SDI	selective dissemination of information
SOULBAG	Southampton University Library Budget Allocation Game
SUNY	State University of New York
SWALCAP	South West Academic Libraries Cooperative Automation Project
UFC	Universities' Funding Council
UGC	University Grants Committee
UKSG	United Kingdom Serials Group
UTLAS	University of Toronto Library Automated System
VALNET	Valley Automated Library Network
VISCOUNT	Viewdata and Interlibrary System Communications Network
WLN	Washington Library Network

Index